FIRE AND FREEDOM

FIRE AND FREEDOM

THE AMERICAN REVOLUTION IN NEW YORK

EDITED BY
THOMAS S. WERMUTH,
DEVIN LANDER,
JENNIFER LEMAK,
AND ROBERT CHILES

With a foreword by Russell Shorto

A *NEW YORK HISTORY* PUBLICATION
THREE HILLS
CORNELL UNIVERSITY PRESS
Ithaca and London
NEW YORK STATE MUSEUM
Albany

First published 2026 by Cornell University Press

Librarians: A CIP catalog record for this book is available from the Library of Congress.

ISBN 9781501786181 (hardcover)
ISBN 9781501786198 (pdf)
ISBN 9781501786204 (epub)

GPSR EU contact: Sam Thornton, Mare Nostrum Group B.V., Mauritskade 21D, 1091 GC, Amsterdam, NL, gpsr@mare-nostrum.co.uk.

CONTENTS

Foreword

Libraries are filled with volumes devoted to the topic of what the American Revolution meant and what it means. There are good reasons for the abundance. Most people would probably agree that the revolution was fundamentally about freedom, but that seems to be where agreement ends. Alas, "freedom" is a word of such scope that it veers toward emptiness. Even when we limit the question to the colonists who rebelled against England in the eighteenth century, figuring out who wanted freedom and exactly what kind of freedom they had in mind is a significant puzzle. Extrapolating that freedom forward in time becomes more complicated with each era, to the point of ultimate incomprehensibility. Unity, too, is far from being a straightforward concept, yet it is often employed matter-of-factly. The pronouncement of the authors of the Declaration of Independence that they represented "one people" was a rhetorical device.

And yet somehow we all think we know what these concepts meant and continue to mean. We know that those eighteenth-century colonists, many of them anyway, wanted freedom from England, freedom to make their own decisions, freedom to tax themselves as necessary rather than submitting to the whims of a distant empire, freedom to choose their own leaders. We know they formed a union, and that Americans ever since have seen themselves as part of it. Americans believe in freedom. "American" is an identity, one that nearly all citizens of the United States seem happy to don, and one that we confidently trace right back to 1776.

This unified sense of American identity is an illusion. These concepts have not meant the same thing to all Americans—not remotely. I would argue that for much of the past 250 years, Americans have used platitudes and symbols to paper over what are in fact profoundly different beliefs. The polarization in American society that seems to be a feature of the 2010s and 2020s in fact goes right back to the beginning.

When we think of the planting of the American colonies in the seventeenth century, New England comes first to mind. And, indeed, the influence of New England, and especially of the power center of Boston, on the future nation was profound. New England's early dominance helped to ensure that English would be the common language of the future nation. As a Puritan stronghold, Boston also contributed Christian nationalism to the nation's fabric. The sense that the United States is fundamentally a Christian nation, undergirded by biblical precepts and with a commandment to propagate the word of God, is shared by tens or even hundreds of millions today.

But New England was not the only power center, and this brings me to the subject of this book: New York and the revolution. Each of the thirteen colonies that pitted itself against Britain and became an American state had its own unique perspective. I would suggest that New York's perspective was, as it were, more unique than others'. Its geographical location gave it a certain prominence and strategic importance, as did New York Harbor and the Hudson River. New York City was a sought-after prize, which the Continental Army under George Washington strove to defend but which the British took with relative ease.

But New York had something else besides, which set it apart from the other colonies: its history. For its first forty years as a European settlement, it was the Dutch colony of New Netherland, and New York City was originally New Amsterdam. That Dutch capital, at the base of Manhattan Island, was a kind of melting pot. In 1643 it was asserted that the settlement's residents spoke eighteen languages, and that at a time when the population was not much more than five hundred. Add in Native and African languages, and there must have been something like twenty-five different languages spoken. The Dutch of the era also pioneered elements of what would later be called capitalism. It is no accident that the center of US finance is associated with Wall Street, which was the northern boundary of New Amsterdam.

In 1664 the English took over the Dutch colony. But the English who achieved that feat were very different from those in New England. The English who sailed into New York Harbor had been on the opposite side of the Puritans in that country's civil war. Ideologically, they were poles apart. Where the Puritans stood for theocracy and uniformity of thought, the representatives of the English monarchy were pragmatists who espoused religious toleration. When they arrived to do battle with the Dutch in order to wrest Manhattan and the rest of

New Netherland away, they found they had much in common with the pragmatic, business-minded, pluralistic people of New Amsterdam. The Dutch there likewise found themselves in alignment with this bloc of English society, so that the two sides created a kind of merger. The new city, New York, became a base for a relatively tolerant, pluralistic, business-minded society, one that ultimately favored secular government.

As the colonies and then the United States grew in power, so did both of these sensibilities: one theocratic and intolerant, the other secular and pluralistic. The US Civil War stands as the greatest testament to what today we call polarization. Reconstruction was doomed from the start, because that polarization was embedded in the country's DNA.

It is no surprise that New York's role in the revolution was complicated. New York was a hotbed of Loyalist sentiment but also of ardent patriots, and plenty of New Yorkers did not like either option, or changed from one to the other and back again. But if confusion is one byproduct of pluralism, another is flexibility. The mixed society that New York inherited from its Dutch predecessor, coupled with an ethos of tolerance and compromise, gave it unparalleled power: to consider new ideas, to adapt, to evolve. A culture of pragmatism and creativity helped New York not just to survive the turmoil of the revolution but to thrive. And that may be New York's biggest contribution to American society.

Russell Shorto

FIRE AND FREEDOM

The American Revolution in New York Revisited

An Introduction

Thomas S. Wermuth

In 1763, news of England's triumph over France in the Seven Years War, a veritable world war fought across North America, Europe, the Caribbean, and even as far off as India, reached the people of New York. From Manhattan to townships up and down the Hudson River Valley, New Yorkers celebrated their victory as well as their royal leader, King George III. Parades and processions of military detachments marched proudly through the streets, banquets and congratulatory toasts were offered, church bells pealed and volleys of cannon fire were discharged. Even though they lived thousands of miles away from England, the people of New York took great pride in celebrating their identity as loyal subjects of the king and of the British Empire. In fact, New Yorkers had fought side by side with the British, battling the French and their Indigenous allies along the province's northern and western frontiers. At the war's conclusion, many in the province could confidently echo James Otis's declaration in 1764: "We love, esteem and reverence our mother country and adore our king."[1]

The celebration was short-lived, however. Just a little more than a decade later, in the summer of 1776, the largest British military force to ever cross the Atlantic, some forty thousand soldiers and sailors and several hundred naval ships and support vessels, sailed into Manhattan Harbor. The goal of this massive army was not to do battle again with the French or some other European adversary, but to subdue the violent rebellion being waged by the very same colonies that just a few years earlier had celebrated their Britishness and fought for their king. For the rest of the year, forces under George Washington battled the invading British armies across New York, in Long Island, Brooklyn, Manhattan, and finally into the Hudson Valley. Washington's army retreated from New York in December, leaving the city and its inhabitants in the possession of the British. For the next seven years, New York City was under martial law and served as the central headquarters and command post of the British Army's attempt to put down the rebellion, and the Hudson River Valley became the war's major battleground.[2]

What had happened in those years that led to such a reversal of affections? Ironically, the very same victory over the French that solidified England's supremacy in North America also revealed a variety of challenges and obstacles that few had anticipated or foreseen. The British government's desire to raise additional revenue to finance the armies stationed along the western border led it to develop a plan to tax its colonists, a proposal not well received in North America. Further, the English victory had garnered for the empire all of the territories east of the Mississippi River, potentially opening this region to land speculators and settlers. This area was already home to thousands of Indigenous peoples wary of any future European encroachment. The British government recognized the threat posed by new settler expansion and sought to control the movement westward by establishing a boundary—the Proclamation of 1763—prohibiting European migration west of the Alleghany Mountains. Although this action was meant to be a temporary response to a challenging problem, it frustrated and angered land speculators and potential settlers.[3]

It was this series of initiatives—new taxes to provide revenue to defend North America, a more robust regulation and enforcement of imperial trade, and limits to western expansion and development—which Parliament considered reasonable and even overdue, that some British Americans questioned and opposed. People living in the colonies had become accustomed to self-governance and a generous amount of autonomy, so these parliamentary measures were viewed with suspicion. Almost immediately, Americans reacted to the proposed initiatives with a mix of political arguments, constitutional challenges, boycotts, and, as was common in eighteenth-century America, protests and raucous crowd actions in the streets. What began as a resistance movement to these new British polices by increasingly angry colonists steadily became a violent rebellion and, in the summer of 1776, a war for independence waged by thirteen of Britain's North American colonies against their "mother" country and their once beloved king.[4]

Over the years, historians have debated the meaning of the revolution, its causes, course, and outcomes, and have even engaged in an ongoing discussion on whether or not the event was truly "revolutionary." In the early twentieth century, Carl Becker articulated what became the dominant interpretation of the revolution for many years. Becker argued that there were two parallel movements at work during the colonists' struggle with Britain: first, "the contest for home rule," and second, the contest "of who should rule at home" once independence was achieved. In what became known as the "Progressive" interpretation, Becker and others asserted that a powerful struggle took place among different socioeconomic groups and classes, with wealthy merchants and substantial property owners battling middling artisans, craftsmen, and laborers for control over the revolution and its outcome.[5]

Although this interpretation held sway for many years, by the mid-twentieth century some historians began to question this view and even challenged the belief that the revolution was a radical event. These scholars argued that the United States' experience with revolution was nothing like those in other parts of the world, such as in France or Russia where brutal "reigns of terror" occurred, thousands were executed or exiled, and large property confiscations took place. In comparison, as interpreted by what has become identified as the "consensus" or "neoconservative" school of history, the American Revolution seemed quite tame and orderly. By the 1950s and 1960s, the prevailing historical interpretation was that, far from being a radical struggle characterized by an attempt to undermine the social order, as the Progressives had theorized, the revolution was actually an attempt to protect democracy in the colonies from an overreaching British government. Daniel Boorstin, the long-serving librarian of Congress and strong proponent of the neoconservative interpretation, even went so far as to declare that the revolution in the United States was "one of the few conservative colonial rebellions of modern times."[6]

Our understanding of the revolution has continued to evolve and broaden as historians have asked new questions, revised old interpretations and studied previously overlooked groups. Since the 1960s, scholarly attention has tended to focus on historical players previously excluded from the revolutionary narrative or seen as peripheral to the revolution— enslaved people of African descent, Native Americans,

Loyalists, women, rural tenants, and others who both affected and were affected by the conflict. Although this widescale reassessment was not limited to the study of the revolution since scholars scrutinized many aspects of the nation's history, its impact was particularly profound to the study of the early United States.[7]

This widening of the historical lens was influenced by many factors, but certainly the social activism of the 1960s and 1970s, with its challenges to traditional sources of power, including the power of the academy, was a powerful variable in the decline of the more "consensus-oriented" interpretation. The civil rights movement, antiwar protests, and the women's rights movement, among other socially progressive causes, revealed the failure of the consensus interpretation to account for the many different social, racial, gender, and ethnic groups that participated in the historical process generally, and in the revolution specifically. Starting in the 1960s and carrying through to today, a robust literature looking at revolutionary history "from the bottom up," in the words of Jesse Lemisch, has recharted our understanding of early US society. New studies on women and gender, race and enslaved African Americans, the laboring and working classes, Indigenous peoples, and others have revealed the important roles these and others played in the revolutionary drama.[8]

As Alan Taylor has argued, this more inclusive and broader examination reveals that the American Revolution had far more in common with other revolutions around the world than many historians had acknowledged. Generally missing from previous studies of the revolution was that large structural changes *did* occur in North America. Emerging state governments confiscated vast amounts of land and property from thousands of Americans who supported the "wrong" side of the conflict. Some sixty thousand Americans loyal to the Crown were forced to flee the colonies (a larger percentage of the population was displaced during the American Revolution than in revolutionary France), and the homelands of thousands of Indigenous peoples were devastated by military invasions.[9] Throughout North America—in New York's Mohawk Valley, Pennsylvania's revolutionary frontier, the southern backcountry— a brutal civil war took place, with many participants using the conflict as an opportunity to settle old feuds and long, simmering grievances, often with vigilante violence.[10] In sum, hundreds of thousands of people in North América were affected by a real social revolution in the 1770s and 1780s.

New York lends itself as an ideal location to study the many facets that characterized the revolution. As Edward Countryman has convincingly argued, "No state experienced the Revolutionary War with greater ferocity or over a longer period than New York." Beginning with the resistance to Parliament's attempt to tax the colonies in the mid-1760s, it was in New York that large crowds rioted, destroyed property, battled with British soldiers, and threatened civil officials attempting to implement British policy. Crowds intimidated merchants and boycotted storekeepers who continued to do business with the British. Rioters in Manhattan paraded through the streets burning effigies of British leaders, while women in the Hudson Valley tarred and feathered suspected Loyalists and Tories.[11]

As political resistance drifted into military rebellion, New York's role became even more prominent. The armed uprising may have begun in Massachusetts, but the conflict soon moved out of New England and focused on New York. From the beginning of the British invasion in the summer of 1776 until the war's conclusion seven years later in 1783, New York served as the war's primary battleground. George Washington spent one-third of the war in and around New York and identified the Hudson Valley region as the "Key of America."[12] With its bustling commercial port at Manhattan, its massive natural transportation system in the Hudson River, and the rich agricultural bounty of the surrounding valley, New York offered what the British felt to be the most promising and strategic option for crushing the rebellion.

It was on the battlefields around New York City in 1776 that US troops had their first major experience of warfare with the redcoats, a campaign that did not go well for George Washington and his army, who were forced to withdraw from the state. It was on the battlefields in upstate New York in 1777 that US forces reversed those earlier defeats and stopped the invading British armies at Saratoga, convincing a skeptical France to enter the struggle in support of the rebellious colonies and changing the direction of the war. And it was in central New York in 1779 that Washington organized one of the largest US forces composed during the war to invade the homelands of the Indigenous allies of the British. The invasion—the Sullivan-Clinton Campaign—succeeded in driving the Haudenosaunee several hundred miles westward across the state to the Canadian border, killing hundreds and burning and destroying dozens of their villages and thousands of acres of rich agricultural land.[13]

No other state experienced both combatant armies stationed within a few miles of each other throughout the duration of the war. With the British occupying Manhattan and the southern Hudson Valley through 1783, US forces were stationed just a few miles to the north along the Hudson River to deter potential British invasions. The New York City market closed to valley farmers, and marauding forces from both armies seized what they needed from farm families throughout the region. The Hudson Valley economy was ravaged, food confiscated, and property requisitioned or destroyed.[14]

On the eve of the revolution, few contemporaries would have predicted New York's rise as the Empire State in the decades following the war's conclusion. But New York City was already a thriving port town, exporting large amounts of wheat, flour, grain, and other agricultural bounty, mostly from the Hudson River Valley and western Long Island. A large part of the city's population of twenty thousand or so worked in the shipping industry: merchants and storekeepers, artisans and mechanics, sailors and laborers, most of whom were free white workers but some of whom were enslaved people of African descent and indentured servants working on the docks and wharves, shipping goods in and out of New York.[15]

The vast majority of New Yorkers (about 90 percent of the approximately168,000 inhabitants) lived not in the city but in the countryside. Most rural residents were members of farm families that worked the land they owned, but a substantial portion of the white population were tenants on one of the great Hudson Valley estates, such as Rensselaerwyck or Livingston Manor. These manors were contentious places characterized by disputed land claims between landlords on the one side and settlers pushing across the New York border from New England on the other. The growing unrest fueled the 1766 rebellion on the Hudson's east bank, resulting in pitched battles between landlords and rebellious tenants. British troops rushed to the manors to put down the insurrection, in some ways portending the conflict on the horizon.[16]

With almost twenty thousand enslaved men and women of African descent living in the province, New York, according to Michael Groth, was "the largest slave society north of the Chesapeake." Much of New York's economic growth was dependent on the forced labor of enslaved men and women who worked in the fields and orchards of their owners. The contradictions of the American Revolution—white Americans fighting for freedom from what they termed British "slavery" while actually enslaving large numbers of Black people—was not lost on New Yorkers, white or Black. During the war, debate began in earnest throughout the North about slavery's future. While some states legislated a quick end to the institution of slavery, New York, far more dependent on enslaved labor and with a powerful slaveholding constituency opposed to manumission, debated its prospects for more than decade after political independence had been achieved.[17]

If the ravages of the war offered challenges to many people in New York, they also offered opportunities to others. Hundreds of enslaved New Yorkers used the chaos of wartime and risked brutal punishment to escape from their enslavers and make their way to British-occupied New York City seeking freedom. Tenants on the Hudson Valley estates used the conflict to again challenge land titles and engage in new uprisings aimed at their landlords. Seizures and confiscations of property owned by Loyalists presented opportunities for tenants and small freeholders to purchase land, sometimes the very same properties they had tilled under lease.[18]

Many groups were damaged by the war, however—some irreversibly. Those who remained loyal to the king and empire are among the most obvious. New York engaged in the largest land confiscation and property redistribution of the United States in the eighteenth century, as the new state government seized several hundred thousand acres from hundreds of Loyalists and others who fled the war and the region. Also affected were the Indigenous peoples in the state. Thousands of Haudenosaunee lived in central New York, tending farms, fields, and orchards. They had observed the outbreak of hostilities with apprehension, wary of becoming involved in the struggle between the two combatants, but well aware that their future was likely to vary dramatically depending on which side emerged victorious. The Haudenosaunee—the majority of whom eventually allied with the British—were severely affected by the war but, as we will see in these pages, were not powerless victims in this struggle.[19]

This book presents a sampling of the new research and scholarship being conducted on New York and the revolution—and the many thousands who participated and are now recognized to have played important and often instrumental roles in the conflict. These chapters reveal the richness and wide-ranging interest of present research, with studies of Loyalism on Long Island, George Washington's military strategy, enslaved African Americans battling for their own freedom, and even the memory of the revolution for later generations, among several other subjects.

The central event connecting all these topics, of course, was the war. While the conflict raged, the apparatus of a state government was being built. Looking at New York's experience, Dillon L. Streifeneder tackles this crucial part of the revolution. Streifeneder argues that New York implemented an ongoing process of structural reform that routinized governance by local officeholders. The institutional framework capable of shaping society remained in place after the Revolutionary War, fostering the emergence of the powerful and vigorous states of the early republic.

Emily Sneff focuses on the circumstances of disseminating the news of independence in wartime New York in the fateful summer of 1776. As news spread after July 4, every active newspaper in the new United States included the Declaration of Independence in their pages. When John Holt printed the Declaration in his *New-York Journal* on July 11, 1776, he formatted the text in two columns within a decorative border and explained that some of his customers had asked him to create a copy of the Declaration they could display in their homes. While people across the United States read the text in their local newspapers and gathered to hear it read aloud at public readings, the reception of the news in New York was decidedly different, because the Declaration reached Manhattan at the same time that British forces were landing on Staten Island, and the Continental army was preparing for an attack. What did it mean to create and display a copy of the Declaration of Independence in a space so quickly transformed into a battleground? Sneff considers the stakes of printing and displaying the Declaration at this precarious moment, when New York was on the eve of British occupation.

New York City's first Great Fire occurred shortly after George Washington's retreat from Manhattan on September 15, 1776, leaving the city in the hands of the invading British forces. The Great Fire has occupied a surprisingly small part of the story of the revolution. It was destructive—burning about a fifth of the city—but as Benjamin L. Carp notes, Americans tried to misdirect investigations into the origins of the fire almost immediately after the event, which seemed to cast aspersions on Americans' wartime conduct. Misinformation muddled contemporary accounts, and scholars who did not know what to make of this dramatic event carried these distortions into the nineteenth and twentieth centuries. These scholars argued that either an accident or apolitical actors, rather than George Washington's men or radical saboteurs, caused the fire. While some writers questioned these conclusions, their voices were largely ignored. Carp offers a fuller treatment of how New York historians shaped the memory of the Great Fire and, by extension, revolutionary New York City, compelling us to consider how much we can still learn about the revolution from the study of this event.

Historians have long debated what truly defined a Loyalist during the American Revolution. Was it a matter of belief, action, or survival? Christopher F. Minty and John Cording use British-occupied Long Island as a case study to explore the complexities of allegiance, showing how political identity was rarely clear-cut. Through the 1778 oath of allegiance, they examine how even known revolutionaries—such as members of the Culper Spy Ring—swore loyalty to the Crown while secretly aiding the American cause. Those revolutionaries' actions raise important questions about whether an oath was a true reflection of allegiance or a strategic necessity in the face of British occupation. By analyzing the choices Long Islanders made under martial law, this chapter challenges the rigid binary of Loyalist versus revolutionary, revealing a world in which political survival often outweighed ideological purity. The article also highlights Long Island's overlooked role in the revolution, showing how its residents navigated the shifting demands of war, occupation, and espionage. Ultimately, Minty and Cording argue for a more nuanced understanding of loyalty, one that recognizes the fluidity of identity in times of upheaval and reexamines how historians define allegiance in the context of revolution.

The Haudenosaunee and their lands were intentionally targeted by the Continental army during the revolution, with the Sullivan-Clinton Campaign destroying their towns, homes, and agricultural fields and devastating Iroquoia. While the Haudenosaunee suffered greatly, they were not politically, militarily, or diplomatically powerless in the postwar period. A lesser-known part of the story is that the Haudenosaunee, especially the Seneca, regrouped and, as Elana Krischer reveals, established new settlements and once again threatened US frontier communities. The revolution's conclusion changed the nature of US westward expansion and, with the failure to displace the Iroquois through warfare, forced the United States to look for different ways to gain control of Seneca land.

Although much of the revolution was fought on New York battlefields, the final major conflict of the war occurred not in New York but in Virginia. Well into the summer of 1781, however, George Washington still envisioned an attack on occupied New York City, not the South, as the logical final step to defeating the British. Iris de Rode focuses on the decision-making process that guided General Washington and his French counterparts, including Comte de Rochambeau and Chevalier de Chastellux, away from a direct assault on the city, as they instead redirected their efforts toward an attack in the Chesapeake. Central to this change in planning was the "Grand Reconnaissance" in northern Manhattan in the summer of 1781, which convinced Washington and Rochambeau to strategically withdraw after better understanding the formidable British strength around the city, and to instead pursue opportunities that had revealed themselves in the Chesapeake.

One of the central stories of the revolution, unresolved during the conflict itself, was the continued existence of the institution of slavery. Some states recognized the contradiction and began to support manumission laws. New York was slow to follow. The revolution raised the question and the promise of emancipation, but it would still be many years before this happened. By focusing on the western frontier region of the state, Lucien Holness examines how emancipation unfolded after the revolution. The legislators from western counties formed after the conflict ended provided the votes needed in 1799 to pass a gradual abolition bill that became law. But even after 1799, the enslaved population in western New York continued to grow. Holness observes how the limitations of statewide manumission groups in the struggle against slavery forced enslaved people to adopt their own strategies to secure their freedom.

As we approach the 250th anniversary of the revolution, the chapters in this book illuminate how wide-ranging this event was. What started as a constitutional and political dispute about "home rule" and taxation became a transformative event that unleashed a host of unanticipated consequences.[20] It is clear in these chapters that a diverse group of New Yorkers—soldiers, Loyalists, Indigenous peoples, and the enslaved, among others—many of whom were previously ignored or viewed as inconsequential, were important participants in the revolutionary process. By bringing these historical actors back into the story, a more complete understanding of the revolution in New York emerges, enriching our knowledge of what the revolution was and what it meant to the many thousands who participated in it.

CHAPTER 1

"The Propriety of a Vigorous Government"

Revolution and the Creation of the Empire State

Dillon L. Streifeneder

February was not a good month for Udny Hay. In fact, the entire winter of 1778–79 proved to be a period of considerable frustration. As the deputy quartermaster general in the Hudson Highlands, Hay was responsible for finding, purchasing, transporting, and storing supplies for the Continental army. By late January, the army's provisions were nearly exhausted, and with the farms in the immediate vicinity barren, Hay had to transport supplies by wagon or sled from more distant magazines. Lacking either, Hay found himself having to impress them—that is, to seize the wagons and associated horse or oxen teams and force their owners to drive them at the government rate.

Impressment, as Hay well knew, was not popular. In New York and elsewhere, it had prompted public outcries of government tyranny and of trampling on personal rights and liberties—the very things many believed had justified independence from Britain. To make this policy more palatable, New York's government had drafted a law that empowered local officials to mediate such transactions, leaving it to their discretion whether impressment was indeed justified. Those discretionary powers in the hands of the local justices of the peace (JPs) were the primary source of Hay's frustration. For to impress the transportation he required, Hay would have to follow state law and plead with a local JP for assistance. As they had many times before, his calls for aid were rejected.

There was, however, a work-around to this predicament. In the case of an "emergency," the law authorized military officials to obtain an impress warrant from the state's governor or commanding general in the vicinity, thereby circumventing the local JPs.[1] Believing that the threshold of an emergency had been met, Hay leaped into action, seizing wagons and teamsters. In doing so, he prompted immediate condemnation. Writing on February 10, Hay informed his superiors that the JPs had "imprisoned a Waggon Master, sent the constable after one of my assistants, and have arrested myself."[2] As Hay learned the hard way, central state capacity was weak and dependent on the cooperation of local magistrates; trying to alter that reality could, and often did, prompt backlash.

This dilemma was far from novel; rather, it was the status quo during the colonial period. Britain's colonial governments had long relied on a host of local officials—some elected, some appointed—to perform an array of duties associated with governance.[3] Unlike modern states with professional civil servants and large bureaucracies, early modern polities relied almost entirely on local officials to implement centralized policies.[4] But as Hay's case demonstrates, this reliance could prove problematic for state authority. It could, and often did, undercut what political scientists refer to as "state capacity," that being the ability of the central state apparatus to carry out and implement its intended policies. State capacity relies on numerous sources, including money, information and knowledge, organizational and administrative structure, and personnel.[5] Just as for states today, the absence or weakness of any of these elements could hinder state capacity.

As Udny Hay's predicament highlights, the linchpin of colonial state capacity in New York was the office of justice of the peace,[6] composed of men who were appointed by the governor with the advice of the Council (usually from a list provided by the province's gentry elite). It was intended that every odd administrative unit of New York's establishment, including precincts, districts, manors, wards, boroughs, and towns, would have a resident JP to act as the leader of a team of other local officers within their respective neighborhood. In this role, the JP would coax or coerce propertied heads of households to help enforce the law (or localized expectations of it) and oversee the lesser elected local officers, including supervisors or aldermen, constables, tax assessors

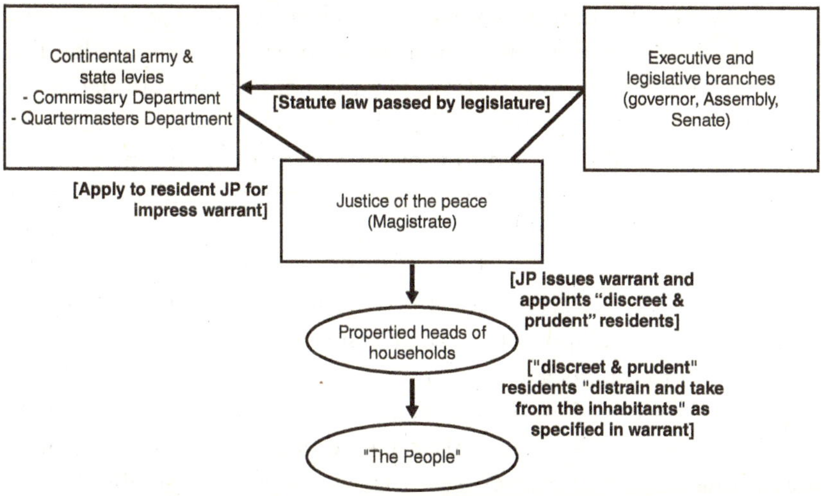

FIGURE 1.1. A simple model of the "colonial state" in New York. Adapted from John L. Brooke, "A Very Simple Model of the Early Modern English State," in *State and Citizen: British America and the Early United States*, ed. Peter Thompson and Peter S. Onuf (University of Virginia Press, 2013), 183.

and collectors, overseers of highways and of the poor, fence viewers, coroners, and clerks, as well as the colony's militia.[7]

Overall, this was a system where centralized authority was, according to John L. Brooke, "radically and fundamentally *embedded*."[8] To implement centralized policies, it relied on the voluntary cooperation of JPs and lesser local officers: Negotiation and accommodation were its defining features.[9] When approached by flexible leaders, this system could provide workable governance over a vast imperial space. But it nevertheless resulted in what Jack P. Greene has described as "a fundamental structural weakness."[10]

When faced with a mid-century demographic explosion and westward settler migration from the Carolinas through the Mid-Atlantic, this weak governing structure, as Christopher R. Pearl's study on Pennsylvania demonstrates, proved increasingly "incapable of addressing community problems."[11] In New York, the government struggled to provide everyday law enforcement, to suppress larger agrarian revolts, or to organize a coherent war effort, and it repeatedly had to apply for British military intervention.[12] Though not the sole cause of the American Revolution, such structural weakness among the colonial governments, Douglas Bradburn argues, certainly "created conditions highly favorable to revolution."[13]

Against this backdrop of weak colonial polities lies an impressive body of work that views the American Revolution, as Oscar Handlin and Mary Flug Handlin put it, "as the moment of the foundation of the state," and a strong state at that.[14] Unlike their weak colonial predecessors that had struggled to provide governance amid internal crises, the thirteen US state governments, according to William J. Novak and Steven Pincus, established a "distinctive and powerful governmental tradition."[15] Directed by revolutionary state legislatures, the state governments asserted control over internal public governance, economy, and development. In their responses to wartime demands, James A. Henretta has asserted, the states "acted in dramatically new ways," passing what Novak and Pincus argue were "powerful statutes regulating almost every necessary aspect of state economic and social life in time of war and transition . . . as extensive as imaginable."[16] The states reorganized local jurisdictions; printed money; sent out diplomats; forcibly removed Native Americans; aggressively policed society; regulated wages, debts, and fraud, the price of goods and services, health and hygiene, licenses, and even building construction; tended to refugees; seized and redistributed property; organized forced labor; and built roads, bridges, and canals, all in the name of the general welfare of the people. After the revolution and into the nineteenth century, this tradition of powerful state action and intervention persisted, with the state governments, as Max M. Edling puts it, serving "as the principal political organization of the American union" well into the twentieth century.[17]

Proponents emphasizing a powerful early American state make a compelling case. Yet one is left to wonder how Udny Hay's arrest by a local JP in 1779 fits within this framework. I believe that Hay's plight at the hands of local authorities helps remind us that while the framework for a "strong revolutionary American state tradition" as described by Novak and Pincus may have emerged by the end of the war, that outcome was in no way guaranteed.[18] Over the course of the revolution, the central state apparatus in New York struggled greatly to implement policy solutions developed in response to complex and urgent problems. As Hay's case shows, enactment did not mean enforcement. Without agents to implement the policies written in the state's laws, the state's capacity would remain just as weak as its colonial predecessor.

That simply passing powerful statutes did not immediately establish a strong American state tradition calls our attention to the internal process of state formation. Existing scholarship, however, largely fails to address that process by jumping over the incredible messiness of the Revolutionary War, leaving our understanding of this critical moment largely incomplete.[19] This chapter examines the problems that nearly eight years of war presented the nascent state governments to explain *how* New York developed the institutional mechanisms that formed the foundations of a strong and vigorous state. That foundation rested on expanding state capacity by reorganizing and reshaping the administrative structure at the state's center—the legislature, governor, council, and supreme court—and by organizing a web of local officials to carry out the state's policies. While the new state's institutions and officers were similar in appearance to the colonial system of governance, wartime exigencies offered a window of opportunity to make significant changes to how that system operated. The state did so by implementing an ongoing process of structural reform to its civil institutions, aimed at routinizing governance by local officeholders, curtailing local prerogative and discretionary powers, and creating a coercive system of oversight to ensure that local magistrates uniformly carried out centralized directives. In doing so, New York established the institutional framework for a strong state tradition that emerged in the early republican period.

From the opening of the military campaign in 1776 until the British sailed away in 1783, New York stood, according to its legislature, as the "principal Seat of War."[20] While kinetic violence did not touch every community across the state, issues including ballooning inflation, a refugee crisis, supplying the army, and suppressing Loyalists did. Historians have pointed to challenges such as these for sparking what James A. Henretta has called "an unprecedented wave of governmental activism" by the state legislatures.[21]

In New York, the legislature passed 324 statute laws over the course of the war. These included establishing a uniform method for tax assessment and collection, codifying election procedures, organizing and regulating the militia, disarming and arresting Loyalists, regulating smallpox and other diseases, providing care for refugees and the families of soldiers killed or disabled in the war, regulating the sale of liquor and public houses, seizing and redistributing personal property, convening and regulating small debt litigation, organizing treaty relations with the Haudenosaunee, and providing for the payment of countless wartime expenses.[22]

Taken together, these statutes served two purposes outlined in the 1777 constitution. First, as Edward Countryman explains, they were intended to end "popular direct action" and extralegal committee governance by demonstrating to the people that the government "could and would respond to popular pressure."[23] As the opening of the constitution explained, the period from 1776 to 1777 had been one of transition. Wartime crisis had, according to the constitution's drafters, "reduced them to the necessity of introducing a government by Congresses and Committees . . . established for the sole purpose of opposing the usurpation of the British Parliament." In other words, these bodies were not intended as a long-term solution for governing. The Provincial Congress and committees, the constitution stated, were merely "temporary expedients, and to exist no longer than the grievances of the people should remain without redress."[24] Second, these statutes were to serve as what the constitution's authors intended as the cornerstone for "erecting and constituting a new form of government and internal police" that would be, according to Novak and Pincus, "strong enough to defeat British imperial authority at one of the heights of its force."[25] The framers of this new government, therefore, intended it to be a "vigorous" one, and the need for a new form of internal police was all the more reason to move quickly to have "our Civil Magistrates appointed and our Courts of Justice opened."[26]

Erecting such a government, however, was a long and drawn-out process shaped by the course of the war. Much of the early legislation did not immediately establish the "vigorous Government" that the state's wartime governor, George Clinton, called for; that required amending legislation and restructuring institutions. Rather than trying to examine this process within what was a vast catalog of early legislation, this section will look at a single policy: the impress. Discussing the Impress Act will help illustrate how New York established effective centralized authority and state capacity over the course of the revolution. In doing so, it highlights two challenges the state faced: first, getting JPs to serve, and second, making the JPs implement statutes uniformly in accordance with the letter of the law.

On April 2, 1778, the legislature passed "An Act for Regulating the Impresses of Forage and Carriages and for Billeting Troops Within this State." In recognizing the need to impress goods and services, the first rendition of this law followed colonial precedent, requiring military officials to apply "to any justice of the peace resident in the town, manor, district or precinct in which such impress is required."

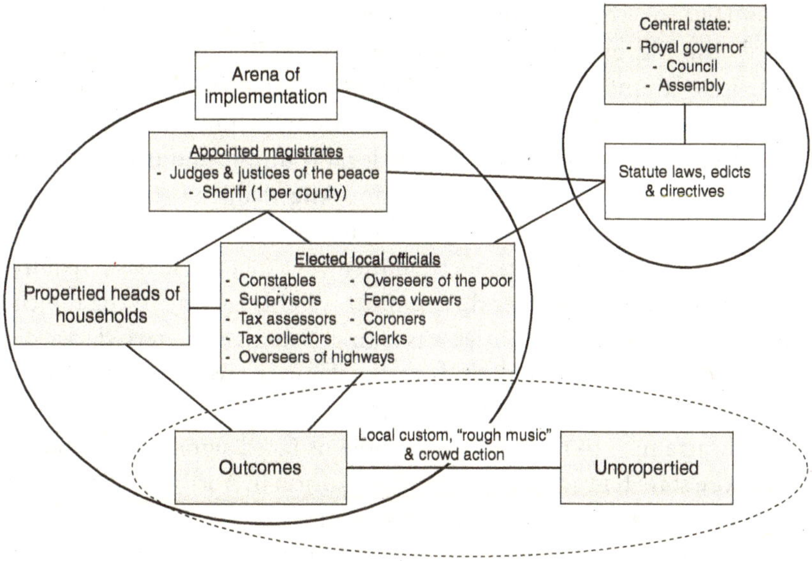

FIGURE 1.2. Implementing the Impress Act, April 1778.

Determining whether impressment was necessary, however, was left up to the JP, not the military. Only if the JP believed the impress necessary would he issue a warrant. If a warrant was issued, an additional element granted the JP further discretionary powers, as the law authorized him "to appoint . . . discreet and prudent inhabitants . . . actually resident in the said town . . . to distrain and take from the inhabitants . . . the quantity of forage to be specified in the said warrant," rather than having soldiers do it. Consequently, propertied heads of households would determine to whom the warrant might apply and how much might be taken by the army. The law made similar stipulations for regulating transportation, again leaving it up to "the judgement" of a resident JP to determine the "number of teams, horses and carriages, with drivers."[27]

To function as designed, this law relied on flesh-and-blood people carrying it out. But as state leaders discovered, the personnel necessary to implement central policies often refused to take on that responsibility. Herein lay the first challenge the state faced in establishing a vigorous government: Many magistrates refused to accept their appointments.

There were several reasons, both novel and predictable, why the state struggled to get JPs to serve. For starters, roughly 40 percent of New York's colonial-era JPs remained loyal to the Crown.[28] Others—while supportive of the revolutionary movement—determined they were simply too old or infirm to continue serving. Both reasons created a significant number of vacancies. While the qualifications to be a JP in New York were less stringent than those in Britain, the expectation remained that JPs should have some legal training, and if not, then at the very least they should have practical knowledge of the law and be in good-enough standing to command respect and influence over their neighbors.[29] Many of the propertied men who met those basic requirements had numerous other duties, most notably serving in the militia. Balancing both responsibilities was taxing, and many preferred to avoid more obligations, particularly because the extra work provided little compensation at the start of the war.[30]

Early attempts to remedy these problems faced significant setbacks. While the state had adopted a new constitution in April 1777, it was not until 1778 that new appointments were made in the counties.[31] When commissions were finally issued, many of the appointees—most already officers in the militia—refused to serve.[32]

Their absence was immediately felt when the army's supply officers tried to execute the Impress Act. In April 1778, Major General Alexander McDougall, the commanding officer in the Hudson Highlands, wrote to Governor Clinton that while attempting to "obtain a warrant from a Justice of the peace" as the Impress Act required, the army struggled in "procuring this article . . . as there are but few, if any Justices qualified."[33] The following month, when trying to obtain wagons to move provisions, Udny Hay likewise informed the governor that "Great inconvenience . . . arises from so few Justices of the peace being Sworn into Office."[34] While Clinton promised Hay that he would "endeavour to have a greater Number of Justices qualified," in October 1778 Hay reiterated his earlier complaint, observing that while "there are many Gentlemen in this State who have been nominated for justices of the Peace," most had "not yett qualified, which neglect is a hurt to the Country in general."[35] As fall turned to winter, further complaints piled up on the governor's desk, with one committee chairman asserting that "the Gentlemen appointed to the magistracy of this County refusing their Commissions" was not just a "Great inconvenience"; it had "Prevented the whole Machine of Government from motion."[36] In response, the governor and council acted aggressively to appoint hundreds of new JPs across the state.[37]

While vacancies persisted, the governor's efforts found willing men to fill many of the offices. Getting those who accepted their commissions to comply with centralized—and often unpopular—decisions, however, proved just as challenging a task. Commenting on this dilemma, Quartermaster General Nathanael Greene shrewdly identified the flaws of many of the early efforts by the states to implement centralized policies. With a provision granting local officials final say on "how much every Farmer shall spare," the army would forever be in want of supplies. For as Greene observed, the local officials judged "from motives of tenderness to their Neighbours," taking "so sparing from the People, that our supplies are very deficient notwithstanding we can see the Country full of Forage."[38]

Greene's comments were based on the lived frustrations of mid-level managers such as Major Cornelius Bogart. In March 1779, Bogart was charged with impressing "Waggons to Ride wood" near Fishkill to provide sick soldiers fuel for their fires. After searching out Justice Wiltsie twice for an impress warrant but not finding him at home,[39] he went instead to Justice Thomas Storm. Justice Storm, however, "Refus'd giving me Any . . . Warrant to impress," justifying his refusal by stating that he did "Strict Justice to the Precinct," as it was "as busy a time as at sowing time with the Farmers" (Storm's neighbors), and that the needs of the army were "not so Urgent as many other things."[40] To Justice Storm (and countless other JPs), his duty was to his tiny precinct, not the wider needs of the state or nation.

Bogart's experience was a common one that winter, and it prompted some officials to try bypassing the JPs. Doing so could lead to increased conflict, as Udny Hay discovered in February. Having initially followed the Impress Act, Hay informed the governor that he had "requested Justice [H]umphrey's assistance and begd he would procure me ten Waggons." Eight days later, however, "not a single one" had appeared.[41] While Hay explained that he had wanted to "avoid making use of Military Force" to acquire the wagons, he found himself under necessity of impressing them to supply the garrisons "very near being out of flour & bread."[42] Informed of Hay's impress, Justice Humphrey—the dilatory JP who had refused to issue warrants on Hay's behalf—leaped into action, arresting and imprisoning Hay, his assistant, and a wagon master. In the aftermath of this squabble, it took the governor's direct intervention to free Hay from jail and quash the local legal proceedings against him.[43]

Observing Hay's plight from afar, Nathanael Greene concisely summarized this debacle. Commenting on Hay's "dispute with the Justices," Greene described the JPs as "Watchmen upon the Tour [Tower]

FIGURE 1.3. *Panoramic View of West Point, New York Showing American Encampments on the Hudson River*, Pierre Charles L'Enfant, August 1782. Library of Congress, Prints and Photographs Division, Washington, DC.

to give the cries to the people," ever ready to rebuff outside interference in their neighborhoods.[44] Being "confident and conceited; obstinate and vindictive," they viewed their communities as little fiefdoms. Noting the "battalion of Constables to carry into execution their devices," Greene acknowledged that it was "difficult for poor honesty to resist their force" and advised Hay to "settle the difference, and bury the hatchet."[45] For as long as the state laws were construed to support the local magistrates, the army needed their assistance, even if it proved frustratingly insufficient.

Incidents like this illuminate a central dilemma for the revolutionary states, one that played out in countless interactions during the war: Where would authority reside? Would the local JPs and other officials whose discretionary powers thwarted centralized agents' efforts to obtain supplies define revolutionary governance? Or would a centralized administration capable of squashing such localism emerge? In New York, this dilemma pushed the state to develop ways to subordinate obstinate magistrates and make them work on its behalf, thereby laying the foundation for a strong postwar state.

Enforcing compliance required multiple approaches, but first and foremost it relied on the legislature to write stricter statutes and establish a more effective system of regulatory oversight to ensure uniformity. The legislature had no sooner passed the Impress Act in April 1778 than officers who relied on it to obtain supplies for the army complained of its inadequacies. But from its shortfalls and those of other statutes like it emerged an important dialogue between policymakers and agents on the ground. That dialogue included talking through both the precise intentions of the statutes and the manner in which agents were expected to act. It was in these conversations that the problems facing the entire war effort and the realization of independence teetered, and it was in this ongoing dialogue that state officials worked through the nuanced challenges of centralized state authority.

In the month leading up to his arrest, Hay had informed the governor of the "extreme trouble" he was having in "Procuring the necessary carriages wanted for public Service," which he did "without deviating from the laws of the State." Hay followed this up with a series of recommendations he believed would fix the flaws in the Impress Act, including establishing a new system for staging wagons and carts along main supply routes, keeping the wagons in repair, establishing "a heavy fine" for those who failed to do so, organizing the wagons into "district brigade[s]" with a JP associated with each, and establishing "Three Gentlemen appointed by the State" whose authority trumped that of the JPs to oversee the entire process. Finally, Hay prescribed that if fines failed to "deter the evil minded from not complying with such wholesome laws," military force might be used.[46]

The governor and legislature took Hay's complaints and recommendations seriously, and on February 3, 1779, Clinton informed Major General McDougall that he was "sensible" of the army's "Troubles," assuring him that "whatever Measures you may be oblidged to take out of the ordinary" for supplying the army, he would "find the Legislature as well as the Executive Authority of the State disposed to put the most favourable Constructions on your Conduct & to render you every Assistance which they can consistently grant." He further informed McDougall that at the last "Meeting of the Legislature, I submitted to their Consideration a Representation of the Difficulties & Distresses under which the army labour" (Hay's aforementioned report).[47] The following day, Clinton sent along the "Resolutions" devised by "The Legislature to obviate the Difficulties experienced in supplying the army," including an approval for appointing additional commissaries and assistants.[48] Here was the legislative process in action, seeking, albeit too slowly, a resolution with the obstinate local officials interfering with supplying the army.

Hay's arrest just days later shows that the legislature had struggled to keep pace with events on the ground. McDougall therefore promptly requested the opinion of State Senator John Morin Scott, one of

New York's leading legal minds, and Egbert Benson, the state's attorney general. As McDougall explained, "The Justices and Constables, will not execute the Law for impressing Teams," readily shown by Hay's actions that led to his arrest. Beyond reiterating an ongoing problem, McDougall wanted clarification on the legal definition of "the Emergency intended by the Act," which would authorize him to issue a "warrant without the aid of a Justice of the Peace, to impress the Teams"—an attempt to get state leaders to explicitly approve bypassing the JPs.[49]

Scott replied rapidly, writing McDougall back the following day; Benson's response took longer, not arriving until the end of March. Both men essentially came to the same conclusion: the statute was quite clear in that it prohibited impresses "on any pretence whatsoever without warrant from a Justice of the Peace." Disappointingly, they would not put in writing what McDougall desired—direct approval to use military force.

Neither response provided an immediate solution to the problems with the act, but they demonstrate an important and ongoing development: the desire and genuine effort by the legislature to amend state laws to ensure effective implementation that would actually solve the problems at hand. While Scott was not willing to stretch the meaning of the existing law to meet McDougall's needs, he informed the general that at that very moment, the legislature had a new "Law on the Anvil" aimed at remedying the problems with the local JPs.[50] Benson sent a similar message, telling McDougall that in the time since he had received McDougall's initial letter, a new bill "for amending the Impress Law" had been passed.[51]

In mid-March, the legislature had indeed passed an amendment, justifying it on account of "disputes" between agents like Hay and local officials like Justice Humphrey. The revised act increased fines for persons refusing to comply with it from five pounds to ten; removed some discretionary powers of the JPs for determining prices, pay, and wages; and established a small financial reward for the JPs and constables for issuing warrants and impressing teams.[52] But it still proved insufficient. In April, Udny Hay informed Clinton, "Though I have tried every possible method which I could devise, since the new Law for Impressing Teams, they have all proved Ineffectual." As Hay noted, he had "attended in the Strictest manner to the Law of the State . . . but all in vain." While he had "wrote the justices" and "beged their advice and assistance in the most humble manner," the JPs had "in an unpardonable degree, Neglected their Duty."[53]

So once again, the act went back to the legislature's "Anvil" for further amendment. In the course of trying to improve the act, the legislature and governor actively solicited advice on how best to alter it, and many officials—including McDougall and Hay—took advantage of this opportunity, channeling their frustrations into a successful campaign for further amendment. In October 1779, it paid off: The amended act placed additional constraints on the discretionary powers of the JPs regarding pay and wages, increased the fines from ten to twenty-five pounds, and bumped up the rewards for JPs and constables.[54]

When these still proved ineffective, Hay urged the legislature to draft a more "coercive Plan," readily providing pages of proposals for further amending the act.[55] And once again, the legislature responded with additional amendments, coming in February and June 1780. These amendments further centralized power, authorizing the "First Judge" in each county to issue a blanket impress warrant, thereby cutting obstinate JPs out of the process, while simultaneously increasing fines for those who still refused to follow the law and offering greater rewards for those who did.[56] By 1780, the law, imposing serious consequences for delinquents, looked quite different from when it was first conceived.

Creating stricter statutes was an important step in curtailing local discretionary power, but just as important was communicating those changes to local officials, and that meant significantly altering and expanding administrative and institutional mechanisms to communicate policies, strictly enforce fines and rewards, and remove from office those who failed to conform. To do so, the legislature—drastically expanded from its colonial predecessor—organized itself into working committees to facilitate specialization regarding the creation of central policy. Those committees were responsible for establishing and maintaining communication with local officials, as well as acting as the top of a tiered system of oversight that ran from the legislature to the counties and then down to each neighborhood.[57]

To assist in this process, New York's revolutionary state relied heavily on written documents.[58] Print copies of the state's laws helped convey state authority into every locality; their absence, conversely, could lead to confusion and undermine central authority. Highlighting the importance of providing local officials with copies of the laws, in December 1778, McDougall complained to one of the state printers, John Holt, "of the great Inconveniency of delaying the publication of the Laws of this State."[59] After explaining that the delay was "occasioned . . . by the Tardiness of the [Legislature's] Secretary and Clerks" in providing him drafts of the laws, Holt promised to send along copies of the requested statutes, as well as "one Paper including the Titles of all the Acts passed" for future reference.[60] Over the course of the war, Holt and Samuel Loudon printed the statutes as individual pamphlets and in "Setts" to provide to officers like McDougall and Hay, and to the legislature. These, in turn, were distributed by the legislature's committees, usually with circular letters that provided additional guidance to every single judge and JP in the state, with even more copies shared with lower-level officials.[61]

For broader reach, the legislature ordered Holt and Loudon to publish the statutes, or excerpts of them, in their newspapers.[62] This served to reiterate the specifics within the laws, but it also identified officers whom the state had authorized to act on its behalf. For example, in the April 12, 1779, issue of *The New-York Journal*, the first column on the front page detailed the "Pay and Wages to be allowed for Teams, Carriages, Horses and Drivers, impressed within this State . . . pursuant to a Law of the State," while also identifying the "first Judge" in each county authorized to sign an impress warrant.[63] By blanketing the space of public discourse with pamphlets and newspapers, the legislature added an additional backstop to rein in wayward magistrates and property-owning householders on whom this system relied.

As the legislature pursued more widespread dissemination of statutes, the executive branch also threw its weight behind establishing a vigorous government. Throughout the conflict, Governor Clinton personally involved himself in the state's effort to enforce the legislature's statutes, repeatedly using the magnitude of his position to convince local officials to comply. Clinton regularly sent out circular letters to the JPs encouraging them to enforce compliance with the statutes, and he also went into the countryside and arranged personal meetings with the JPs. In May 1779, for instance, Hay wrote to Nathanael Greene of how he had failed to procure the necessary "number of Waggoners" to transport supplies in Dutchess County. Already burdened with drafts for the militia, the justices had refused Hay's request to draft more men to serve as teamsters. Governor Clinton found an immediate solution and promptly intervened. Using his powers as commander in chief, he suspended conscription for men identified as teamsters. Immediately after, the Governor arranged for "two meetings of the justices . . . at both which he gave his attendance." Following the meetings, the justices agreed to impress the teams requested by Hay, thereby securing the army its transportation and ensuring local compliance with state laws.[64]

By 1780, these efforts had had a notable impact. Describing the state's revamped network of officials in action in a series of letters, Hay detailed how he had established a system of express riders that connected him "with the Justices of the peace, the Commissarys and the Forage masters."[65] Upon receiving word from a commissary that flour was ready at a mill or storehouse, Hay explained that "an express [rider] must be immediately sent to the nearest Justice to request he will order out sleighs for its immediate transportation." Having learned his lesson in earlier quarrels with the JPs, Hay noted that he was "allmost constantly informing them of our situation, returning their thanks for past favours, and earnestly soliciting a continuance of their wonted Zeal."[66] Hay also stated that he had reached out beyond the justices, regularly writing circular letters "to the Inhabitants in General" as well as "some of the other principal civil officers of the State . . . requesting their influence" in acquiring supplies.[67]

This new system, of course, did not solve the unsolvable wartime problem of eighteenth-century supply and transportation.[68] Scarcity of provisions still persisted, and New Yorkers remained reluctant to part with their property. Yet this should not obscure the significant change that occurred with the relation between local officials and centralized state authority. Commenting on this change in a letter in March 1780, Hay wrote that although he was "totally destitute of public Forage," the justices of the peace had come through for him. It was his belief that affairs were improving, due "in no small degree on the Harmony that subsists betwixt the inhabitants of this State (particularly the Justices of the Peace) and myself."[69]

New York's experience of revolution demonstrates how waging a war to secure independence pushed the state to consolidate power and challenge local authority and autonomy long resistant to centralized directives, while simultaneously expanding the state's capacity to develop and implement policies to solve complex, urgent problems. That war helped create a "vigorous government," however, is not unique to the case of New York, or to the American Revolution: War has often led to an expansion of state power. But what would the end of war bring regarding that power? A long view of the American experience, Gary Gerstle observes, has shown "an equal determination to scale those forces back after conflagrations ended."[70] Would that similarly be the case with New York's revolutionary state?

That state power might be dismantled after the conclusion of the revolution was certainly a possibility. Stirred by revolutionary ideology holding "that sovereignty no longer came from the top down," as Laura F. Edwards writes, many of the states relinquished emergency wartime powers, locating matters of public governance locally. Below the Chesapeake, according to Edwards, "Revolutionary-era constitutions decentralized the institutional structures of government," and from the 1780s into the 1840s, deeply entrenched localism triumphed over uniform legal doctrine "articulated by professionally trained lawyers in written texts."[71]

But that is not what happened in New York at war's end, at least not in the sense of reversing or stopping the state's regulatory and developmental legislation and its reach across the state.[72] As the new nation pondered what would happen next, the response in New York and its Northern neighbors differed starkly from that in the South, setting the regions on a diverging trajectory regarding state activity in the postwar years and antebellum period.[73] In the North, developmental states emerged that harnessed private interests in the name of public good to encourage industry, economy, and internal improvement, resulting in expansive government undertakings—New York's construction of the Erie Canal chief among them.[74]

Binding this system together was an impressive regulatory apparatus established during the revolution. While still based on local offices, this body, in the aftermath of Shay's Rebellion in neighboring Massachusetts, was restructured through a series of statute laws that tightened control over local offices, creating a more orderly system of governance that had greater penetration into the countryside. Then, in 1788, the state abolished the chaotic jurisdictional mosaic of towns, precincts, districts, and so on, instead dividing the state into sixteen counties (with more to follow), each with neatly organized towns reminiscent of New England's arrangement. Shortly thereafter, further statutes required that each town have a resident JP (this was increased to four by the end of the century) and instructed the JPs to "preside" at town meetings and to regulate the actions of all other local officials, doling out fines for those who failed to comply.[75]

These statutes proved highly effective at creating conformity, as was apparent in the deeply controversial 1792 gubernatorial election. Since the revolution, elections had been closely regulated, with statewide canvassers readily tossing out ballots when local officials failed to follow standardized procedures.[76] In the contested election of 1792, according to Alfred F. Young, the central issue "of the dispute was simply whether the officials of three counties had observed the letter of the law in returning the election ballots to the secretary of state at New York City."[77] Per the 1787 election statute, the state "spelled out in great detail the procedures for taking and reporting ballots," with specific requirements for how to fold the paper tickets, what type of lockbox should be used, how to bind the box following the election, and the manner in which the ballots were to be presented to the Senate for counting.[78] In 1792, local officials in three counties failed to follow those directions, and so the state canvassers "by a vote of seven to four rejected the ballots from all three counties,"[79] securing George Clinton the governorship for his sixth term.

Even though Clinton's Federalist opponents "breathed fire," according to Young, they accepted the election results.[80] This was possible in part because John Jay's defeat in 1792 and his subsequent victory in 1795 occurred amid routine rather than crisis politics. That was made possible primarily by the state's ability to establish stable civil institutions through the framework of a "vigorous government." While local officials were never completely under the thumb of central control, New York became a state that strove to be, as the Council of Revision put it, "governed by the laws alone, and not by the discretion of the magistrates," a state many soon likened to an empire.[81]

CHAPTER 2

"Fix It Up, in Open View"

The Declaration of Independence in Wartime New York

Emily Sneff

On July 4, 1776, John Holt printed a warning to his customers. It was only after "much difficulty," he wrote, that he had been "able to publish any paper" that week. Readers of *The New-York Journal; or, the General Advertiser* would have to make do with a single sheet of news. Holt's workforce had been depleted—"all his hands having been taken on public service"—and he had to hope that his customers would excuse "all omissions and defects" in his newspaper.[1] It was a tense time in New York City. British ships were gathering in the harbor and the Continental army was preparing for an attack.[2] Increasing numbers of people were evacuating Manhattan—a task that would have required Holt to either break down and transport his printing press or leave it behind in his Water Street office and risk the British forces seizing it. Holt must have worried that the truncated July 4 issue of *The New-York Journal* might be his last. But then came "the most important event that ever happened to the American Colonies, an event which will doubtless be celebrated through a long succession of future ages": the Declaration of Independence.[3]

John Holt celebrated the news of independence in his *New-York Journal* on July 11, 1776. When his readers opened their newspaper—restored to four pages—they would have seen the Declaration of Independence filling an entire page, surrounded by a border of ornamental type. They also would have seen another note from Holt: "*The Declaration of the United States of America, is inserted in this paper, in the present form to oblige a number of our Customers, who intend to separate it from the rest of the paper, and fix it up, in open view, in their Houses, as a mark of their approbation of the* INDEPENDENT SPIRIT *of their Representatives.*"[4] In the very next issue of *The New-York Journal*, on July 18, Holt told his customers that it was "impossible to carry on his Business." Once again, he portended the end of his newspaper, for want of "Provisions, Candles, and many other Necessaries, and especially of Money."[5] In these three issues of *The New-York Journal*—on July 4, 11, and 18, 1776—John Holt printed three messages, each set off with brackets or a manicule, or pointed hand, to catch the reader's eye. Holt's suggestion that readers could split their newspaper in two and post the Declaration of Independence in their houses with pride was sandwiched between his concerns that he might never furnish his readers with another issue.

This chapter examines the Declaration of Independence in wartime New York, the decisions that political officials made, and John Holt's role in disseminating the news. In the summer of 1776, the Declaration was printed in every active newspaper in the United States, but Holt's *New-York Journal* stands out. Most printers included the Declaration in the regular columns of their newspapers. In some papers, the Declaration was front-page news, and in others, it could be found in the interior pages. A handful of printers, including Holt, formatted the Declaration on a single page, using wider columns or ornamental type borders to give the text more prominence. But Holt was unique in directing his readers to do something with his newspaper. He was the only printer who encouraged his customers to separate out the Declaration from the rest of the issue and "*fix it up, in open view, in their Houses.*" Holt's location makes this directive all the more remarkable. His predictions that the July issues of *The New-York Journal* might be his last were premature, but only slightly.[6] Within weeks, Holt, his competitors, and many of his customers had to flee from the advancing British forces. New York City became a Loyalist stronghold—a place where it was almost as if the Declaration of Independence had never been published.[7]

When the Continental Congress declared independence from Great Britain, there were four active newspapers in New York City: Hugh Gaine's *New-York Gazette* on Mondays, John Anderson's semiweekly *Constitutional Gazette* on Wednesdays and Saturdays, and John Holt's *New-York Journal* and Samuel Loudon's *New-York Packet* on Thursdays.[8] Anderson's and Loudon's newspapers were new on the scene—in print for less than a year before the Declaration of Independence—while Gaine's and Holt's were long established. The British royal coat of arms adorned the top of Holt's newspaper until June 1774, when he opted for a design made famous two decades earlier by Benjamin Franklin: a snake, in multiple pieces, with the rallying cry "UNITE OR DIE," modified from Franklin's "JOIN, or DIE."[9] Holt was the first newspaper printer in the colonies to make such a change, and he went a step further in December 1774 with a custom masthead ornament. In the center of a circling snake—bearing the motto "United Now Alive and Free, And Thus Supported, Ever Bless Our Land, Firm On This Basis Liberty Shall Stand, Till Time Becomes Eternity"—there was a pole, resting on the Magna Carta, supported by outstretched arms, and topped with a liberty cap.[10] *The New-York Journal* developed a reputation as the "receptacle of every inflammatory piece that is published throughout the continent," as one critic put it. One of Holt's supporters retorted, "Let patriotic be a substitute for inflammatory."[11]

John Holt filled his weekly newspaper with essays and articles on the escalating conflict with the British government and its impact on New York. In almost every issue of *The New-York Journal* in the first half of 1776, Holt apologized to his readers and correspondents for omitting certain articles and advertisements for want of room. He occasionally added his own perspective on the latest news. In May, John Dunlap's Philadelphia newspaper confirmed rumors that tens of thousands of German soldiers would be joining the British side of the war. Dunlap, referencing the king's promise to send commissioners to reconcile with the colonists, added a note to his readers: "*Oh* GEORGE! *Are these thy commissioners of peace and reconciliation?*"[12] Holt, in his newspaper, added, "*However, we fear them not—Their treachery, is all we have to fear.*"[13]

Later that month, Holt reported that the Continental Congress passed a resolution recommending that each of the colonies "adopt such government as shall, in the opinion of the Representatives of the people, best conduce to the happiness and safety of their constituents in particular, and America in general."[14] The New York Provincial Congress responded by calling for an election, whereby the colony's electors could authorize representatives "to take into consideration, the necessity and propriety of instituting such new Government" and, if agreed on, "to institute and establish such a government as they shall deem best calculated to secure the rights, liberties and happiness of the good people of this colony."[15] Each county's election needed to be held in time for deputies to report to New York City by Monday, July 8.

Holt printed a letter from "Columbus" to the electors of the city and county of New York, stressing that the election of representatives to form a new government was "a matter of the highest importance to our future happiness and prosperity, as well as to the rights and liberties of the United Colonies in general." To any readers who worried that taking such a step would be, in effect, a declaration of independence, Columbus answered that "if the measure be necessary to preserve us from a thousand evils that are ready to break in upon us, without it, it ought instantly to be adopted, though the enemies of our land should stigmatize it with a name which they, and they only, think a term of reproach."[16] The election in New York was a measure to ensure the consent of the governed, at a time when popular opinion was shifting and British forces were rapidly approaching New York Harbor.

Meanwhile, in Philadelphia, the Continental Congress was working on a different schedule. The Virginia delegation to the congress had received new instructions from Williamsburg that empowered the colony's representatives to propose three new documents: a declaration of independence from Great Britain, a plan of confederation among the thirteen colonies, and a plan for treaties with foreign powers, especially in Europe. On June 7, Richard Henry Lee put forward three resolutions to this effect. The first resolution articulated "that these United Colonies are, and of right ought to be, free and independent States, that they are absolved from all allegiance to the British Crown, and that all political connection between them and the State of Great Britain is, and ought to be, totally dissolved."[17] The next day, the New York delegates who were in Philadelphia—William Floyd, Francis Lewis, Robert R. Livingston, and Henry Wisner—sent an anxious letter to the New York Provincial Congress by express rider. They expected that, "very shortly," Congress would debate "the question of independance."[18] The only instructions they had dated from April 1775, shortly after the first shots of the war were fired at the Battles of Lexington and Concord. The New York delegates in Congress were supposed to vote "for the preservation and re-establishment of American rights and priviledges, and for the restoration of harmony between Great Britain and the Colonies."[19] They were not sure if they could—or should—vote for independence.

The consent of the governed was at the core of the New York delegates' concern, and when the New York Provincial Congress responded a few days later, they agreed. The "good people of this Colony," they stated, had not, "in the opinion of this Congress, authorized this Congress, or the Delegates of this Colony, in the Continental Congress, to declare this Colony to be and continue independent of the Crown of Great Britain." Now the electors could give "their sentiments relative the great question of independency" by choosing representatives who supported the measure. The Provincial Congress told the delegates in Philadelphia that the people of New York would be consulted at "the earliest opportunity."[20] But in the meantime, the delegates in Philadelphia were left in the lurch.

The Continental Congress decided to postpone the debate on independence until Monday, July 1, and during this three-week deferral, the situation in New York City changed dramatically, as recorded in the pages of John Holt's newspaper. The expectation of British ships caused a flurry of activity to support the Continental army. Holt printed a recruitment notice for the "aged Friends of the American Cause"—men over the age of fifty, which included Holt himself—to bear arms "in defence of the lives, liberties and fortunes" of generations of New Yorkers to come.[21] *The New-York Journal* was filled with advertisements showing the transient and martial quality that the city was taking on, including a plea for axes, spades, and shovels needed to build fortifications.[22]

Then the New York Provincial Congress learned about a plot, meant to sabotage the Continental army and timed to coincide with the arrival of the British forces. The conspiracy involved the destruction of both the powder magazines and the bridges that connected Manhattan to the rest of New York, as well as the assassination of General George Washington and his officers. On June 21, the Provincial Congress issued a warrant for the arrest of the mayor of New York, David Mathews, on charges of "dangerous Designs and treasonable Conspiracies."[23] A detachment of Continental army soldiers surrounded Mathews's home in Flatbush, Brooklyn, at one o'clock in the morning and took the mayor into custody. Mathews claimed that the lead conspirator was William Tryon, the royal governor of New York, who was living on the HMS *Duchess of Gordon* in the harbor. But it was Thomas Hickey, one of Washington's life guards, who paid the highest price for his participation in this plot. On June 28, a crowd of twenty thousand people gathered to see Hickey hanged for treason.[24] The day before, John Holt told his readers that "a most wicked, unnatural and treasonable conspiracy against the lives of multitudes, and the liberties of all the inhabitants of the American Colonies" had been foiled. He did not have the full story yet, but he promised that "as soon as a particular account can be collected, it will be inserted."[25] But there was no space for the plot in his next issue, on July 4, as it was shortened to just two pages.

Two of New York's delegates to the Continental Congress, John Jay and Philip Livingston, were also members of the New York Provincial Congress, and that was where they were in June 1776. Both men were assigned to a committee to investigate the conspiracy against the Continental army. But at the end of June, the Provincial Congress granted Livingston's repeated requests to go to Philadelphia.[26] He arrived after the Continental Congress resumed the debate about independence on July 1.[27] While Livingston traveled to Philadelphia, Jay made a quick trip to Elizabethtown, New Jersey, and the Provincial Congress made a significant move without him. A British invasion seemed imminent, and the Provincial Congress worried that the "tumult and confusion incident upon such attack" would make it difficult for them to continue their work in New York City and would put their records at risk.[28] They decided to relocate both the congress and the planned constitutional convention to White Plains, in Westchester County.

John Jay worried that the New York Provincial Congress's decision to relocate, combined with Philip Livingston's decision to go to Philadelphia, would cut short the investigation of the conspiracy and create more opportunities for mischief by New Yorkers who remained loyal to the king. Jay wrote to his colleague in Philadelphia, Robert R. Livingston, about his "great mortification" upon returning to New York on July 1 and learning about the Provincial Congress's "precipitate ill advised Retreat."[29] After sending this letter to Philadelphia, Jay received an urgent message from Edward Rutledge, one of South Carolina's delegates to the Continental Congress. It was Rutledge who had pushed to postpone the debate on independence until July 1. He sent two pleading letters to Jay—one on June 8, the other on June 29—trying to convince him to come to Philadelphia.[30] Rutledge did not think it was the right time for the colonies to declare independence from Great Britain, and he believed that Jay agreed with him. "I know full well that your Presence must be useful at New York," Rutledge wrote, "but I am sincerely convinced that it will be absolutely necessary in this City."[31] Unfortunately for Rutledge, his letters found Jay "engaged by plots, conspiracies, and chimeras dire." Jay regretted that "Governor Tryon and the devil" had kept him from attending the Continental Congress at this critical moment.[32]

On July 1, when the Continental Congress resumed the debate over whether to declare independence, the New York delegates in Philadelphia prepared to abstain from the decision. Francis Lightfoot Lee wrote a letter to his brother, Richard Henry Lee, who had returned to Virginia to participate in their home colony's constitutional convention. Lee told his brother that a preliminary head count had shown that ten colonies would support independence. Two colonies—South Carolina and Pennsylvania—still dissented. "N. York did not vote," Lee explained, "not being empower'd." But Lee was hopeful that the new convention in New York would "do the business" of declaring support for independence.[33] By the morning of July 2, twelve of the thirteen colonies were in agreement. And although public support for independence seemed to be on the rise in New York—especially after the revelations about the conspiracy against George Washington and the Continental army—the newly elected constitutional convention was not set to meet until the following week.

The New York delegates wrote in desperation to the Provincial Congress on the morning of July 2. "The important Question of Indepen[den]cy was agitated yesterday," they explained, "and this Day will be finally determined." They had the Provincial Congress's directions from earlier in June. But they anticipated that "new doubts and difficulties" would arise if every colony except New York voted for independence. "What Part are we to act after this Event takes Place," they asked, if "every Act we join in may then be considered as in some Measure acceding to the Vote of Independency, and binding our Colony on that Score." The delegates worried that the "immediate safety" of their colony would be at risk, at the worst possible time, if they could not vote freely for measures that would support the war effort. They asked the Provincial Congress to send their "earliest Advice and Instructions" on how to participate in Congress without violating their constituents' consent.[34] Later that day, Henry Wisner wrote a short note to cover his colleagues' letter. "Since Writeing the enclosed," Wisner explained, "the question of independance has Been put in Congress, and carried in the affirmative without one dissenting vote."[35] New York abstained.

The New York delegation did not receive any word from their home colony-turned-state before the next critical vote, to approve the Declaration of Independence, on July 4. They abstained once again, even though Robert R. Livingston had been part of the committee that drafted the Declaration. The rest of the Continental Congress seemed hopeful that, when the elected representatives to the constitutional convention met in White Plains the following week, they would approve the Declaration. Massachusetts delegate Elbridge Gerry wrote that, "most probably," New York would "join in the measure, and then it will be entitled the unanimous declaration of the thirteen United States of America."[36] Gerry's Massachusetts colleague Robert Treat Paine was not as confident. He wrote that the Declaration was "voted by twelve colonies, agreeable to the sense of the constituents, and New-York was silent, til their new convention (which sits next week) express their assent, of which we have some doubt."[37] Even before the news of independence reached New York City, people there were aware that their delegates in Philadelphia were in a lonely minority. In *The New-York Journal* on July 4, John Holt noted that New York was likely to be the last of the thirteen colonies to declare support for independence. This prediction was crammed into the same columns as a report that British ships were descending on New York Harbor like a "swarm of Locusts, escaped from the bottomless pit," as in the book of Revelation in the Bible, as well as Holt's admission that his two-page newspaper had been extremely challenging to produce because his laborers were pitching in to defend the city.[38]

On July 4, after the Continental Congress—minus New York—approved the Declaration of Independence, they sent a manuscript copy of the text to John Dunlap, whose printing office was a few blocks from the Pennsylvania State House, now known as Independence Hall. Dunlap produced broadsides of the Declaration, poster-sized sheets with the text formatted in a single wide column under the title, "IN CONGRESS, JULY 4, 1776. A DECLARATION BY THE REPRESENTATIVES OF THE UNITED STATES OF AMERICA, IN GENERAL CONGRESS ASSEMBLED." When these broadsides came off Dunlap's press, the Declaration of Independence was still not unanimous.

John Hancock, the president of the Continental Congress, set to work sending out John Dunlap's broadsides of the Declaration of Independence to each of the United States, as well as the divisions of the Continental army. On July 6, he enclosed a Dunlap broadside in a letter to the New York Convention. Hancock wrote that "although it is not possible to foresee the Consequences of Human Actions," the Continental Congress had determined that it was "necessary to dissolve all Connection between Great Britain & the American Colonies, and to declare them free and independent States." Hancock directed state officials to proclaim the Declaration "in the Way you shall think most proper" and "in such a Manner, that the People may be universally informed of it."[39]

The New York Convention was therefore faced with two immediate, interconnected decisions that took priority over their mandate to establish a new government: They needed to determine whether to support the Continental Congress's decision to declare independence and, if so, how to share the news with the people of New York. On Tuesday, July 9, in White Plains, the convention reached a quorum. As soon as the representatives presented their credentials, they turned to the question of independence. They had received a copy of the Declaration from the New York delegates in Philadelphia and listened as the text was read aloud. Later that afternoon, they resolved "that the reasons assigned by the Continental Congress for declaring the United Colonies Free and Independent States, are cogent and conclusive." It was "cruel necessity" that had rendered independence "unavoidable." Still, "we approve the same," the representatives agreed, "and will, at the risk of our lives and fortunes, join with the other Colonies in supporting it."[40] The vote was unanimous, and accordingly, so was the Declaration of Independence.

The representatives to the New York Convention decided that there should be public readings of the Declaration throughout the state, beginning at their meeting place, the Westchester County courthouse in White Plains, on Thursday, July 11.[41] They resolved that five hundred copies of the Declaration should be printed, and that these broadsides should include the convention's resolution in support of independence and their instructions for publishing the Declaration. The convention also wrote a lengthy letter to the Continental Congress, announcing their decision, and another shorter letter to John Hancock after it received his July 6 letter enclosing another copy of the Declaration.[42] When the news of the New York Convention's support of independence reached Philadelphia on July 15, one delegate, John Alsop, was shocked. "As long as a door was left open for a reconciliation with Great Britain," Alsop wrote, he was "willing and ready" to serve New York in Congress. But the convention had "closed the door of reconciliation" with their approval of the Declaration. "I must beg leave to resign my seat," Alsop stated.[43] He left Congress before he received a response from the convention and, apparently, without telling his colleagues he had resigned.[44] The convention's representatives were "surprised to learn" that independence—a "measure which they conceived necessary" to strengthen the United States—"should disgust any gentleman."[45] They "cheerfully" accepted Alsop's resignation.[46] The worries over New York's abstention quickly faded in the face of unanimity.

The representatives in the New York Convention in White Plains were the first people in the state to hear the Declaration of Independence, on the morning of July 9.[47] Later that day, in Manhattan, the Continental army listened as the Declaration was read aloud by order of General George Washington. That evening, a crowd of people—perhaps soldiers, perhaps civilians—tore down the gilded equestrian statue of King George III that had sat on Bowling Green since 1770.[48] Most of the lead from the statue was carted off to be melted down and cast into bullets that could be fired back at the British forces. Since the end of June, the number of British ships gathering in New York Harbor had grown exponentially, and an even larger fleet of reinforcements and hired German soldiers was still to come. New York's belated support for independence was not widely reported in newspapers, but these other events—the reading of the Declaration to the Continental army, the destruction of the king's statue, and the increasing British presence in the harbor—were described in detail, alongside the Declaration of Independence and accounts of other public readings. The newspaper printers in New York, and especially John Holt, played a significant part in the dissemination of this information.

John Holt's delight at the news of independence emanated from the pages of his *New-York Journal*, making his newspaper stand out from those of his competitors. John Anderson was the first printer to feature the Declaration of Independence; it appeared on the first two pages of his octavo-sized newspaper on Wednesday, July 10.[49] Holt and Samuel Loudon printed the Declaration in their newspapers the next day, and Hugh Gaine included the Declaration in his July 15 issue.[50] In his celebration, Holt got a few details wrong. He said that the "first instant," July 1, was the "auspicious day" when the "Representatives of the Thirteen United Colonies, by the providence of God, unanimously agreed to, and voted a Proclamation declaring the said colonies FREE AND INDEPENDENT STATES," glossing over the fact that New York's delegates had abstained from the vote. Holt expected that the day would "doubtless be celebrated through a long succession of future ages, by anniversary commemorations, and be considered as a grand Æra in the history of the American States"[51]—which has proven true for the Fourth, rather than the First, of July.

John Holt then provided his customers with a thorough—and decidedly biased—account of what had happened in Manhattan on July 9. First he explained that the Declaration of Independence was read at the head of each brigade of the Continental army and was "received with loud huzzas, and the utmost demonstrations of joy." Then he described the destruction of the statue of the king that evening: "The equestrian statue of George III. which Tory pride and folly raised in the year 1770, was, by the Sons of Freedom, laid prostrate in the dirt, the just desert of an *ungrateful Tyrant*!" Holt reported that the lead from the statue would be turned into bullets, "to assimilate with the brain of our infatuated adversaries." He quoted a gentleman who witnessed the destruction and, thinking back on the beginning of the king's reign and John Milton's epic poem, *Paradise Lost*, "exclaimed in the language of the Angel to Lucifer, '*If thou be'st he; but ah! how fallen? how chang'd*?'"[52] Holt also scoffed at the members of the British Parliament who had thought that taxing the colonists would work in their favor. He believed that, to "gain a peppercorn," Great Britain "lost an Empire." His account was reprinted in other newspapers—including in London.[53]

Below his vivid description of the destruction of the king's statue, Holt included his instructions to his customers to separate out the Declaration of Independence on the opposite page and "*fix it up*."[54] The back of the page with the Declaration was filled with advertisements as well as Holt's typical "Poet's Corner" at the top of the left column. The poem he selected for this issue began with a call for public patriotism:

> FREEMEN, if you paint for glory,
> if you sigh to live in story,
> if you burn with patriot zeal;
> Seize this bright auspicious hour,
> Chase those venal tools of power,
> Who subvert the public weal.

The first line of the refrain was a timely "Huzza! Huzza! Huzza!"—the same words that echoed from the crowds that listened as the Declaration of Independence was read aloud. But nearby on the page, there was a reminder that the term "freemen" was understood to be exclusive. Holt advertised a reward of ten dollars for the recovery of Jack, a thirty-five-year-old enslaved man who had self-emancipated. His enslaver, Jacob Wilkins, described Jack as a "square well built fellow" who had been born in Guinea and spoke "broken English." The advertisement suggested that Jack might be "sculking in the country, or among the troops." He had supplied himself with an extensive wardrobe and absconded with his enslaver's gun and a broadsword, determined to fight for his own freedom.[55]

After John Holt printed the Declaration of Independence in his newspaper, he used the typesetting for another purpose: a broadside. Hugh Gaine also printed a broadside of the Declaration of Independence, and evidence suggests that Samuel Loudon did, as well.[56] But it was Holt who fulfilled the New York Convention's order for five hundred broadsides.[57] This was a significant undertaking, given that just one week earlier, Holt had advised his customers that his laborers had abandoned him and he could barely manage to print a single sheet of news. Holt's wife, Elizabeth, almost surely assisted in the process of printing *The New-York Journal* and the broadsides for the New York Convention.[58] Holt likely brought in any apprentices or journeymen that he could, given the circumstances of the war. But he was also efficient with his printing process. He adapted the typesetting from the newspaper, moving the title into the center of the page and doubling up the border of ornamental type. And, most importantly, he included the convention's resolutions, dated July 9 in White Plains. He emphasized the representatives' unanimous decision to concur with the "Reasons assigned by the CONTINENTAL CONGRESS, for declaring the United Colonies FREE AND INDEPENDENT STATES." Holt's extract from the convention's minutes included the printed signature of Robert Benson, one of the convention's secretaries. Assuming that Holt printed the full number of five hundred copies requested by the New York Convention, only 1 percent of the broadsides that came off his press in mid-July 1776 survive today.[59]

In both his broadside and his newspaper, Holt made decisions that were unique among the printers of the Declaration of Independence in the summer of 1776. He chose to place the New York convention's resolutions, explaining the representatives' support for independence and their plans for spreading the news, at the top of his broadside, above the Declaration. When officials in Rhode Island and Massachusetts ordered batches of broadsides to be sent out across their respective states, the printers that fulfilled those orders put the relevant resolutions at the bottom of their broadsides, below the Declaration.[60] As for newspapers, Holt was not the only printer who chose to format the Declaration on a single page. On July 16, in Exeter, New Hampshire, Robert Luist Fowle printed an extraordinary, single-sheet issue of his *New Hampshire Gazette* with the Declaration of Independence.[61] He had some space at the bottom of the third column of text and included an advertisement of things for sale in his printing office, including copies of *Common Sense* and writing paper and quills, but otherwise, the

Declaration filled the page. A few days later in nearby Portsmouth, New Hampshire, Benjamin Dearborn organized the Declaration in three skinny columns under a wide, bold title on the last page of his newspaper, *The Freeman's Journal.*[62] But neither of these printers gave any suggestion to their readers that their newspapers should be treated like broadsides and posted up.

Unfortunately, there is very little evidence of how people used John Holt's newspaper printing of the Declaration of Independence. The note in his July 11 issue indicates that he designed his newspaper to "oblige" a number of customers who wanted, essentially, a broadside of the Declaration for the price of their regular newspaper. He appealed to people who wanted to celebrate the "*INDEPENDENT SPIRIT*" of New York's representatives. But he did not specify which representatives: the delegates in the Continental Congress who had abstained from voting for the Declaration of Independence in obedience to their instructions, or the men who had been elected to form a new government for New York and made it their first matter of business to support the Continental Congress's decision. From the scant number of surviving copies of *The New-York Journal*, it is difficult to tell how many of his customers actually posted the Declaration. There are no notes scribbled in the margins of the page or remnants of adhesive on the back of the page to serve as testimony of what people did with John Holt's newspaper in July 1776.

Meanwhile, Holt's broadsides were delivered to the New York convention and sent out to different towns in New York and used for public readings. If his broadsides were ready before July 18, then perhaps one was used for the public reading at city hall in New York. Holt described this reading in his newspaper a week later. A crowd of "true Friends to the Rights and Liberties of America" attended the reading and "signified their approbation by loud acclamations." Then the wooden coat of arms was taken down from the courthouse, "torn to pieces and burnt," and the painted portrait of King George III was removed from the council chamber and similarly broken apart and burned. Another coat of arms, in stone, "was thrown to the ground and broke to pieces." Through all this destruction, "the people testified their approbation by repeated huzzas."[63] From Holt's description, it is hard to know how many people gathered for this public reading and destruction of the king's symbols. Three weeks earlier, an estimated twenty thousand had attended the public hanging of Thomas Hickey. But because people left the city in droves and the ones who stayed behind prepared for a British invasion, it is difficult to imagine tens of thousands of people turning out for a public reading of the Declaration in mid-July. The rhetoric of the essays and articles that appeared in Holt's newspaper in these critical weeks in the summer of 1776 reflect fears that the "true Friends" of the United States were threatened by their neighbors who still supported reconciliation with Great Britain and would seize the opportunity to support the approaching British forces.

Everywhere the Declaration of Independence was printed in 1776, it was part of a context specific to that moment and place, and this was especially true in New York. The last colony to express support for independence was also the first to see a major battle after July 4. The columns of neatly arranged type in John Holt's newspaper and broadside belie the stresses on his printing office caused by the arrival of British ships from late June through July and into August. The New York printers who created newspapers and broadsides bearing the words of the Declaration of Independence, including Holt, fled the city just weeks later. Still, as the United States commemorates its 250th anniversary in 2026, it is worth thinking about Holt's instructions to his readers to post the Declaration of Independence "*in open view, in their Houses*"—in the face of a British invasion—"*as a mark of their approbation of the* INDEPENDENT SPIRIT *of their Representatives.*"

The Declaration of Independence was a galvanizing force in New York, despite the concurrent threats from British forces and their supporters who had planned to sabotage the Continental army. In the span of a month, the concern of the delegates in the Continental Congress and the New York Provincial Congress over whether their constituents supported independence was erased by the resolution, proudly presented at the top of Holt's broadside. The people had not voted for independence directly, but they showed their approbation through iconoclastic acts and huzzahs at public readings. And if they numbered among John Holt's customers, then perhaps they displayed their unique issue of *The New-York Journal* in their homes—that is, until they needed to evacuate.

CHAPTER 3

Raking the Ashes

The New York City Fire in Historical Memory

Benjamin L. Carp

Washington Irving wrote his satirical *History of New York* in 1809 about the seventeenth-century Dutch seaport. His pseudonymous alter ego, Diedrich Knickerbocker, suggested that cities best show their greatness when "they burst forth in some tremendous calamity—and snatch as it were, immortality from the explosion!" Irving had grown up next door to calamity: He was born in April 1783, blocks from the ruined part of New York City known as Canvas Town, a slum of brick husks topped with sailcloth. He was the youngest sibling in a family that had lived through the British occupation of Gotham. "Knickerbocker" wrote that the history of New York is "worthy of being pondered over attentively, for it is by thus raking among the ashes of departed greatness, that the sparks of knowledge are to be found, and the lamp of wisdom illuminated." As the city began a century of breathtaking growth, the ash rakers of New York's revolution had only just begun their work.[1]

Colonial New York City had been the headquarters of the British American Empire, an important center of culture and an economic powerhouse. For most of 1776, New York City was the central focus of the warring forces of the American Revolution. After several months of occupation by George Washington's army, Lower Manhattan was occupied by British troops on September 15; six days later, on

September 21, several saboteurs set fire to the city but left surprisingly few traces. The wind diverted the fire to the west, but one-fifth of the buildings were left completely in ruins, including Trinity Church, the Lutheran Church, and the customs house. Thousands of people lost their homes. The scar of Canvas Town remained on the downtown landscape for years after the war. Once New Yorkers rebuilt, they characterized the fire as a shocking but minimally important prelude to the city's eventual rise. As a matter of history, they treated the Great Fire as a trivial curiosity and then forgot it entirely. The event is still largely unknown to the general public, yet it deserves greater attention. The Great Fire ought to destabilize traditional understandings of the city's past and remind us of the disruptions wrought by people from all walks of life. By more closely examining the chaos and conflict that characterized New York City's revolutionary history, we can revise more traditional narratives of the American Revolution that tend to exclude New York's story.[2]

Setting fire to New York City is not as edifying a story as the signing of the Declaration of Independence; instead it was one of the events of the American Revolution that "don't fit neatly into the prevailing narrative of the rise and progress of liberal freedom," as Vincent Brown writes. Yet the Great Fire of 1776 may well have been the radical act of disempowered dissidents—ordinary soldiers (including a mixed-race man), their field officers, and civilians, including at least one woman. Dozens of British and Loyalist eyewitnesses, and even some rebels at a distance, all agreed that rebels set the fire deliberately. Witnesses saw the fire break out in several places at once, discovered incendiary materials throughout the city, and caught (and killed) a few saboteurs in the act. Yet the British Army launched half-hearted inquiries in 1776 and 1783 that yielded little in the way of results, so the evidence about the origins of the Great Fire remained in dispute.[3]

Confronted with allegations that the fire was deliberate, Americans in the army, the press, and Congress deflected them with a disinformation campaign. The founding generation, as well as subsequent historians, largely followed their lead, arguing that the Great New York Fire of 1776 was caused either by an accident or by apolitical miscreants. New York historians, while acknowledging the physical impact of the fire, nonetheless contributed to the campaign of muddling the fire's origins, diminishing its significance, and keeping it out of the public memory. As Alfred F. Young argues, "The American Revolution was not a plebeian revolution, but there was a powerful plebeian current within it." Like the Boston Tea Party, the fire may well have been a destructive expression of popular protest that later generations of "patrician historians" needed to sanitize, to use Clifton Hood's term.[4]

This chapter argues that for more than 150 years after 1776, patriotic and patrician historians of New York underestimated the historical significance of the story of the Great New York Fire of 1776 with silence, minimization, and redirection. By the middle of the twentieth century, historians generally decided that the evidence was insufficient to make bolder claims. Some historical writers dissented from the argument that the fire had no political meaning, but their voices were largely overwhelmed by a more patriot-friendly story. History writers collectively concluded that Americans were not guilty of radical wartime misdeeds, a conclusion that protected the reputation of the nation and the city. By looking at how generations of historians shaped the public memory of the fire, we can begin to appreciate how much more there is still to learn about New York's revolutionary history and the different strains and currents within it.

New York struggled to develop its local history, but the city's growth eventually spurred its leaders to take an interest in crafting a local past that would serve its future. Until the middle of the twentieth century, Hood writes, "social and economic elites" mostly produced "patrician histories" of the city, and they were reluctant to cheapen the city's reputation. By the late nineteenth century, these patrician historians had conjured a nostalgic colonial past and "turned this fictive Old New York into a haven that affirmed elites' identity and their role as guardians of American heritage." Such accounts made little mention of social and political upheaval or "other unpleasant events," because they wanted to connect to a romanticized past that preceded modern infrastructure, recent immigration, and social contestation. Hood concludes, "Because the rise of New York was a source of anxiety as well as of pride, historians tried to make urban development seem less threatening by maintaining that New York City had changed slowly, steadily, peacefully." The Great Fire of 1776—a calamitous rupture—came into this narrative only because it had destroyed Old New York so that the modern city could spring up in its place. Patrician writers wanted nothing to do with a history of revolutionary New York that showed its social, political, and violent struggles.[5]

When focusing on the Revolutionary War itself, New York historians were forced to make their arguments from a place of insecurity. Many rural Americans looked askance at the nation's seaport cities, regarding them as hotbeds of Toryism, British occupation, vice, crowd actions, and concentrations of mercantile wealth and foreign influence: Thomas Jefferson famously referred to "the mobs of great cities" as "sores" on the body politic. Boston and Philadelphia could, however, each make robust claims to patriotic participation in the revolution. New York City, by contrast, had an image problem. During the war, greater New York City saw more retreats than victories. Occupied by the British Army from 1776 to 1783, Manhattan fit poorly into a patriotic national story. New Englanders criticized the city's residents for their dilatory patriotism and emphasized the presence of Loyalists in New York; their critiques infused later history writing, which was also heavily influenced by New England writers. New York's complex history of ethnic diversity and factional politics did not lend itself easily to what Michael Hattem calls the "simplistic good-versus-evil narratives" of the nineteenth century.[6]

Yet New York City and its environs boast a fascinating story of calamity, civil war, skullduggery, espionage, treason, Black liberation, and sabotage during the American Revolution. It was a region where violence and property destruction were endemic and political allegiances were contingent. Prior to the middle of the twentieth century, a few studies did pay sustained attention to the British occupation.[7] Only since the late 1990s, however, have scholars sufficiently emphasized New York's stories of disaffection, suffering, captivity, privation, and destruction.[8] As these more complex interpretations emerge, and as public historians wrestle with ways to share those stories with a larger audience, it is worth reexamining how earlier generations of writers shaped the history of revolutionary New York. The Great Fire created problems for local historians because it exposed some uncomfortable truths about the American Revolution, but the ambiguity of its origins also allowed these writers to preserve the reputation of the city and the Patriot cause.

In 1776, Loyalists and the British in New York reported that the rebels had deliberately started the fire (figure 3.1). Within days, the Americans in rebellion began working to suppress this story. They had made much of British destruction of American towns, and they hoped to protect the reputation of their army. The Continental army, Congress, affiliated newspapers, and other allied correspondents therefore obfuscated the causes of the fire and propagated distortions about it. These sources intentionally cast doubt on Loyalists' accounts. By the time national histories of the American Revolution and biographers of Washington looked at the archival record, it was filled with motivated

FIGURE 3.1. The European engraver who made this image used British newspaper accounts to tell the story. Franz Xaver Habermann, *Representation du feu terrible a Nouvelle Yorck*, [1778?], Eno Collection of New York City Views, Miriam and Ira D. Wallach Division of Art, Prints, and Photographs, New York Public Library.

writings that exonerated Americans—particularly their commander in chief—of wrongdoing. Some of these accounts went beyond disclaiming any knowledge of the fire or writing it off as an accident; a few well-placed sources introduced arrant falsehoods. Newspapers, for instance, suggested that the British themselves had done the job, while John Sloss Hobart, a member of the New York Provincial Congress, wrote that British soldiers, "having been promised the plunder of the town in case of conquest, . . . have set fire to the town." To deflect blame for the fire, Hobart reported, General William Howe's soldiers threw suspected incendiaries into the flames (which was partly true) or slit their throats (which was not true at all). It served the cause of independence to propagate atrocity narratives about the British for the purposes of mobilizing public opinion, and the British helped these narratives by burning several North American towns throughout the war.[9]

Once the British evacuated in 1783, New Yorkers regarded the fire as part of their general accounting of the British occupation. The Reverend John Rodgers, leader of New York City's First Presbyterian Church, preached a thanksgiving sermon on December 11. He castigated the British for "wantonly burning our towns," including the destruction of more than fifty church buildings throughout the United States. Though he stopped short of accusing the British of "*designedly*" burning lower Manhattan, he concluded—"after all that malice has said to the contrary"—that "the fire was occasioned by the carelessness of their people, and they prevented its more speedy extinguishment." The word was out among returning New Yorkers who had supported the revolution: Only a person of "malice" would promote the Loyalist version of events. The Great Fire was merely an act of carelessness and neglect, patriots argued, and the British, not the Americans, had wantonly destroyed North American towns. The elite New Yorkers who supervised the memory of the American Revolution hoped to perpetuate the wartime portrayal of the Americans as more virtuous than the British in their conduct of the war.[10]

The earliest British histories of the conflict followed the lead of General Howe's report to Lord George Germain, blaming rebel "wretches" for the Great Fire of 1776, while subsequent histories pointed to George Washington himself.[11] It took a few years before Americans contributed their own histories, and once they did, they repeated the propagandistic accounts that had emanated from American partisans during the war. William Gordon wrote a national history that drew on local evidence, which was published in London in 1788 and later in New York City. Gordon had met with Washington a few weeks after the fire and then corresponded with him. Though eyewitnesses believed that Americans allied with the rebellion had set fires in several places at once, Gordon insisted that the fire had a single point of origin: "The fire broke out at a dram shop, close in with the waterside; on Whitehall slip," he wrote, maintaining that the reports of multiple outbreaks were "erroneous." A man named Griffiths, who saw the fire from Bergen, New Jersey, told Gordon that the fire was "merely accidental, and the probable consequence of the sailors having been suffered to go on shore the day before to regale and frolic." While Gordon also blamed wind, dryness, wooden building materials, the city's depopulation, and broken firefighting equipment, he particularly ensured that readers would conjure an enduring image of tippling British sailors at Whitehall Slip. In national histories like Gordon's and biographies of Washington, it made little difference whether readers believed that the fire was an accident or was set by deluded enthusiasts or miscreants, so long as it was not attributed to the Continental army. As David Van Tassel characterizes the historians of this period, "The revolution was an event to be defended and glorified, and the men who participated in it must needs be seen as heroes." To characterize the people who burned New York as drunks or "wretches" robbed them of intent and safely separated them from the heroic narrative of the revolution.[12]

Early writers about New York City tried to focus on the growing seaport and the contributions it might make to the new nation's success. The Duke de la Rouchefoucault-Liancourt, who traveled to the United States in the 1790s, spoke with local residents to add a flavor of history to his observations. After talking with New Yorkers, he learned, "the best part of the town . . . was, as the Americans say, burnt by the English, and, according to the English, by the Americans"; regardless, by 1795, "this quarter of the city has been rebuilt since the peace, and is now one of the handsomest parts in it." In 1807, United States Senator Samuel Latham Mitchill wrote only that the area around Bear Market "had been consumed by fire, while it was in possession of the enemy." These early writers had little to say about the fire, perhaps deciding that it was better left forgotten.[13] By contrast, communities around New York City had no trouble acknowledging fires that the British had set: They wrote elegies, held inquiries, made restitution to sufferers, and challenged politicians on their responses to British depredations.[14]

Fifty years after 1776, when most eyewitnesses to the American Revolution had died, the desire to commemorate the revolutionary generation gained new urgency. David Grim, a German-born Loyalist tavern keeper who integrated into federal New York City as a wealthy merchant, died in 1826. His remembrance of the Great Fire, like Gordon's history, suggested that the blaze had a single point of origin at a wooden house on Whitehall Slip, "then occupied by women of ill fame," and that the flames then spread via the wind. Grim also drew a map showing the burned section of the city as a contiguous area (figure 3.2). He stated that the fire had claimed 493 houses, all "inferior houses to the present." His strangely precise figure was lower than most contemporary estimates, which—along with his denigration of eighteenth-century house construction—served to minimize the fire's effect. Grim asserted that British troops arrested "several decent citizens" but then released most of them; he made the redcoats sound quick to judge these prisoners without proof. Grim was not offering the history of violent incendiarism that his Loyalist contemporaries witnessed. Instead, as a city father, he told a story that separated "decent citizens" from the vicious and "inferior."[15]

FIGURE 3.2. Martha Lamb incorporated David Grim's account and reproduced his manuscript map for her three-volume history. "Map of Great Fire 1776," in Martha J. Lamb, *History of the City of New York: Its Origin, Rise and Progress*, vol. 2 (New York, 1880), 136, Picture Collection, Miriam and Ira D. Wallach Division of Art, Prints and Photographs, New York Public Library.

The banker-historian John Fanning Watson of Philadelphia discovered Grim's reminiscences in manuscript during a visit to New York in 1828, and he published them in 1830. The fire of 1776, he wrote, "excited a fear at the time, that the 'American Rebels' had purposed to oust them, by their own sacrifices, like another Moscow. It is however believed to have occurred solely from accident." Abram Brower, a resident, told Watson a secondhand story that wood shavings in a board yard on Whitehall Slip had first kindled the flames.[16] Through paraphrase and reprintings, the tale of "Old David Grim" appeared in at least twenty historical works over the course of the nineteenth century.[17]

Although the revolutionary generation was passing on, historians had now cemented Gordon's interpretation and Grim's account into their assessment of the Great Fire. As historians repeated the patriotic version of events, the accumulated weight of those repetitions became so massive that it became difficult for later scholars to avoid their gravitational pull. Gotham swelled to more than a million people by the end of the nineteenth century, and audiences took an increasing interest in crafting a local past that would serve the city's future. Subsequent generations of historians, taking their cues from previous primary and secondary sources, replicated the patriots' strategies for shaping local memory of the fire: They either exaggerated British misdeeds in order to overshadow the destructive act the Americans had committed, or they minimized the damage so as to rob the Great Fire of any historical significance.

During the nineteenth century, local historians revived a discussion of British atrocities during the fire, either by emphasizing British misdeeds or by inventing them. They described aggressive British officers beating New Yorkers with their swords and thereby hampering firefighting efforts, or noted the "helpless patriots" whom the soldiers had killed on the spot. Writers drew attention to the "women of ill fame" at the "low groggery and brothel" or "place of revelry and debauchery" where the fire supposedly started. Some said the fire was caused by the British soldiers' wives—"careless gypsies" and "half drunken beings"—having left pine boards sticking out of a fireplace. These historians argued that there was no proof that Americans had set the fire, and they stressed that British wartime behavior was comparatively worse.[18]

Among another strain of patrician historians, the fire's insignificance dovetailed with boosterism about the city's growth. John Pintard had helped establish the New-York Historical Society in 1804. Echoing Gordon and Grim, he argued in 1826 that the fire was, "undoubtedly, accidental," caused by "drunken sailors" at Whitehall Slip. Perhaps participating in what the scholar Michel-Rolph Trouillot calls "formulas of banalization," Pintard also dismissed the fire's damage; indeed, he lamented that the fire had not burned all of Lower Manhattan so that surveyors could replace it with a geometric grid. Like Rouchefoucault, he focused on the city's beauteous progress.[19] In 1827, James Hardie gave much the same account as William Gordon's but added another marker of the city's progress: "They had not then a FIRE DEPARTMENT so well organized as we have, at present."[20] In the wake of another devastating "Great Fire" in 1835, the *New York Sun* also minimized the 1776 fire, arguing that the thousand homes lost "were mostly of little value . . . and the whole loss was estimated at less than one million of dollars."[21] The fire itself was not as important as the buildings that replaced the ruins and the systems that New Yorkers had developed to combat destructive fires.

By the mid-nineteenth century, historians could consult dozens of newly available sources about the Great Fire in published collections. In a sketch of Trinity Church, the Reverend William Berrian printed contemporary accounts by the Anglican ministers Charles Inglis (a direct eyewitness to the fire) and Robert Auchmuty, both of whom also attested to the abuse that Loyalists suffered at the hands of rebellious New Yorkers. The Irish emigrant Edmund Bailey O'Callaghan, after supporting the Lower Canada Rebellion (Guerre des Patriotes) and fleeing to the United States, became a New York state archivist and printed Inglis's letter to London as well as Governor William Tryon's letters to Lord George Germain. Peter Force, the printer and archivist, included Edmund Burke's speech about a female incendiary, General William Howe's report, a letter by the Loyalist exile Samuel Curwen, and numerous items from British and United States newspapers, as well as important correspondence by George Washington and congressional committees. After the Civil War, David Thomas Valentine's *Manual of the Corporation of the City of New York* published many of these items together in a piece titled "The Great Fires in New York City in 1776 and 1778," with important statements from the two sides of the conflict and from local, national, and British historians. The full battery of British accusations was now available for researchers in the United States; William Gordon and David Grim no longer stood alone.[22]

Even after looking at the newly available evidence, most historians were still unwilling to characterize the Great Fire as part of the city's radical and insurrectionary past. Early national historians had cautiously argued only that the accusations against Washington were unfounded, while other writers were unsure, but mid-century historians such as Benson J. Lossing, George Bancroft, and others insisted that the fire was an accident.[23] Clifton Hood found the histories by Mary L. Booth and Martha J. Lamb to be "exceptional" for their willingness to address the Negro Plot of 1741 or the city's ethnic and racial diversity more generally, yet these writers echoed the patricians when it came to the Great Fire of 1776. After receiving encouragement and manuscript materials from local historians and archivists, Booth argued forcefully in 1859, "Several of the citizens were also arrested and imprisoned on the charge of being accessories to the deed, but the accusations were not sustained, and they were afterward acquitted of the charge. No evidence exists, indeed, to prove that the origin of this fire was anything else than purely accidental, or that the suspicions of the British officers had any foundation." Booth implied the existence of a formal trial and acquittals, for which evidence is scant, and dismissed the accounts of British eyewitnesses.[24] Two decades later, Martha J. Lamb wrote that although the fire "was generally attributed to incendiaries," the arrests "elicited no proofs of guilt," and she concluded with evidence from Grim and Brower.[25] Well into the nineteenth century, historians clung strongly to the patrician notion of American innocence with regard to the Great Fire. They hoped to keep revolutionary New York in the patriotic fold—to tell a story in which the authority was obeyed, order was maintained, and property was preserved.

Other historians were cautiously intrigued by the idea of a deliberate fire, though few committed such ideas to print before 1870. In part this was because historians rarely incorporated a Loyalist perspective. As Eileen Ka-May Cheng writes of the revolution's generation of historians, "Writing at a time when national bonds were still tenuous, it was necessary to portray the Revolution as a unanimous uprising against tyranny." Nevertheless, a travel memoir published in 1834 did echo the Loyalists' views. George Rapelje was born on Crown (Liberty) Street in August 1771. His father was Rem Rapelje, and his mother's brother was Theophilus Hardenbrook; during an anti-Loyalist crowd action on June 12, 1776, local supporters of the rebellion had subjected both men to extreme physical torture by riding them on rails through the town. George Rapelje wrote that one of his rebellious relatives warned his mother (Eleanor, called Nelly) to flee the city, saying, "I assure you it is the intention of General Washington to fire the city, if it falls into the hands of the British army." According to Rapelje, the plan was common knowledge among the rebels. Afterward, however, the British examined suspects and "no satisfactory account of the conflagration could be given." Nevertheless, "the general opinion was, that the fire originated from design." Rapelje's memoir stands out as a published Loyalist perspective on the Great Fire, but it was not a history of the revolution, and no historians of the city's revolutionary history have ever cited it.[26]

Americans finally gave more of a hearing to the Loyalists in the late nineteenth century. The attorney Edward Floyd DeLancey published Judge Thomas Jones's *History of New York During the Revolutionary War* in 1879, many decades after the original author's death in 1792. Jones had married Anne DeLancey (sister to Edward's grandfather), served as a justice in colonial New York's Supreme Court, and became a Loyalist exile. In his manuscript, which he wrote in the 1780s, Jones shared none of David Grim's evident desire to make amends and integrate by telling a patriot-friendly tale of the Great Fire. Instead he accused the New York Provincial Convention of authorizing Continental troops "to burn the city of New York" if necessary. He agreed with other Loyalists that the rebels had burned the city on September 21, 1776. Like Rapelje, he explained why no perpetrators were ever named: "In the hurry, no affidavits could be taken or even memorandums made" of the captured incendiaries, so "no specified charge could be laid against any one in particular." Jones noted the irony of the Americans' complaints about British incendiarism—"Who burnt a fourth part of the city of New York . . . ? The Americans"—and asserted that they had done the same at Norfolk, Long Island, White Plains, Hoboken, Weehawken, and Quebec. In the end, he maintained, "the burning of towns in times of war, in all civilized nations, is a usual practice," hardly worth Americans' furious, one-sided condemnations of the British for their inhumanity.[27]

By the time Jones's words were published, New Yorkers had also begun to seriously consider the Loyalists' charge against the Americans. William Leete Stone Jr. was a Brown graduate with training in Germany, whose father was also a historian. Stone wrote in 1872, "It would seem . . . as if the firing of the city—though given up by Washington and [General Nathanael] Greene—was still cherished by some of the residents of the city." He drew from Grim's account but also mentioned multiple outbreaks, captured incendiaries, and combustible materials, as mentioned in British and Loyalist accounts. "For ourselves, we are inclined to believe that the fire was the result of deliberate design," he argued, without "much room left for doubt." Stone noted the contradictory nature of the primary sources and the fact that "it was found impossible to obtain legal proof sufficient to fasten the act upon any particular individual." In the aftermath of the Civil War, new attitudes about wartime destruction had probably inspired a fresh look at the Great Fire. As Clifton Hood writes, a new "memory culture" had emerged, "emphasizing destructive warfare" and "a messianic belief in devastation as necessary for redemption." This new perspective still may not have endorsed arson as one of the "weapons of the weak" used by radicals, but it at least had more sangfroid about the possibility.[28]

William Henry Shelton was a Civil War artillery lieutenant from Ontario County, New York, who later became a printmaker and illustrator. As curator of the Morris-Jumel Mansion in Upper Manhattan, where Washington lived in September 1776, Shelton believed that Americans—particularly New Englanders—had conspired to burn

New York. As he wrote in 1916, "Plans for wreaking vengeance on the invaders had gone so far among the troops that Washington was powerless to stem the current." On the eve of the fire, Washington "was not uninformed of the determination in certain quarters to burn the city." The consequent fire was the "unofficial and unsuccessful, but intensely patriotic attempt of a few young officers of the Continental army," including (he mistakenly believed) Nathan Hale, who were willing to "die in the attempt." Shelton was intrigued by the reports of British officers and Loyalists that appeared in London newspapers; he also noted hints in the writings of Tench Tilghman (Washington's aide-de-camp) and General Gold Selleck Silliman. Regardless, "a curtain of silence fell over the disaster, that was never broken during Washington's life." Shelton believed that "there has long been a persistent purpose among the writers on Nathan Hale to suppress any documents that might in any way connect him with the great fire." Hale's role, he insisted, had been obscured by "a half-century of silence and another half-century of pious fables." Shelton was wrong about Hale, but he nonetheless highlighted important primary sources that blamed New England saboteurs.[29]

New controversies over the revolution emerged during the Progressive Era. A few years after Shelton published his book, a group of isolationists and nationalists initiated a controversy over New York City school textbooks. Even to omit Hale's name from the books, they argued, was unpatriotic. The Hale that conservatives wanted, of course, was not Shelton's incendiary but an innocent, Yale-educated schoolteacher with a famous valediction about patriotic self-sacrifice. The public memory they sought could not have incorporated the social profile of the saboteurs who burned New York, who probably included a tavern keeper, a woman, and several rank-and-file soldiers, one of whom was mixed-race. Nor would they have tolerated any suggestion that Washington's officers had ordered the burning of New York. Perhaps in response to the Hale controversy, in a 1926 article in the *New York Times*, Shelton made clear that Washington would have disapproved of his men setting fire to New York. Still, in 1929, he reiterated, "The story of Americans participating in the burning of New York has been suppressed in all American histories from that day to this."[30]

As David Van Tassel writes, "The long age of the amateur historian had ended" by 1884, yet patrician historians of the early twentieth century were still eager to minimize the burning of New York City. They worked hand in hand with the preservationists who, as

Randall Mason writes, "were 'imagineering' a consensus history of the city" that was "narrow, paternalistic, largely authoritarian, and rigorously 'on message'"; they fostered "norms of patriotism and respect for powerful institutions and people while admitting few dissenting narratives." And so, despite the "wreck left by fire," wrote Rufus Rockwell Wilson, the New Yorkers of the 1780s "faced the future with stout hearts." Henry Collins Brown, founder of the Museum of the City of New York, also wrote in 1917 about Canvas Town: the "dumps" and "shanties" that "were erected temporarily in lower Broadway" after the Great Fire, which "gave the noble thoroughfare a decidedly poverty stricken appearance." He mocked the grocers and artisans who lived on lower Broadway in 1785 as "squatters," "nondescripts and hucksters," compared with illustrious families such as the Livingstons, Varicks, and Gracies, who replaced them by 1793. The fire, if anything, had been a blessing, because it made way for progress and improvement (figure 3.3). The message was clear: Old New York had to die so that new New York could be born.[31]

As Great Britain and the United States became close allies in the twentieth century, New York City celebrated its last official Evacuation Day in 1916. New Yorkers from older families now had more disdain toward newly arrived immigrants than they had toward any Loyalist ancestors they might have previously suppressed. Because of the Anglo-American alliance, the civil war aspects of New York's war years still fit poorly in the national narrative, if for different reasons. Noting that the city had preserved less of its colonial landscape than Boston or Philadelphia, New Yorkers rushed to erect monuments, nail plaques to walls, and restore historic houses. The revolution now had a few local places to express public history, yet revolution-era New York City remained underappreciated.[32]

After the Great Fire's 150th anniversary, historians of New York City had another resource available: the fifth volume of I. N. Phelps Stokes's *The Iconography of Manhattan Island.* As Max Page writes, Stokes was simultaneously responsible for preserving knowledge of "Old New York" as a collector and destroying the city's landscape as a developer. In addition to numerous sources from past compilations, Stokes's volume reprinted several witness testimonies—most of them by Britons and Loyalists—from a 1783 commission ordered by the British general Guy Carleton to investigate the fire. A Canadian historian had donated these testimonies to the New-York Historical Society in 1890. In 1931, Oscar T. Barck Jr. was one of the first scholars to refer to these records,

FIGURE 3.3. Henry Collins Brown's description of St. Paul's Chapel was reverent. In an accompanying image he shows it dwarfed by the Woolworth Building, and in his description of that building he assured readers that they would never forget ascending to its tower balcony. "St. Paul's Church and Park Row—Woolworth Building on left, Municipal Building on right, in distance," in Henry Collins Brown, *New York of To-day* (Old Colony Press, 1917), 147.

which lean decisively toward the theory that the Americans deliberately burned New York. Yet Barck shared none of the collection's details with readers, or any quotations, and he came away unimpressed: "The investigation proved nothing since it was held too long after the fire. . . . No decision was reached, but it was generally agreed that the city had not been fired through any official American order." He concluded, "Discounting highly-colored rumors, it would seem that the inception of the fire was accidental," adding, "The significance of the fire was not, therefore, political or military."[33] Thomas Jefferson Wertenbaker also thought that "the evidence of incendiarism laid before this committee is unconvincing," and he concluded in 1948 that "the origin of the fire remains to this day a matter of doubt." He believed that the appointment of the Carleton Commission was itself an indication that the British were reconsidering their initial accusations. In spite of Stone's or Shelton's attempts to question the consensus, the myths and minimizations that began as American propaganda remained mostly impervious to new evidence.[34] Most scholars, even after World War II, preferred to demur, equivocate, or offer an ironic wink rather than take the British accusations of incendiarism seriously, though they did do much more to incorporate a more "plebeian current" in their treatment of New York City's revolutionary history.[35]

The semiquincentennial of United States independence is also the semiquincentennial of the military campaigns of 1776 that took place in New York, as well as that of the Great Fire. Generations of writers have dismissed the calamity as a parochial sideshow, an entertaining but unsolvable mystery, or even a propitious demolition that made way for progress. Yet future scholars ought to confront this story—and other uncomfortable parts of this history—directly, and they ought to nourish the sprouts of public memory that give New Yorkers a truer picture of their revolution. Historians now incorporate a wider range of perspectives in their writing, they no longer minimize the violence of the American Revolution, and they have made the war and its ragged edges more central to the nation's early history. We can now offer not just a more plebeian perspective but also narratives of Black and Indigenous people, women, ordinary soldiers, captives, and Loyalists. Certainly since the bicentennial, audiences have learned from such stories that the revolution did not quite live up to its stated ideals. Yet historians have not yet exhausted the possibilities of recasting the revolution as what Stephen Conway calls a "people's war" that reshaped the lives of many different actors.[36]

For 250 years, Americans have hardly given New York City's revolutionary history its due. Nor have New Yorkers done enough to understand how the country's largest city contributes to the story of the war for national independence. Historians still have more ash raking to do to reinterpret the past and dust off some of the nation's most occluded stories. The results will light the lamp of wisdom by yielding a history that is not just more inclusive, but more disruptive.

Chapter 4

Long Island Loyalties

Unveiling the Oath of Allegiance During the Revolutionary War

Christopher F. Minty and John Cording

Writing to General George Washington from Huntington, New York, on September 10, 1778, Thomas Wickes explained that William Tryon, New York's royal governor, had assured "the torys and Friends to Government" that British reinforcements numbering "at Least ten thousand" would soon arrive in New York. Wickes, however, had heard different intelligence. "Its the Oppinion of our Friends on the Island and in Newyork," he told Washington, "that they are Preparing to Leave Newyork." Wickes was not sure what to make of Tryon's statements, but he knew that Tryon was attempting to mobilize Long Islanders to the British cause. With his letter to Washington, Wickes enclosed "a Copy of the Oath that Tryon obliges the Inhabitants to take, or to Pay five Pounds and Quite the Island Imediately." The oath asked residents of Southold, New York, to swear "to bare faith and true Allegance" to King George III and "that he Will not directly or Indirectly openly or Secretly, aid, abet, councel, Shelter or Conceal, any of his Majestys Enemys, and those of his Government, or Molest or betray the Friends of Government but that he will behave himself Peaceably and Quietly, as a Faithful subject of his Majisty and his Government."[1]

Writing to the British secretary of state for the colonies, Lord George Germain, Tryon reported proudly on September 5, 1778, that the oath had been "administered to all the inhabitants on the North side of the Island."[2] Of course, Tryon's statement was not entirely accurate. Many Long Islanders had already fled by that time, many of them—some 3,500 or so—to Connecticut.[3] Still, Tryon's work had been productive. He detailed that he had given Long Islanders a choice, "either to take the Oath or remove with their families and furniture to Connecticut," and he added that "not one of the whole chose the latter, even the hotest Rebels said my proposal was generous, and took the Oath, which convinces me that the acrimony of opposition is much softened by the late concessions of Government."[4]

A major in the First Regiment of Suffolk County militia and a member of the New York General Assembly, Wickes sent a copy of that oath to George Washington. Since late August 1778, Wickes had served as a faithful purveyor of intelligence, writing to Washington on August 25 and 27 to update him on Tryon's movements and intentions.[5] But Wickes's intelligence trailed off by the time Tryon returned to Long Island in early October 1778. "Having in a second Excursion brought all the Inhabitants on the East End of Long Island, as far as Montaulk Point, under an Oath of peaceable behaviour to His Majesty's Government, (and with good humour,)," he wrote to Germain, "I acquainted Sr Henry Clinton therewith, and that I now only waited to receive his Orders to Act under his Command." Tryon was proud of his efforts on Long Island, and he sought to replace his gubernatorial appointment with "a Military one in Exchange."[6]

Tryon soon submitted a lengthy list of names from Brookhaven,[7] Southampton, East Hampton, Huntington, Smithtown, Islip, and Southold. All together, Tryon reported that 2,677 Long Islanders were administered the oath of allegiance. The oath, which matched the one that Wickes had submitted to Washington, was dated November 24, 1778, and included farmers, cordwainers, weavers, millers, tailors, shipwrights, hatters, carpenters, and more. Male members of families signed. Fathers and sons signed. (No women were administered the oath.) There were Hawkinses, Conklings, Wellses, Blidenburghs (Blydenburghs), Wheelers, and L'Hommedieus. There were men in their seventies and boys in their teens. There were also members of the Culper Spy Ring, including Phillips, Austin, and Nathaniel Roe Jr. and Selah Strong, as well as Culper associate Nathan Woodhull.[8]

The Culper ring comprised a network of spies and couriers and has come to attract greater attention from those interested in the American Revolution and the history of intelligence and espionage.[9]

The ring formed in autumn 1778 to fulfill George Washington's need to support Vice Admiral d'Estaing by relaying information to him about the movements of the British fleet around New York. Thinking d'Estaing's intelligence needs had not been met, Washington created the Culper ring. Major Benjamin Tallmadge managed the ring under the alias John Bolton. Abraham Woodhull, who was the ring's chief intelligence gatherer, used the name Samuel Culper. As the ring developed to suit Washington's needs and wants, more people were brought on board, including Robert Townsend, who used the alias Samuel Culper Jr. Prior to Washington looking toward Yorktown and beyond, the Culper ring provided Washington, then a capable spymaster, with critical intelligence on British activities in and around New York.[10]

Some members of the Culper ring—revolutionaries, or Patriots—took the oath of allegiance to George III and Britain. By most historians' definitions, that act would make them Loyalists. But considering their other activities during the Revolutionary War in the Culper ring, these men were no Loyalists. They took the oath of allegiance to ensure that they could remain on Long Island, in order to continue their Culper activities, which had just started. And they were not alone. Others on Long Island who were and have been considered revolutionaries took the oath of allegiance to Britain as well.

The behavior of these individuals offers an interesting perspective on Loyalism, voluntarism, and revolutionary activities during the American Revolution. Many historians have struggled to define "Loyalist" or to answer the question "What is a Loyalist?" In an often-cited piece, Edward Larkin concedes that "determining who was a loyalist and under what conditions can be very difficult." Indeed, he acknowledges that "most loyalists were deeply ambivalent about the Revolution," adding, "A loyalist was an American who favored reconciliation with Great Britain during conflicts that began with the Stamp Act and concluded with the War of 1812."[11] Larkin's definition is straightforward, but it does not indicate how we should understand people's feelings toward reconciliation. Stretching Larkin's definition, to be considered a Loyalist, an American would have to indicate their desire for reconciliation through actions or words. Using that framework, it would not be altogether surprising to consider people who took the oath of allegiance Loyalists. They publicly reported their desire for reconciliation and their steadfast commitment to and support of Britain's rule over the rebelling North American colonies.

Other historians have tried to answer the same question that Larkin answers, with varying degrees of success. Maya Jasanoff describes Loyalists as a group of people who had "a shared allegiance to the king and a commitment to empire," while Liam Riordan and Jerry Bannister describe them as a group that had a shared "body of thought, opinion, and self understanding."[12] But as Emma Stapely writes, "What goes unchallenged . . . is the assumption that Loyalism exists in a binary with Patriotism that is defined in opposition to an apolitical 'neutrality.'"[13]

The behavior of Patriot oath takers further complicates this narrative. These men took the oath of allegiance, and they did so not despite their revolutionary status but probably because of it. Culper members, for example, sought to maintain their cover to ensure that they continued intelligence gathering. They, along with their Patriot colleagues, also presumably sought to stay in their homes with their families. In other words, it was an effort to maintain their status quo. It was an act of survival.

There is a magnetic pull toward Manhattan for historians, whether they write about Patriots, Loyalists, or the British Army.[14] Aside from New York City, Long Island was occupied by the British for longer than any other area in the rebelling thirteen colonies turned states. Due to the often-scattered nature of extant sources related to Long Island, Long Island's significance to the war has long been underappreciated. During the occupation, the local population endured hardships, including confiscation of property, quartering of troops, and restrictive measures imposed by the British authorities. The island's economy was also affected as it became a focal point for military activity rather than trade and agriculture. Important communications often passed between Long Island and Connecticut, too, delivering key intelligence to revolutionary forces. As Charles Lee told George Washington in early 1776, Long Island was "a more capital point than ever," and he added that without Long Island, the British would "find it almost impossible to subsist." British forces appreciated its importance, too, with one observer writing that after they had retaken control of the island, he believed, "the Game is almost over."[15]

Even though it made up two-thirds of eastern Long Island, Suffolk County has received less historiographical attention than Kings or Queens Counties. Measuring ninety miles long and thirty-four miles wide, it had over six hundred miles of coastline and was home to around thirteen thousand people. The lack of research on this area is unsurprising. Its road networks were poor, its towns were not particularly prosperous, there were no newspapers, and its inhabitants did not leave behind voluminous records. Researching Suffolk County requires piecing together diverse information from multiple sources.

Examining Long Island in any degree of depth presents other challenges as well. It is a vast area, with few large, accessible repositories. Documents are available in local historical societies and libraries, but access is limited.[16] This chapter offers insight into one aspect of Long Island's history during the American Revolution. It begins with an overview of Long Island and the Revolutionary War up to the administration of the oath of allegiance in November 1778. It then introduces known members of the Culper ring and other Patriot Long Islanders before offering an assessment of how the oath of 1778 affects historians' understanding of Loyalism, voluntarism, and allegiance. Finally, we call for an increased need to judge loyalties with understanding and nuance.

Long Island During the American Revolution

Political loyalties during the Revolutionary War were partly a creation of the region's colonial and religious history (see figure 4.1). The creation of colonial Long Island was fraught with political discourse. In the early 1600s, Puritans settled there to contain Dutch colonial expansion

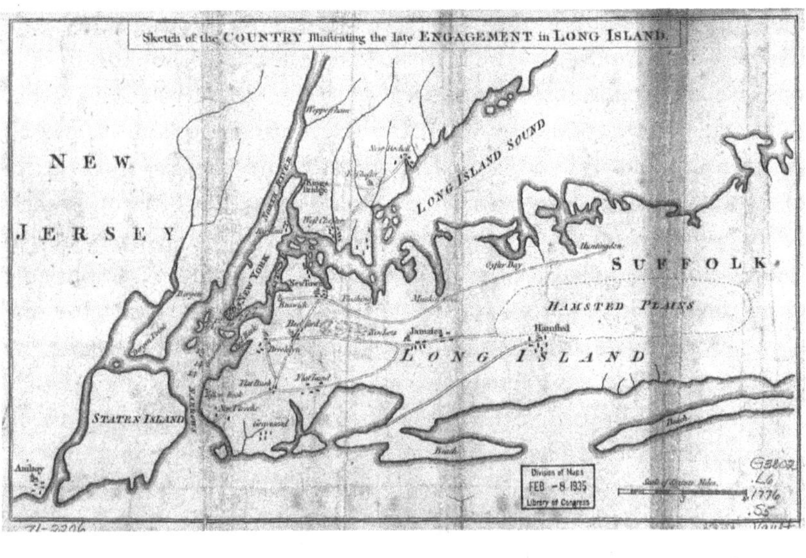

FIGURE 4.1. "Sketch of the country illustrating the late engagement in Long Island" [London, 1776], G3802.L6 1776.S5, Geography and Map Division, Library of Congress.

in Manhattan. They used their connections to New England to secure eastern Long Island, modeling their own towns off Connecticut-style villages and even submitting themselves to Connecticut's government in the mid-1600s.[17] In many ways, Long Island, especially its easternmost areas, was more like New England than like New York City, and Long Islanders formed deeper connections with Connecticut through commercial and familial ties.[18]

This strained relationship between Long Island and the rest of New York resulted in many towns creating homogeneous communities that promoted New England living, in which the Presbyterian Church was a large factor.[19] The creation of such communities, with the goal of preserving local identity in the face of outside influence, exposed behavior within Long Island communities that was both beneficial and detrimental to residents during the Revolutionary War. Long Islanders were content with the political situation of early 1770s America. Many areas of their lives were somewhat unrestricted, and they could act with considerable freedom. Put simply, there was no incentive to alter a government that had no qualms with the autonomy of Long Island residents. This, however, changed with the 1774 Coercive Acts, especially the Massachusetts Government Act, which brought that colony under parliamentary control. Many viewed the legislation as a direct threat to their homogeneity and autonomy. Just as in other areas throughout New York, and indeed the Eastern Seaboard, Long Islanders formed political committees to protest Parliament's attempted reorientation of the British Empire. They, too, opposed Parliament's measures and sought to have them reversed.[20] After the First Continental Congress, committees circulated the Continental Association, and they expected signatures from all white males ages sixteen to sixty. Committees also kept two lists: those who signed and those who did not. The Continental Association was a document that, when signed, pledged allegiance to the Continental and Provincial Congress as well as the revolutionary cause. Those in favor of the association mobilized wide-ranging, broad-based support for their cause and were fully prepared to push people out of their inward-looking, self-contained communities if they refused to sign. In Suffolk County, those who refused were ostracized, and beginning in the spring of 1776, nonassociators had their weapons confiscated by the county militia.[21]

Adherence to and support of the Continental Association was extraordinarily high in Suffolk County, higher than in other areas not only in New York but across the colonies. John G. Staudt attributes this to the area's history of "socio-economic aversion towards New York's royal government," as well as its relative "geographic isolation." Long Islanders had long been separated from outsiders, and people had generally adopted similar views. It was no different here. Roughly and only around 8 percent of the eligible population refused to sign the Continental Association. This was due in part to the Long Islanders' history of conformity: People fell in line because they and their family members had done so.[22]

Indeed, in Suffolk County, protests developed quickly into revolutionary ferment. When New York's assembly refused to appoint delegates to the Second Continental Congress, Suffolk's committees met at Riverhead and appointed five men to represent them at New York's provincial convention, which had usurped the assembly's political power. On April 20, 1775, with strong representation from Suffolk County, delegates were appointed for the upcoming congress. This political support soon turned into military support. Historically, Suffolk's farmers had not experienced a well-organized military system, but as the war developed, Long Islanders enlisted. This was in part due to British operations elsewhere in the colonies. Between the summer and fall of 1775, hundreds of heads of cattle and thousands of sheep were seized from the tip of Long Island (Gardiner's Island, Fisher's Island, Plumb Island, and Montauk Point) to support the British Army and Loyalists in and around Boston.[23] The British, believing it was their property to seize during war, mobilized Long Islanders against them. Suffolk County reorganized its two militia battalions into three militia regiments and one regiment of minutemen. The rebranded militia regiments had most of Suffolk's troops, whereas the minutemen were the county's elite fighters. By July 1775, these men were charged with protecting Long Island against the British foragers. In February 1776, over two thousand men—nearly 75 percent of the county's eligible population—had been enlisted in the local militia, and some militia units were raised in places that had never had one before.[24]

The Declaration of Independence was read publicly throughout Long Island on July 22, 1776. In Huntington, for example, crowds gathered on the village green to witness the spectacle, and as the document was read across the island, it mobilized Long Islanders. Indeed, most of the island supported the revolution, but circumstances soon changed. The British targeted New York City and Long Island, and while Long Island militias participated in the Battle of Long Island (also known as the Battle of Brooklyn), they could do little to prevent the British invasion. Between July and September 1776, over three hundred Royal Navy ships, hundreds of cannons, and over forty thousand soldiers, sailors, and marines arrived in New York. It would be the largest British military expedition until the invasion of Normandy in World War II.[25] As Lieutenant Colonel Robert Hanson Harrison told John Hancock at eight o'clock at night on August 27, the Americans were entirely "unequal to the force they had to contend with." As such, Harrison went on to say, they had "sustained a pretty considerable loss—At least many of our Men are missing."[26] On August 29, 1776, the British occupied Long Island and New York City. At Washington's war council on that date, it was "Unanimously agreed" that US forces would "Leave Long Island & Its Dependencies."[27]

The British Army recognized Long Island's significance for several reasons, the first of which was the island's strategic location. Long Island's proximity to New York City—also under British occupation—made it a vital geographic feature in controlling the region. Alongside its status as a major commercial center, Manhattan had become the center of British military operations in North America. Long Island provided a natural barrier to protect the city from attacks from the Continental army, and it allowed the British to control access to key waterways, including the East River and the Hudson (North) River. Indeed, those waterways proved crucial to the British who were moving troops and supplies. Long Island's occupation also helped the British secure Manhattan, almost acting as a buffer zone, making it difficult for the Continental army to regain the city or the area. Indeed, the British fortified key positions on Long Island, ensuring their grip on the region and protecting New York from potential attacks. With relative security, the British focused on broader campaigns without worrying about the security of their vast stronghold.

Equally important, Long Island's fertile farmland and agricultural output proved valuable to British troops. Local farms provided grains, livestock, and other provisions that supported the British Army, thereby reducing the burden of importing supplies from other colonies or Britain. In turn, controlling these supply lines disrupted the Americans' supplies, weakening the Americans in the process. Also, Long Island's geography was significant. Surrounded by the Atlantic Ocean, New York Harbor, and Long Island Sound, it was an almost ideal location for the Royal Navy to operate. The near dominance of the British at sea allowed them to use the island as a base for their ships, which could be anchored in the relatively calm waters of the sound and the harbor.

From this position, the British could block US trade routes, enforce a naval blockade, and transport troops effectively and quickly along and up the coast. Those waterways also enabled the British to conduct amphibious landings and evacuations as needed, giving them considerable mobility compared to the Continental forces.

The victory put Long Island under full occupation by the British Army. No other area throughout the colonies was put under martial law for longer than Long Island, including Manhattan, and it became a cornerstone of British strategy during the American Revolution. The island's location, naval advantages, economic resources, and loyal population, and the inability of the Continental army to defend it, made it a vital asset for the British in their efforts to suppress the rebellion. Its control allowed the British to maintain dominance in the region and provided a platform for further military actions throughout the war. Almost as soon as the British gained control of Long Island, revolutionary leaders were removed from local committees and replaced with more Loyalist-leaning citizens. As Jonathan Trumbull Sr. told George Washington from Lebanon, Connecticut, on September 5, 1776, "Since our Troops retreated from the West End of Long Island the Militia have disbanded themselves, laid down their Arms, and are making Submission to Genl How, and . . . all Ideas of Opposition *there* are at an End." Writing to Washington on September 11 from Saybrook, Connecticut, Lieutenant Colonel Henry Beekman Livingston reported on "the Malitia of Southold." He noted that about 150 had deserted, "haveing heard that long Island was given up to the Enemy." Moreover, Livingston detailed how the British were neutralizing any threats on the island, at least in theory, by administering an oath of allegiance to Long Islanders. According to Livingston, people in East Hampton and Southampton had "almost universally taken the Oath of Allegiance" to George III. Equally important, that oath had been administered by Abraham Gardiner, a member of the East Hampton Committee of Correspondence and a signer of the Suffolk County Association.[28]

On September 4, John Adams offered an equally gloomy perspective, writing to his wife, Abigail, "Our Affairs having taken a Turn at Long Island and New York, so much to our Disadvantage, I cannot see my Way clear, to return home so soon as I intended." He went on: "I hope, the Disasters at Long Island, and New York will not dispirit our People."[29] Writing on the same day to Samuel Cooper, Adams offered another bleak assessment: "Our Generals, I fear have made a Mistake in Retreating from Long Island. I fear they will retreat from the City of New York next." He added, "These are disagreable Events. I dont like these Measures. I wish there was more firmness. But let not these Things discourage. If they get Possession of New York, Long Island, and Staten Island—these are more Territory than their whole Army can defend—this Year. They must keep their Force together. The instant they divide it they are ruined."[30]

Gardiner's oath was administered to hundreds, if not thousands, of Long Islanders. On August 23, General William Howe issued a proclamation offering pardons and protections to loyal Long Islanders who had been "forced into rebellion." He also encouraged them to "take up arms for the restoration of order and good government within this Island."[31] Six days later, Brigadier General William Erskine issued a proclamation, calling on Long Islanders to surrender their firearms and provide British forces with cattle, horses, and wagons. Erskine added that if Long Islanders did not fall in line, British forces planned to "waste the property of the disobedient, as persons unworthy of his Majesty's clemency."[32]

The British enjoyed successes too. By the end of September, it was reported that "a great number of men" had signed up to fight for the British, and Long Islanders had supplied the British Army with "large quantities of Stock, throughout the Island, for their support." And by mid-October, there was chatter of "a Battalion of Tories" on Long Island.[33]

Governor William Tryon had sought to firmly reestablish and legitimize his, George III's, and Parliament's authority over Long Island's residents. Various towns in Suffolk County administered "voluntary Declarations" from those towns' respective committees. From Brookhaven (i.e., Setauket), a declaration was administered on October 23. It read, "We the Committee of the County of Suffolk, being assembled by Permission of his Excellency the Honorable William Tryon, Esq; Governor of New-York, and the Territories depending thereon in America, do hereby reject the Orders of Congresses and Committees, and totally refusing Obedience to them, revoking all our Proceedings under the Congress, and being desirous to obey the legal Authority of Government rely upon your Excellency's Clemency, hoping that you will pass by our former Conduct, and gracious pleased to protect us agreeable to the Laws of this Province."[34]

On November 24, 1778, Tryon finalized the list of Suffolk County residents who had taken the oath of allegiance.[35] The circumstances under which Long Islanders lived during the British occupation motivated their behavior. Different types of people signed the list, including those who had supported and were continuing to support the American cause. Members of the Culper spy ring, who were perhaps among the most prominent Patriots on Long Island, were among the oath takers. Not only did Culper ring member Selah Strong take the oath of allegiance, so, too, did various members of the Roe family: Nathaniel Jr., Phillips, and Austin Roe. The Roe family held particularly important roles within the Culper ring. Writing to Brigadier General Oliver DeLancey on December 21, 1780, from Flushing, Queens, Nehemiah Marks, a rambunctious Loyalist with deep family ties to Manhattan, identified members, or at least supporters or associates, of the Culper ring: Nathaniel and Phillips (Phillip; Philip) Roe. The brothers, of Drowned Meadow (now Port Washington), were "villin[s]" who had assisted Caleb Brewster in transmitting intelligence across Long Island Sound. They had separate roles and responsibilities. Nathaniel Roe Jr. provided intelligence, while his brother Phillips supported the ring through provisions and supplies.[36] Meanwhile, it was from Austin Roe's tavern that Brewster routinely traveled around sixty miles to Manhattan, carrying messages from Robert Townsend and the Culper ring to forward to George Washington.

These men were not the only Patriots who took the oath of allegiance. Long Islanders who had signed the Continental Association were among their ranks too. In Brookhaven, William Brewster, a captain in the militia, signed the Continental Association but later took the oath of allegiance. Daniel Mulford, an ensign in the militia, did the same. So, too, did Josiah Satturly (Satterley), Robert Homan, William Brewster Jr., Jonathan Jones, Justis (Justus) Overton, Benjamin Overton, Nehemiah Hulse, and others.[37] In Islip, Israel Howell, a farmer born in 1742, signed the Continental Association in May 1775. Three years later, he took the oath of allegiance. Like Howell, Islip residents Jonas Wheeler, John Mowbray (Moubray), Caleb Sexton (Saxton), Micah Wheeler, Samuel Oakley, and others signed the Continental Association but later took the oath of allegiance.[38]

This pattern—signing the Continental Association and later taking the oath of allegiance—was repeated in other areas outside Brookhaven and Islip. For example, the Continental Association was administered in Southold on June 23, 1775. John Corwin, the first name listed on the association, was born in 1738, and he was a farmer. In 1775 he would be considered a Patriot. Three years later, when he took the oath of allegiance, he would ordinarily be considered a Loyalist. With him, the following men replicated his behavior: Barnabas Wines, Thomas Wines, Jonathan Pike, Henry Pike, Micah Howell, Edmund (Edmond) Howell, Joseph Mapes, John Gardiner (Gardinier), and others.[39] In East Hampton, John Chatfield, Elias Conkling, Jeremiah Conkling, Abraham Gardiner, Abraham Mulford, Hunting (Huntling) Miller, John Stratton, Benjamin Stratton, Samuel Parsons, John Dayton, and others all signed the Continental Association but later took the oath of allegiance. John G. Staudt has reported that "the Association was signed by every man to whom it was presented." Many of these men took the oath of allegiance.[40] In Smithtown, Jedediah Mills, Epenetus Smith, Zophar Wheeler, Jacob Longbottom, John Gerrard, Selah Hubbs, Abner Smith, James L'Hommedieu, and others did the same.[41] Perhaps most significant, in Southampton, Daniel Howell, chairman of the Committee of Correspondence, reported on August 1, 1775, that "all the males in the Town of *Southampton*, from sixteen years and upwards, have signed the Association, excepting Mr *Elisha Paine* and *John Cook*."[42] Three years later, 544 men took the oath of allegiance, including John Cook (but not including Elisha Paine).[43] In Suffolk County, 91 percent signed the Continental Association. The number of those who took the oath was similar.[44]

Of the men who signed these ostensibly contradictory documents, no real patterns emerge. They were of varying ages and occupations. Some signed the documents as families, while others did not. Living under martial law, with British soldiers stationed among them or at least nearby, affected Long Islanders' everyday lives, and their actions often reflected their desire to maintain some degree of equilibrium and normalcy. For those who took the oath, doing so meant putting aside their political and, perhaps, moral convictions. They had to prioritize their way of life. And this practice was not exclusive to Long Island, either. The British administered an oath of allegiance to thousands of men in Manhattan in early 1777. Among those who took the oath were Peter Van Brugh Livingston Jr., the son of prominent New York Patriot Peter Van Brugh Livingston. Christopher Kilby Allicocke took the oath as well; he was the son of Joseph Allicocke, who had at one time led New York City's Sons of Liberty but was later targeted for his alleged Loyalist sympathies. Gerard G. Beekman, hailing from a prominent Patriot family, also took the oath of allegiance.[45]

Those who were in the Culper spy ring and adhered to this pattern are extreme examples of what Donald F. Johnson has described as "ambiguous allegiances." Those people are often held up as exemplary revolutionaries, or Patriots—people who fought against British rule through intelligence and espionage, risking their lives in the process. But neither their behavior nor that of Long Islanders was unique. This behavior was also replicated in other areas throughout the thirteen colonies, and it may not be an understatement to say that Americans' allegiances during the revolution were fluid throughout the conflict in all areas. There is, however, a key similarity between colonial Americans: Where the British Army was present, inhabitants' Loyalism emerged, one way or another.[46]

The British Army, Hessians, and Loyalist troops spread throughout Long Island, and ships from the Royal Navy patrolled Long Island Sound and the South Shore. As Patriots lost political control, the British reestablished themselves. Huntington became the base of British operations in Suffolk County until the end of the war. Oliver DeLancey's Loyalist battalion fortified the area, erecting magazines and building a gated wall as a checkpoint, and a campground formed in the town center. The British established at least six fortifications elsewhere in Suffolk County, creating the environment in which Culper spy ring members lived and operated. The forts that the British created—Fort Slongo, for example—soon became targets for their espionage.[47]

Yet the British enjoyed neither universal success nor control of Long Island. In June 1780, nearly two years after the oath of allegiance had been administered, Governor James Robertson issued a proclamation ordering Long Islanders within Suffolk County to cut down trees on the estates of two prominent revolutionaries, William Floyd and William Smith. Those who performed these services were to be compensated. As the Loyalist historian Thomas Jones reported, however, "Not a labourer turned out; not a stick of wood was cut; nor did military execution ever take place." He went on to observe that "the proclamations of Generals and Governors were become mere farces. The loyalists laughed at them, the rebels despised them, and by both they were held in contempt." Jones highlighted another way that Long Islanders protested and challenged British rule: through inaction. Their refusal to follow gubernatorial proclamations, at least for Jones, was another means by which the revolution was allowed to continue and expand. Indeed, Jones viewed the proclamations and oaths that were administered as entirely ineffective, writing, "The American rebellion was the first (I believe) in the universe attempted to be crushed, and reduced, by proclamations." Instead, Jones believed, military action should have been swift and severe: "It would have saved the lives of at least 100,000 brave men." And that action, Jones argued, should have started as soon as the British retook New York, including Long Island.[48] The British military and gubernatorial powers disagreed, viewing declarations, oaths, proclamations, and petitions as effective means to mobilize support.

Oaths of Allegiance and Loyalism

At least some British forces had seemingly eradicated revolutionary sentiment on Long Island. They had mobilized people in support of the restoration of parliamentary rule through oaths of allegiance and reorganized the island's political and military makeup. But through the Culper ring members' actions, another picture emerges: Long Islanders' public pronouncements did not always match their private sentiments. And someone's having taken an oath of allegiance does not automatically mean they were a Loyalist. And yet, for historians of Loyalism, oaths of allegiance are often significant documents. They can serve as firm, reliable evidence of an individual's politics during the American Revolution. But when members or associates of the Culper ring took the oath, their public statements of allegiance, when compared to their private activities, complicate matters considerably. These men were not and should not be seen as Loyalists.

How, then, should historians work with documents such as oaths of allegiance? It is probable that the Culper members or their associates are in the minority, but in swearing allegiance to the Crown, they maintained their secretive profile as members of an insurgent revolutionary spy network. They concealed their true loyalties to protect themselves and their families and to facilitate their intelligence-gathering activities. This act of taking the oath, while outwardly a declaration of loyalty to Britain, was in fact a calculated move to maintain secrecy and continue their covert support of the American cause.

This duality challenges the straightforward categorization of individuals as Loyalists or revolutionaries based solely on documents they signed. People who were true Loyalists often signed the Continental Association. People who were revolutionaries often took the oath of allegiance. Their actions underscore the fact that allegiance during the Revolutionary War moved along a spectrum depending on one's personal circumstances. Pragmatic choices often came before firm ideological pronouncements. For historians, this raises important questions about the reliability of such documents as indicators of true loyalty.

Allegiance during the war was often shaped by necessity, survival, and strategy. For many, swearing an oath of allegiance was a way to avoid suspicion, persecution, or even death. By taking the oath, the Culper members and their associates were able to blend into the local populace, gather intelligence, and relay information, all while maintaining the appearance of loyalty to the Crown.

This complexity, often underappreciated or unrecognized, requires historians to approach and handle documents such as oaths of allegiance and Loyalist petitions with caution. Rather than taking oaths at face value as definitive indicators of Loyalism, it is essential to consider the broader context in which they were taken. The motivations behind the oaths varied, sometimes wildly, from genuine loyalty (e.g., an Anglican minister) to reluctant compliance or even deliberate deception. The Culper ring example highlights how appearances could be manipulated for strategic purposes, revealing the limitations of relying solely on these documents to assess an individual's or a region's Loyalism.

Loyalist studies requires a deeper examination of the personal, social, and political pressures faced by individuals. Traditionally, it has relied heavily on documents such as oaths of allegiance to identify individuals who supported the Crown. But it is not that simple. Scholars who study Loyalism must adopt a more content-sensitive and -focused approach when evaluating loyalty during the Revolutionary War. Rather than viewing loyalty as a binary choice—either for the Crown or for independence—researchers must consider the fluidity of allegiance and the many factors that influenced individuals' decisions. This includes understanding the pressures, threats, and strategies that may have led someone to take an oath of allegiance to Britain, even if they did not support that cause.

The implications of this for Loyalist studies are profound, as they push the field to move away from rigid classifications and toward a more dynamic understanding of the war and the people who engaged in it. This approach, however, not only provides a more accurate picture of the complexities of loyalty during the war but also helps us to better appreciate the diverse experiences of those who lived through it. By acknowledging the limitations of documents such as oaths of allegiance and recognizing the strategic choices people had to make, scholars can develop a richer and more inclusive narrative of the revolutionary era, one that respects and understands the complexities of human behavior in times of crisis.

The same levels of caution should be used for documents such as the Continental Association or oaths of allegiance to the United States. They do not always provide a complete picture of individual motivations or true allegiance. Just as with Loyalist studies, the study of Patriotism must account for the complexities of human behavior and the fluidity of allegiance in a time of social and political upheaval. Documents that purportedly identify individuals as Loyalist or revolutionary should be considered as part of a larger, more complex tapestry of actions, decisions, and circumstances shaping those individuals' political views. The field must move beyond seeing the war in binary terms and simplistic definitions based on single or narrow documents and adopt a more holistic and context-aware approach. By doing so, scholars, genealogists, historians, and the public can better appreciate and understand the diverse and often contradictory experiences of those who lived through the Revolutionary War, providing a richer and more accurate picture of this pivotal period in US history.

Chapter 5

From Defeated People to Sovereign Nation

The American Revolution in Seneca Country, 1779–94

Elana Krischer

On July 5, 1779, Lieutenant Thomas Blake, along with the soldiers under the command of Major General John Sullivan, commemorated America's Declaration of Independence. The soldiers made a series of toasts, including "Civilization or death to all savages."[1] Blake recorded these toasts during the Sullivan-Clinton Expedition through Iroquoia, a military campaign during the American Revolution whose purpose was destroying Haudenosaunee towns, homes, agricultural fields, and orchards.[2] Iroquoia refers to the homelands of the Haudenosaunee, a confederacy of distinct but related Native nations: the Mohawk, Oneida, Onondaga, Cayuga, Seneca, and Tuscarora (see figure 5.1). Although the expedition targeted the Mohawk, Onondaga, Cayuga, and Seneca for allying with the British, this chapter will focus on the Seneca experience.[3] With the expedition, George Washington sought to suppress the movements of British-allied Haudenosaunee raiders, who, as the Declaration of Independence complained of all Native nations, were considered "merciless Indian Savages, whose known rule of warfare, is an undistinguished destruction of all ages, sexes and conditions."[4] These Haudenosaunee wreaked havoc on the edges of Iroquoia, disrupted the settler economy, and caused supply problems for the Continental army.[5] Most importantly, Washington wanted the expedition to allow Americans to claim

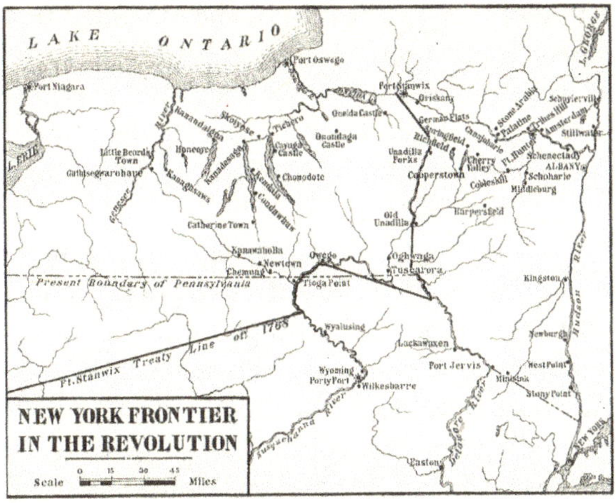

FIGURE 5.1. Map of the New York frontier during the revolution, 1912. Instructional lantern slides, ca. 1856–1939. Series A3045–78, No. 730. Department of Education, Division of Visual Instruction, New York State Archives, Albany.

Iroquoia once the war ended, thereby replacing the "savages" with American settlers.[6] While Sullivan and his forces brought destruction to Iroquoia, the expedition's goal of claiming Haudenosaunee lands for the United States through warfare was unsuccessful.[7] Although many postwar treaties included land cessions, a series of treaties signed by the Seneca and the United States in the 1780s and 1790s created legal protections that allowed the Seneca to mitigate settler expansion and protect their sovereignty.

Eleven years later, Seneca leaders Cornplanter, Half Town, and Big Tree remembered the expedition. In a speech to President Washington, they stated, "When your army entered the country of the Six Nations, we called you the town-destroyer; and to this day, when your name is heard, our women look behind them and turn pale, and our children cling close to the necks of their mothers."[8] While the Seneca remembered the expedition with fear, these Seneca leaders articulated in the same speech, as Seneca leaders would for the entirety of the nineteenth century, that Seneca land claims were legitimate and that they were a sovereign people. According to these leaders, it would not be possible for settlers to take their lands, because "all the land we have been speaking of belonged to the Six Nations, no part of it ever belonged to the king of England, and he could not give it up to you. The land we live on our fathers received from God, and they transmitted it to us for our children, and we cannot part with it."[9] The campaign resulted in significant Haudenosaunee property and agricultural damage, as well as a refugee crisis during the winter of 1779–80, but the settler narrative of Haudenosaunee erasure that developed during the expedition clashed with the Seneca narrative of their sovereignty and the reality of competing land claims on the ground.

The ways in which Native communities successfully negotiated post-revolutionary upheaval deserves greater attention because larger narratives of US history have Native people "exit the stage" at the end of the colonial era. Looking beyond the destruction and population loss of the American Revolution and focusing instead on the continuity of Seneca landholding and political power turns this narrative of erasure on its head. The American Revolution is often portrayed as a moment of permanent decline for eastern Native nations, especially the Haudenosaunee, whose postwar communities Anthony F. C. Wallace has referred to as "slums in the wilderness."[10] Older scholarship asserts that divisions within Haudenosaunee communities marked the end of the confederacy and therefore of Haudenosaunee military and diplomatic power. Histories of the Sullivan-Clinton Expedition in particular highlight the creation of politically powerless Haudenosaunee refugees and the forced circumscription of Haudenosaunee mobility. Famine and epidemics followed the campaign, which led to significant population loss.[11] But rather than the American Revolution representing the "end" of Haudenosaunee history, the motivation to acquire Native land during the war through campaigns like the Sullivan-Clinton Expedition shows that the revolution should be viewed as the beginning of US settler colonialism and western expansion. England's North American colonies were also built on settler expansion, but the American Revolution marks an acceleration of this process, as it was the first time that colonial leadership acted independently of Britain's restrictions on settler expansion. Additionally, US settler colonialism is not something that was simply imposed on Native people; rather, it required protracted negotiations in which the Haudenosaunee were vital diplomatic actors.

The end of the war changed the nature of US expansion. The failure of the expedition to result in territorial acquisition forced the United States to look for more complex ways to make claims to Iroquoia. Additionally, the Continental Congress funded the Sullivan-Clinton Expedition, but state leaders called for its execution, and state militias provided much of the manpower. The military conquest of Iroquoia, in which state and federal governments worked together, fell apart after the war. This in part created the first conflicting claims over Seneca lands in the postrevolutionary era. The conflict between state and federal interests played out through treaties with the Seneca and between settler groups in the 1780s–90s, and the outcomes of these treaties sometimes unintentionally created legal protections for the Seneca against settler encroachment and helped shape the existing Seneca narrative of continuous sovereignty.

The war put in motion events that created additional protections for Seneca territory that did not always exist for other Haudenosaunee nations.[12] The military campaign forced the Seneca to settle or resettle lands closer to the eastern shore of Lake Erie, which became marked by conflicting claims in the postwar period and provided a new legal landscape from which the Seneca protected their lands. The end of military engagement and other postwar factors, including US debt, national instability, and conflict between individual states, meant that the United States had to construct new forms of US expansion from the ground up. For the remainder of the eighteenth century, New York, the United States, and private individuals had to engage in frequent treaty negotiations and spend hundreds of thousands of dollars to extend control over only a portion of the Seneca territory that the expedition had intended to claim. The use of military force during the revolution did not move the western boundary of white settlement in New York and restructured rather than destroyed the land base from which the Seneca asserted their sovereignty throughout the nineteenth century. Rather than serving as the catalyst for the disintegration of Seneca society, the campaign marked the slow and unsteady beginning of US expansion.

The Sullivan-Clinton Expedition

Before the American Revolution, Iroquoia included most of what is now New York state and extended from north of the modern Canadian border into modern-day Pennsylvania. The Seneca, the westernmost of the Haudenosaunee nations, lived in towns along the Genesee River and around the Finger Lakes (see figure 5.2). The region was made up of rich agricultural lands, where the Haudenosaunee grew crops such as corn, beans, squash, watermelon, and cucumbers and maintained large orchards. The Haudenosaunee subsisted in part on these foods, which were grown and distributed by Haudenosaunee women.[13] By the outbreak of the American Revolution, the Haudenosaunee had experienced

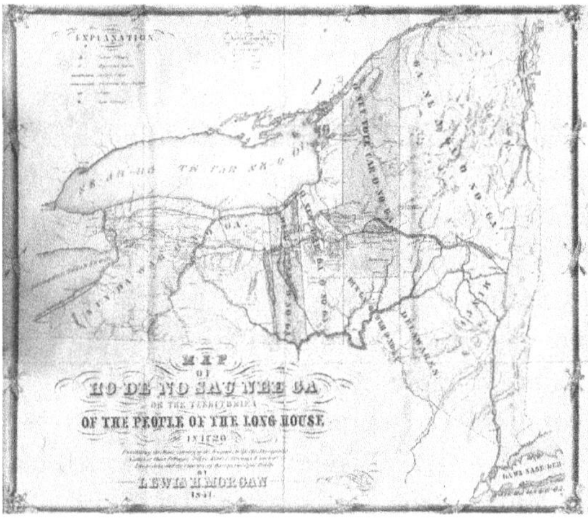

FIGURE 5.2. Depiction of Haudenosaunee territories circa 1720, created by early anthropologist Lewis Henry Morgan in the 1850s. Seneca territory is labeled "Nun-da-war-o-no-ga" from the middle of the Finger Lakes to Lake Erie. Buffalo & Erie County Public Library, Buffalo. https://nyheritage.contentdm.oclc.org/digital/collection/VHB001/id/8122/rec/1.

hundreds of years of interactions with European imperial powers but had so far resisted major Euro-American settlement or incursions into their rich territory.

Haudenosaunee resistance and British imperial policy prevented colonists and their leaders from having any real knowledge of the Haudenosaunee landscape, so "only a few Euro-American travelers and missionaries caught imperfect glimpses of this landscape as it existed prior to the Revolution," according to Chad Anderson.[14] Colonists were so unfamiliar with the terrain that before the campaign, Washington wrote to Brigadier General Lachlan McIntosh that in order to determine the feasibility of such an expedition, the army should first ascertain "whether the Country is generally level or hilly, dry or swampy."[15] The heart of Iroquoia was such a mystery to colonists that they lacked even the most basic understanding of the terrain. Major Jeremiah Fogg, while on the expedition, noted that "here the English in the course of the last war, attempted to establish a post beginning a picket fort, but were compelled to desist, as the savages declined having any civilized people get a foothold in their territories. . . . [E]very precaution has been taken to prevent a survey of the country."[16] Sullivan, in his report to John Jay, complained that maps of the territory "serve not to enlighten but to perplex."[17] Settler groups wanted to claim this land, but first they had to gain knowledge of it.

In addition to Haudenosaunee resistance in limiting settler knowledge of their territories, at the end of the Seven Years' War, Britain issued the Proclamation of 1763 in response to growing multinational Indigenous resistance west of the colonies. This proclamation prevented colonial governors from granting a "Warrant or Survey, or pass Patents for any Lands beyond the Heads or Sources of any of the Rivers which fall into the Atlantic Ocean."[18] Individuals were not to settle west of the boundary line that ran along the Appalachian Mountains, and private land purchases from Native nations and individuals were illegal.[19] Colonists wanted to expand into western lands, but territorial expansion on the scale they desired was not possible under British rule. The American Revolution, therefore, provided colonists with the first opportunity to claim Haudenosaunee lands.[20] The US campaign was the first attempt by the new nation to construct its own expansion, as the colonists rejected Britain's restrictions on settlement. The Continental army's actions, as well as its views on the Haudenosaunee and their lands, reveals much about American attitudes toward Native culture and sovereignty, and about plans for future expansion and nationhood.

New York Governor George Clinton called on Washington to carry out a campaign against the Haudenosaunee, as he found it "impossible to secure the Frontier Settlements against the Depredations of the Enemy" with New York militiamen alone.[21] British-led expeditions and raids, such as the 1778 raids near Wyoming, Pennsylvania, and Cherry Valley, New York, drove Washington to support the campaign.[22] Raiding had gone back and forth for years leading up to the expedition; however, exaggerated stories of Haudenosaunee brutality helped fuel support for a more strategic response. Once appointed to lead the expedition, Sullivan wrote to Washington that "the expedition is undertaken to destroy those Indian nations."[23] In order to ensure this outcome, the Continental army planned to invade Iroquoia using three separate routes. In the spring, Colonel Goose Van Schaick destroyed the center of Iroquoia at Onondaga. Then, throughout the summer, Colonel David Broadhead, General James Clinton, and General John Sullivan led their troops through the Allegheny, Mohawk, and Susquehanna Valleys.[24]

On May 31, 1779, Washington instructed Sullivan to carry out "the total destruction and devastation of their settlements, and capture of as many prisoners of every age and sex as possible. It will be essential to ruin their crops now in the ground & prevent their planting more. . . . [P]arties should be detached to lay waste all the settlements around . . . that the country may not be merely *overrun*, but destroyed."[25] The expedition, which Barbara Graymont describes as "warfare against vegetables," was not a sideshow to the American Revolution but one of Washington's main priorities.[26] According to Rhiannon Koehler's estimates, the Continental Congress allocated 85 percent of the government's budget to the expedition.[27] The Haudenosaunee were major players in the revolution, and the Americans recognized them as both a military threat and a threat to future expansionist goals. For Americans, it was imperative that the Haudenosaunee be removed from the war altogether.

Destroying Haudenosaunee settlements was not just a military strategy but a way to punish the British-allied Haudenosaunee and eradicate the population to make way for future white settlement. Continental soldiers targeted future Haudenosaunee food stores during harvest season, which they knew would bring destruction far beyond the end of the revolution. Sullivan noted that "there were fields of corn, the most extensive that ever I saw with great quantities of potatoes, pumpkins, squashes, and in short every other thing which any farmer could produce—the whole of which was destroyed root and branch."[28] The use of warfare to seize land was not unprecedented. Since the colonial era, Indian wars had allowed European colonial leaders to make claims to the lands of defeated Native nations.[29] With this logic, if the Americans won the war, they could take Haudenosaunee lands as compensation and through conquest, a claim that New York and national leaders later made.[30] Targeting the food supply so aggressively made this expedition different and more intentional, however. While American leaders had very limited knowledge of Iroquoia prior to the expedition, they knew that the Haudenosaunee were agriculturalists, and those western lands remained valuable to land speculators. The land speculation company associated with Washington's family was interested in lands the Haudenosaunee claimed in the Ohio River Valley. Additionally, land surveyors accompanied the expedition, and six of Sullivan's officers were also land speculators. Immediately preceding the expedition, these officers invested $10,000 each in an "association" that sought land from whichever state would end up controlling Iroquoia.[31] National expansion and public and private financial gain rested on the outcome of the expedition.

Leaders and soldiers who were a part of the campaign were acutely aware that their actions would result in starvation and displacement.

Dr. Jabez Campfield, a military surgeon on the expedition, observed, "I very heartily wish these rusticks may be reduced to reason, by the aproach of this army, without their suffering the extreems of war; there is something so cruel, in destroying the habitations of any people, (however mean they may be, being their all) that I might say the prospect hurt my feelings."[32] Washington's orders, and the observations of men on the campaign, show that Washington wanted the Haudenosaunee to become so desperate that they would have to flee to western British forts. Washington wanted the army to "chastise and intimidate the hostile nations . . . and do them every other mischief, which time and circumstances will permit."[33] To do so, Washington directed Sullivan to push "the Indians to the greatest practicable distance from their own settlements" and make "the destruction of their settlements so final and complete as to put it out of their power to derive the smallest succor from them in case they should ever attempt to return this season."[34] Washington and Sullivan did not see the Haudenosaunee merely as allies of their enemy, but as "savages" who needed punishment.

In their journals, soldiers and officers simultaneously discussed the abundance of Haudenosaunee crops and the development of Haudenosaunee towns while imagining how much more productive a future US settlement would be. Lieutenant Robert Parker wrote that he wanted to see "the opening prospects of future greatness which we may reasonably suppose is not far distant, & . . . those deserts that have so long been the habitation of beasts of prey & a safe asylum for our savage enemies, converted into fruitful fields, covered with all the richest productions of agriculture, amply rewarding the industrious husbandman by a golden harvest."[35] At the same time, many soldiers and officers were awestruck by how much Haudenosaunee-grown food they saw. Major John Burrowes wrote that "the land exceeds any that I have ever seen. [S]ome corn stalks measured eighteen feet, and a cob one foot and a half long. Beans, cucumbers, watermelons, muskmelons, cimblens are in real plenty."[36] Iroquoia was already productive in the ways Parker imagined, but because the Haudenosaunee controlled it, the development and production of that land were illegitimate.

Even when Sullivan asked his soldiers to subsist on half rations because of supply issues, the soldiers hardly noticed, because they supplemented their diets with Haudenosaunee food. Sullivan announced to his men that they would receive "half a pound of flour and half a pound of meat, and half allowance of salt per day" while they were "in this country which abounds in corn and every kind of vegetable."[37]

Soldiers knew that the expedition would not have been possible without Haudenosaunee crops. Dr. Jabez Campfield observed that "the army must have droped the prosecution of this expidition long ago had not the corn, beans, &c., which it found from place, subsisted it."[38] Despite direct observations of Haudenosaunee agricultural practices, those on the expedition perceived Native peoples as uncivilized and their land claims as trivial. Sullivan himself, in response to an Oneida man concerned about US land claims, said he believed that Congress would allow the US-allied Oneida to continue to hunt in the area as long as it "would not interfere with our settlement of the country, which I believed would soon take place."[39] The war was not over, and US leaders and soldiers could not have envisioned how western expansion would unfold. But the fact that the expedition's purpose was to negate Haudenosaunee claims to their homelands and make way for US expansion was clear to those on the expedition.

Soldiers often expressed racial assumptions and enacted racial violence against the Haudenosaunee during the campaign. Major Jeremiah Fogg wondered "whether the God of nature ever destined that so noble a part of his creation should remain uncultivated. . . . [H]ad I any influence in the councils of America, I should not think it an affront to the Divine will, to lay some effectual plan, either to civilize, or totally extirpate the race."[40] In 1779, Fogg expressed the assumptions that would animate US expansion for the rest of the nineteenth century. Americans assumed that Native lands were uncultivated despite direct observation of agricultural practices. That Native people had to become civilized or be exterminated so the United States could claim their lands for settlers who would cultivate it properly remained at the heart of settler narratives. Just as proponents of expansion believed during the era of manifest destiny, Fogg saw this plan as "Divine will."[41] Some officers on the expedition took these beliefs and enacted them on Native bodies in violent ways that were not typical of battle. Lieutenant William Barton wrote that he and a group of soldiers found "dead Indians" and "skinned two of them from their hips down for boot legs; one pair for the Major the other for myself."[42] The Sullivan-Clinton Expedition was not just a small campaign to move forward the goals of the American Revolution. It represented American feelings toward Native peoples and shows what US expansion looked like in its most extreme form.

The campaign itself resulted in few combat casualties, but the destruction of food stores forced the Haudenosaunee to suffer through the harsh winter of 1779–80 as refugees at Fort Niagara, where starvation, illness, and freezing temperatures killed more Haudenosaunee people than soldiers did during the campaign.[43] The Haudenosaunee did not remain refugees for long, and some Seneca returned to the destroyed villages near the Allegheny and Genesee Rivers, while others stayed the winter at the fort and in the spring established or reestablished settlements at Buffalo Creek, Tonawanda Creek, or Cattaraugus Creek, or under Cornplanter's leadership along the Allegheny River.[44] Buffalo Creek especially became a thriving center for the Seneca, as they quickly reestablished agricultural fields and took precautions to protect their corn stores while the war continued.[45] The Haudenosaunee did not remain dependent on the British, and while some settlements were pushed further west because of the expedition, Iroquoia still remained separate from the United States.

The end of the American Revolution meant that the United States could no longer mask its efforts to claim Haudenosaunee land through military conquest. Sullivan failed to carry out Washington's vision of the total destruction of Iroquoia and the removal of the Haudenosaunee from the war. After the 1783 Treaty of Paris ended the war, American leaders sought new ways to dispossess the Haudenosaunee. In part relying on colonial precedent, the United States and New York looked to punish the Haudenosaunee further in postwar negotiations and force large land cessions. The United States also wished to resolve conflicting land claims between individual states and establish its primacy in Indian affairs. These postwar issues, brought about in part by Sullivan's failure to seize Haudenosaunee lands, created conflicting claims to Iroquoia in ways that protected Seneca sovereignty.

Treaty Making

After 1783, the United States expanded through treaty making rather than military force, as independence and nationhood both limited the United States and provided it with new forms of dispossession. Native nations previously signed treaties with European powers, but treaty making provided the United States its first chance to construct new legal mechanisms of dispossession. Many settler groups made claims to Iroquoia and tried to assert their right to control land after the war, and in these many diplomatic encounters in the 1780s and 1790s, conflicting claims arose that marked Seneca lands with often unforeseen legal protections. The postrevolutionary negotiations show not only state and federal officials piecing together elements of US expansion, but also renewed Seneca resistance that ultimately ensured the continuity of Seneca sovereignty.

After the American Revolution ended, the United States maintained the aggressively expansionist rhetoric and actions toward Native nations that had animated the Sullivan-Clinton Expedition. The United States aimed its Confederation-era land policies especially toward Native nations that had sided with the British. The Treaty of Paris did not include Native allies, and this omission allowed the federal government and New York state to treat the Seneca as defeated peoples due to their alliance with the British.[46] At the end of the war, Philip Schuyler, a general and a New York state senator, among other titles, informed the Haudenosaunee of the United States' victory. Schuyler told the Haudenosaunee that "as we are the Conqueror . . . we claim the lands and property of all the white people as well as the Indians who have left and fought against us."[47] The Americans failed to claim Iroquoia during the Sullivan-Clinton Expedition, but they won the war and intended to use their victory to justify territorial conquest.

The Confederation government acted aggressively based on its belief that defeated Native nations would willingly cede land to the United States, and in the 1784 Treaty of Fort Stanwix, US commissioners dictated the terms of a "peace" treaty to the "Senecas, Mohawks, Onondagas, and Cayugas."[48] The terms of this treaty, and other treaties forced on Native nations during this period, were based on the assumption that the United States not only had won the war and could now make claims to enemy lands, but had inherited the right of discovery to the lands ceded by Great Britain in the Treaty of Paris, which were largely Native territories.[49]

The United States framed the land cessions at Fort Stanwix as a benevolent gesture. Washington wrote that because many Native Americans allied with Britain during the war, "so, consequently, with a less generous People than Americans they would be made to share the same fate; and be compelld to retire along with them beyond the Lakes."[50] The Committee on Indian Affairs agreed with Washington that Native Americans could not "have any reasonable objections against the establishment recommended," since they were "aggressors in the war" and must "make atonement for the enormities which they have perpetrated."[51] The US commissioners expressed that the federal government did not have to let defeated peoples remain on the territories "conquered" during the American Revolution at all.[52] The Seneca and others who sided with the British remained within the "boundaries" of the United States only because the federal government *allowed* them to. The end of the war prevented Americans from taking Seneca lands through military conquest, but the narrative of Haudenosaunee violence that fueled the Sullivan-Clinton Expedition during the war justified postwar US land claims.

The Treaty of Fort Stanwix reduced and bounded Haudenosaunee territory for no monetary compensation, but with a promise of "protection."[53] The Seneca ceded to the United States a small tract of land near the Niagara River as well as their claim to lands in the Ohio Valley.[54] Unlike previous treaties, this one delineated the lands *not* given up by the Haudenosaunee, rather than the lands transferred.[55] This shift in approach indicates that the United States believed that all land extending to the Mississippi River belonged to that nation, and that the federal government could reserve lands to Native groups if it felt so inclined. Federal officials interpreted what they inherited from Britain as broadly as possible, allowing the United States to make claims to larger territories and restrict the boundaries of Native nations.

The Treaty of Fort Stanwix signaled a continuation of US land claims that began with the Sullivan-Clinton Expedition. With this treaty, the United States intended to limit Haudenosaunee movement and political alliances with the British in Canada and other Native groups to the west. It also attempted to establish the Confederation government as supreme in Indian affairs, facilitate western expansion, and provide a means to pay back the war debt.[56] This early expression of US Indian policy inflated the power of the United States to make a real claim to the lands between the Appalachians and the Mississippi River. But the treatment of Native peoples as conquered peoples did not reflect the economic or military power of the debt-ridden and diplomatically weak postwar United States, and this aggressive strategy soon proved ineffective as Native groups grew resentful of Confederation policy.

In the same era, many of the thirteen states had to resolve the issue of western land claims. The states' actual settlement did not extend as far inland as their claims, and many states even claimed land to the Pacific coast. Massachusetts and New York both claimed Iroquoia and beyond, despite white settlement being restricted mostly to the eastern half of the modern state of New York. The claims of Massachusetts and New York stemmed from conflicting seventeenth-century colonial charters that granted the same land to two separate colonies. One land grant, from Charles I to the Massachusetts Bay Colony in 1628, included all "the maine lands from sea to sea."[57] The other, granted to the Duke of York in 1664 by Charles II, claimed much of the same.[58] To resolve this conflict, commissioners from Massachusetts and New York met in Hartford, Connecticut, in 1786. In the agreement, which became known as the Treaty of Hartford, Massachusetts granted to New York "the claim, right and title . . . to the government, sovereignty and jurisdiction of the lands."[59] In return, New York granted to Massachusetts "the right of preemption of the soil from the native Indians, and all their estate, right, title and property (the right and title of government, sovereignty and jurisdiction excepted)."[60] The agreement represented a plan for the settlement and incorporation of Iroquoia into the United States. The preemption right, or first right of purchase, meant that only Massachusetts could purchase land from the Haudenosaunee within that territory. Massachusetts could then extinguish Haudenosaunee title via treaty and sell the land or sell the preemption right. Unlike the Northwest Territory, in which states could enter the union only after meeting the requirements laid out by the 1787 Northwest Ordinance, the land between Seneca Lake and the eastern shore of Lake Erie, which was mostly Seneca territory, would immediately become a part of New York upon extinguishment of Native title. The existence of the preemption right rested on the assumption that Haudenosaunee decline and New York's expansion were inevitable.

The preemption right, in addition to being a legal mechanism of dispossession, also became a commodity, which Massachusetts sold to private individuals who later sold it to land speculation companies.[61] In these transactions, Massachusetts did not sell the land itself—only the right to purchase land from the Seneca. Unlike the resolutions of many other Confederation-era state claims to western lands, in which the federal government acquired the preemption right, this conflicting claim resulted in the creation of a right that put a critical step of Seneca dispossession in private hands.[62] Although preemption limited Native rights by preventing Native nations from choosing whom they could sell their land to and by assuming that Native title was inevitably temporary, the legal entanglement created by the preemption right to Seneca lands complicated state and federal claims to Seneca lands.[63] That the right was privately held meant that these companies and individuals often had to rely on their own resources to dispossess the Seneca. The Treaty of Hartford additionally stipulated that a representative from Massachusetts be present at any treaty involving the preemption right.[64] The preemption owner would have to convince the Seneca to meet in council and coordinate with both state and federal officials to facilitate a land sale. Private and government interests only occasionally aligned during the late eighteenth and nineteenth centuries, which frustrated coordination efforts. Purchasing land from the Seneca would require significant time, money, and chance. The Sullivan-Clinton Expedition pushed the Seneca farther west into the territory that fell entirely under this preemption right. The reorganization of Seneca settlements during the war, as destructive as that process was, changed the landscape from which the Seneca asserted their sovereignty and provided additional protections that other Haudenosaunee communities lacked in the nineteenth century.

Canandaigua

The Seneca and other Haudenosaunee nations remained resentful of the Treaty of Fort Stanwix and aggressive Confederation-era policies into the 1790s. Paired with other postwar issues for the new nation, such as war debt, Native resistance to US expansion, and the internal issue of divided sovereignty, Seneca complaints over Confederation-era land cessions made the Seneca central to the United States' diplomatic decisions. During this time, Native nations in the Northwest Territory that most ardently contested US land claims chose to stave off US expansion by forming the Northwestern Confederacy to make war against the United States, while most Haudenosaunee, who still remembered the violence of the Sullivan-Clinton Expedition, largely chose to protect their sovereignty through diplomacy.[65] Federal leaders were aware that the Haudenosaunee could easily have joined the Northwestern Confederacy and become a military threat, so the United States diplomatically engaged the Haudenosaunee throughout the early 1790s.

President Washington knew that the United States needed to make peace with the Haudenosaunee. Seneca leaders traveled to Philadelphia to explain their grievances over Fort Stanwix and other land cessions. Washington said to Seneca leaders Cornplanter, Half Town, and Big Tree "that it is my desire, and the desire of the United States, that all the miseries of the late war should be forgotten, and buried for ever."[66] Washington wanted the Seneca to know that it would not be the policy of the United States under the new Constitution to allow for such aggressive land sales, and stated "that these evils arose before the general government of the United States was established, when the separate states, and individuals under their authority, undertook to treat with the Indian tribes respecting the sale of their lands."[67] Washington then urged the Seneca leaders to prevent young Seneca men from joining the Miami, who refused to make peace with the United States. The Seneca wanted Washington to help them secure their lands, but the US needed help from the Seneca just as much.

The United States had to cater to Seneca demands, and in exchange the Seneca agreed to negotiate with the Northwestern Confederacy and maintain peaceful relations with the new United States.[68] As the war between the Northwestern Confederacy and the US progressed during the early 1790s, the Haudenosaunee gained more diplomatic leverage over the US. By 1794, the US still had not defeated the Northwestern Confederacy, and Secretary of War Henry Knox feared that the war would drag the new nation into another conflict with Britain, in part due to the proximity of remaining British forts to the conflict. He wrote to General Anthony Wayne in April 1794 that "the present state of European affairs as connected with the commerce of this country threatening to involve us in the general war require in the most forcible manner that we Should if possible make peace with the Indians in order to prevent such an undue portion of our strength and wrath from being appropriated to an object of less importance than some other which may probably occur."[69] Recognizing Seneca sovereignty and addressing the Seneca's concerns over land loss could save the United States from diplomatic and financial ruin.

To appease the Haudenosaunee and secure them as allies, the United States negotiated the Treaty of Canandaigua with the Haudenosaunee in November 1794. Seneca leader Red Jacket expressed to the Quakers in attendance at the council that he worried that another treaty would be used to deceive the Seneca. He said to US Commissioner Timothy Pickering, "You white people have increased very fast on this island, which was given to us Indians by the Great Spirit; we are now become a small people, and you are cutting off our lands, piece after piece—you are a very hard-hearted people, seeking your own advantages."[70] But the political and diplomatic situation for the United States had changed since the 1780s, so despite Red Jacket's fears, Canandaigua was a diplomatic success for the Seneca.

Canandaigua returned some of the lands lost at the 1784 Fort Stanwix Treaty, delineated the boundaries of Seneca and other Haudenosaunee lands, restated the United States' intention to be supreme in Indian affairs, and recognized Seneca sovereignty.[71] The treaty declared that "the United States acknowledge all the land within the aforementioned boundaries, to be the property of the Seneka nation; and the United States will never claim the same, nor disturb the Seneka nation, nor any of the Six Nations, or of their Indian friends residing thereon and united with them, in the free use and enjoyment thereof."[72] The Seneca immediately saw the importance of such a treaty, and the United States' promise to protect Seneca lands provided the Seneca with an outlet for their grievances in conflicts with New York state and land speculators. The recognition of their lands and sovereignty by the United States became an important tool to check US expansion.[73] As the Seneca contended with the growth of US settlement, they invoked the Treaty of Canandaigua each time a settler group argued for Seneca dispossession, and Seneca representatives later cited the treaty's terms to protect their lands in court. The Seneca saw legitimacy in their own land claims because, as Red Jacket stated during the negotiations, the land was "given to us Indians by the Great Spirit." Now the United States recognized their claim to it as well.

Fifteen years after the Sullivan-Clinton Expedition, the United States still had no real claim to most of Iroquoia and even recognized Seneca sovereignty over part of the area (see figure 5.3). The recognition of Seneca sovereignty by the United States added to the Seneca's narrative of self-determination, but the Seneca did not believe that the

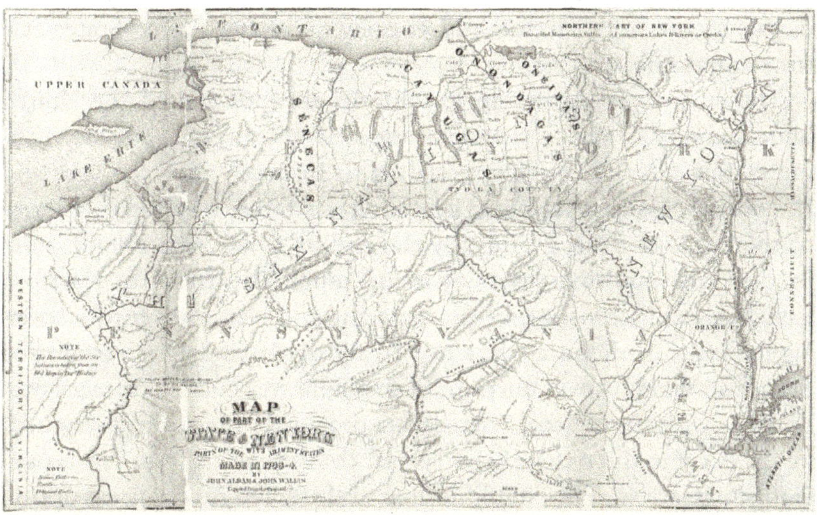

FIGURE 5.3. "Map of Part of the State of New York with Parts of the Adjacent States," 1793–94, Series A0448-79, Recorded Indian Treaties and Deeds, 1703–1871 (bulk 1748–1871), vol. 1, p. 45, New York State Archives, Albany.

United States granted them sovereignty. Rather, the Haudenosaunee nations that participated saw the treaty as an agreement between two sovereigns with mutual obligations.[74] The Haudenosaunee were sovereign and had established the basis of their sovereignty in relation to European powers long before they signed the Treaty of Canandaigua. Yet the treaty became the basis of many Seneca land claims and was at the center of many Seneca arguments against settler claims.

While the Seneca clung to narratives of their continuous sovereignty, settler groups continued to perpetuate the narratives of Native savagery and the illegitimate nature of Haudenosaunee land claims long after the Sullivan-Clinton Expedition. These settler narratives continue to have implications for understandings of Haudenosaunee history today.[75] The Sullivan-Clinton Expedition was largely remembered as successful despite its tactical errors, and Sullivan was remembered as the victorious hero who brought progress to the wilderness that was Iroquoia. In 1879, standing in the field where the Battle of Newtown occurred during the expedition, Reverend David Craft addressed the audience that was there to celebrate the centennial. Craft remembered the expedition as a "historical epoch" that "at a single stroke . . . solved the question, whether the American Indian . . . was longer to stand in the way of human progress."[76] This settler narrative, pervasive enough to warrant a centennial celebration, ignores the fact that the Haudenosaunee's willingness to participate in negotiations at Canandaigua secured the survival and sovereignty of the United States at a time of national uncertainty.

The end of the American Revolution abruptly halted the United States' ability to claim Haudenosaunee lands through military conquest. Instead, the conflicting claims to Iroquoia after the war, and the postwar issues the young United States faced, resulted in a series of treaties over Seneca lands. By the end of 1794, Seneca lands were marked with multiple layers of legal claims. The Treaty of Hartford gave Massachusetts the preemption right and New York future sovereignty and jurisdiction, while the Treaty of Canandaigua recognized Seneca sovereignty over portions of the same area and US primacy over dealings with the Seneca. These layers provided protections for Seneca lands, became the basis of the Seneca counternarrative to US expansionist narratives of inevitable decline, and allowed for the interruption of US expansion.

With the Sullivan-Clinton Expedition, the United States attempted to facilitate expansion into Iroquoia. Although British colonial rule influenced US colonization, 1779 marked the beginning of the United States' aggressive push for more lands through Native dispossession. The American Revolution did not mean permanent decline for the Seneca, however. The end of the war marked a shift in US expansion whereby settler groups had to find new ways to make claims to Iroquoia. For every assertion of Native disappearance, the Seneca held strongly to their narrative of sovereignty, which after 1794 was reinforced by federal recognition.

As the 1790s continued, the United States was forced to rethink expansion. With peace with the Haudenosaunee established, and immediate threats from the Northwest Territory dampened, settler groups used the legal mechanisms of dispossession they created in the 1780s to make claims to Seneca lands on the ground. These claims would not be easy to make, as the Sullivan-Clinton Expedition intended, but had to be constructed from the ground up. Over the next century, settler groups had to spend real time on Seneca lands and expend hundreds of thousands of dollars to facilitate land cessions. While the pressures of US expansion only increased in force and form at the end of the eighteenth century, so, too, did Seneca survivance and creative reorganization to protect Seneca sovereignty into the future.

Chapter 6

"The Last Desperate Struggle"

Leaving New York Behind and Paving the Way to Victory at Yorktown

Iris de Rode

New York City stood as a pivotal hub of military and political activity during the American Revolution, yet its critical role in shaping the war's decisive events in the summer of 1781 remains underexplored. At the heart of this transformative period was a monumental decision faced by General George Washington and his French allies: to launch a direct assault on the heavily fortified British stronghold in New York or to pivot southward toward Virginia. The choice to prioritize the southern campaign not only averted a potentially catastrophic confrontation but also set the stage for the decisive victory at Yorktown in October 1781—a triumph that secured US independence and cemented the battle's place as one of the Revolutionary War's defining moments. Historians have often characterized this decision as a bold and impulsive gamble by Washington and his French allies. Other narratives suggest that Washington was either persuaded or manipulated by his counterparts, with French General Jean-Baptiste Donatien de Vimeur, Comte de Rochambeau, frequently credited with steering him toward the southern strategy. Some argue that Rochambeau influenced French Admiral François-Joseph Paul, Comte de Grasse, whose decision to sail to the Chesapeake Bay allegedly forced Washington's hand. Others suggest that de Grasse acted independently.[1] Such interpretations, however, oversimplify the intricate dynamics in play.

Most importantly, they overlook two Frenchmen who played an indispensable yet largely forgotten role behind the scenes: Major General François-Jean de Beauvoir, Chevalier de Chastellux, and French Ambassador Anne-César de Beuzeville, Chevalier de La Luzerne.

This chapter draws on insights from unpublished materials housed in the private papers of Chastellux. These newly examined documents—including correspondence, operational reports, and strategic analyses—highlight the critical overlooked contributions of Chastellux and La Luzerne as indispensable intermediaries and advisers in shaping allied strategy.[2] Their counsel to Rochambeau, Washington, and de Grasse was deeply rooted in intelligence gathering conducted through the winter of 1780–81, including the often-overlooked Grande Reconnaissance of New York, initiated by Chastellux.[3] This reconnaissance laid the groundwork for the eventual pivot to Virginia. Beyond their strategic contributions, Chastellux and La Luzerne worked to maintain the fragile cohesion of the French-American alliance, a task requiring diplomatic finesse and a nuanced understanding of the differing objectives of the two nations. The decision-making process itself spanned an entire year—far longer than the commonly portrayed timeline of a few weeks or even days—and was fraught with challenges. Conditions for attacking the British were rarely favorable, as the Franco-American forces struggled with weak troop numbers, scarce resources, and persistent uncertainty. Reinforcements promised by their respective governments were slow to arrive—if they arrived at all—forcing Washington and Rochambeau to rely on creativity, adaptability, and patience. Washington, Rochambeau, and de Grasse, guided by Chastellux and La Luzerne, avoided acting impulsively. They deliberately kept their options open, methodically analyzing each possibility until every piece of their complex chessboard became clear.

Although elements of the decision-making process had been initiated as early as the autumn of 1780, it was during the six-week Philipsburg Encampment in July and August 1781, located in present-day Hartsdale, New York, that the allied strategy fully coalesced. Unlike the three-week Yorktown campaign, these six weeks marked the longest continuous period of shared command, as the subsequent six-week march to Yorktown often saw the allies operating separately. During this time, the French did not coerce Washington into adopting a southern campaign. Instead they pursued a careful diplomatic approach that aligned with their shared strategic vision while preserving the chain of command and the unity essential to their partnership—one in which both sides relied on each other to secure victory. Washington, in turn, demonstrated exceptional leadership marked by patience, pragmatism, adaptability, and a willingness to draw on the counsel of experienced strategists. By reexamining the events and individuals who shaped this pivotal period, this chapter presents a more nuanced understanding of the southern pivot—not simply as a military decision but as a master class in coalition strategy that ensured the revolution's success. It also reframes New York not merely as a potential French-American military target, but as the site where arguably the most consequential decision of the revolution was made.

The Triumvirate: Rochambeau, La Luzerne, and Chastellux

By 1780, five years of war had pushed the Continental army to the brink of collapse; it was plagued by dwindling resources, low morale, and acute manpower shortages. The formal entry of France into the conflict in 1778 marked a turning point. For the struggling American cause, French support was a lifeline, while for France, the alliance was

FIGURE 6.1. Jean-Baptiste Donatien de Vimeur, Comte de Rochambeau (1725–1807), by Charles Willson Peale, from life, ca. 1782. Courtesy of Independence National Historical Park, Philadelphia.

FIGURE 6.2. Anne-César de Beuzeville, Chevalier de La Luzerne (1741–91), by Charles Willson Peale, from life, ca. 1782. Courtesy of Independence National Historical Park.

FIGURE 6.3. François-Jean Beauvoir, Chevalier de Chastellux (1734–88), by Charles Willson Peale, from life, ca. 1782. Courtesy of Independence National Historical Park.

a calculated geopolitical maneuver as much as an ideological gesture. Having suffered defeat in the Seven Years' War, France sought not only to weaken British dominance but to reassert its global power, restore its prestige, and secure commercial advantages. France's first two naval campaigns in 1779 ended in failure. Determined to redeem the nation's fortunes, Louis XVI sent 5,500 troops under General Jean-Baptiste Donatien de Vimeur, Comte de Rochambeau, to Newport, Rhode Island, in July 1780. Backed by Admiral Charles-Henri-Louis d'Arsac de Ternay's fleet, Rochambeau's mission was to collaborate with General George Washington and mount a decisive challenge to British supremacy. Reinforcements of 2,000 additional troops and a larger fleet were promised to follow, as France knew that control of the seas would determine the campaign's success.

For France, this effort was more than a military operation; it was a test of national honor and a chance to reaffirm its global influence. The allied command structure reflected a careful balance between unity and operational autonomy. Washington held supreme command over all French-American land forces, ensuring strategic cohesion, while Rochambeau retained authority over the logistics, discipline, and movements of the French troops. His orders from Louis XVI strictly forbade dividing his forces and permitted a retreat to the Caribbean if necessary. Meanwhile, the French navy, including the one based in Newport, operated independently, adapting to maritime conditions while supporting joint operations, ensuring flexibility amid the war's evolving challenges.[4]

The arrival of French soldiers and officers on North American soil was not without its challenges. Cultural, social, military, and linguistic divides, coupled with lingering American suspicions of foreign intervention, posed significant threats to the fragile alliance.[5] Recognizing these potential pitfalls, Louis XVI's ministers, informed by the counsel of the Marquis de Lafayette—who had returned to France to brief the king in his capacity as major general of the Continental army—carefully prepared for these challenges. Acting as an intermediary between Washington's army and the French government, Lafayette emphasized the importance of avoiding the missteps that had marred earlier Franco-American collaborations. In response, the French ministers selected leaders with the diplomatic finesse and strategic vision necessary to bridge these divides. General Jean-Baptiste Donatien de Vimeur, Comte de Rochambeau, was an ideal choice to command the French expeditionary forces. His patience, tact, and military brilliance enabled him to navigate the complexities of this transatlantic partnership. Supporting him was his third-in-command, François-Jean de Beauvoir, Chevalier de Chastellux. A seasoned officer, Enlightenment author, and skilled diplomat, Chastellux was uniquely suited to bridge the cultural and strategic gaps between the allies. His fluency in English and his familial connection to Lafayette further enhanced his effectiveness as a liaison between the French and American forces. Equally vital to the success of the alliance was Anne-César de La Luzerne, France's ambassador to the United States. Arriving in Philadelphia months before Rochambeau, La Luzerne worked tirelessly to strengthen the Franco-American partnership. From his position at the heart of the Continental Congress, he mediated between French and American priorities, secured critical resources, and resolved logistical challenges. His frequent visits to Newport underscored his dual role as diplomat and strategist, as he provided both counsel and direct intervention to ensure the cohesion of the alliance.[6]

Together, Rochambeau, Chastellux, and La Luzerne formed a triumvirate of leadership, each contributing distinct yet complementary skills to the Franco-American alliance. Their shared experiences during the Seven Years' War fostered trust and mutual understanding, which seamlessly transitioned into the revolutionary theater. In Newport, Rochambeau and Chastellux conducted joint military exercises that promoted tactical unity and camaraderie among French and American troops. Simultaneously, social engagements with local elites softened cultural barriers and bolstered the alliance's public perception. At the same time, La Luzerne's deft diplomacy anchored the partnership, skillfully aligning Louis XVI's strategic ambitions with the revolutionary objectives of the fledgling republic. This convergence of military precision, diplomatic expertise, and shared purpose overcame initial tensions, laying a robust foundation for a partnership that would deepen and prove decisive in the months ahead.

The Hartford Conference: Washington and Rochambeau's First Meeting

The Hartford Conference, held from September 20 through 22, 1780, marked the first meeting between General George Washington and General Rochambeau to devise a unified strategy against the British. Chastellux, originally scheduled to attend, was unable to participate due to the looming threat of a British attack on the French forces in

Newport. Alexander Hamilton and the Marquis de Lafayette served as interpreters and recorded detailed notes of the discussions. These talks occurred at a critical juncture in the war. In the North, New York City remained the British Army's stronghold under General Henry Clinton, its formidable defenses and ample supplies posing a daunting challenge. Meanwhile, Washington's Continental army struggled with dwindling resources, severe manpower shortages, and fragile morale. In the South, the situation was even more dire. British forces under General Lord Cornwallis had captured Charleston in May 1780, consolidating control over much of the Carolinas and threatening Virginia. General Nathanael Greene waged a resourceful campaign of attrition in the region, but the theater teetered on the brink of collapse. The survival of the Continental army—and the revolution itself—demanded bold, coordinated action between Rochambeau and Washington.[7]

At Hartford, Washington proposed an ambitious plan to strike New York City with coordinated French-American forces supported by the French fleet. He viewed the city as central to breaking British control in North America with a "decisive blow." While sharing Washington's desire for a decisive campaign, Rochambeau raised significant concerns. French troops, weakened by illness after their transatlantic voyage, were not yet battle ready. Logistical constraints and British naval dominance near Newport further limited their capacity. Most critically, Rochambeau had received no confirmation from Versailles about the anticipated land troop reinforcements or fleet, making it impossible to commit to a major offensive. Rochambeau also expressed a preference for a southern campaign, which appeared more feasible given British strength in New York. Historical accounts, however, often overstate Rochambeau's advocacy for the southern strategy while overlooking Washington's initial pragmatism. From the outset, Washington understood that the final decision would depend on manpower and naval support, allowing for a potential pivot southward if necessary. Both leaders recognized the interdependence of their roles and the importance of careful balancing and diplomacy. Rochambeau relied heavily on Washington's leadership—not only for coordinating US troops but also for Washington's intimate knowledge of the terrain and his ability to secure local support. At the same time, Washington knew that the revolution depended on French expertise, manpower, and naval superiority. Finally, at Hartford, both generals acknowledged the urgent need for reinforcements. Rochambeau dispatched his son, the Vicomte de Rochambeau, to Versailles to appeal for additional troops and resources, while Washington and Rochambeau jointly petitioned Congress to rally support from the states. With winter approaching, they agreed to await further developments before making final decisions, reflecting their shared commitment to pragmatic and cautious leadership.[8]

Shortly after the Hartford Conference, the revolution was shaken by General Benedict Arnold's betrayal. His plot to surrender West Point to the British, which also included plans to capture Washington and French Ambassador La Luzerne, could have devastated the United States' cause. Arnold's defection destabilized the Continental army and sowed mistrust while alarming French officials about the fragility of US leadership. This betrayal underscored the deep challenges facing the revolution and the vital importance of unity and trust within the alliance.[9]

Chastellux's Reconnaissance and Diplomacy

Amid the prolonged wait for reinforcements from France and Congress, François-Jean de Chastellux took proactive steps to address the challenges facing the Franco-American alliance. Recognizing the French army's limited understanding of the North American theater, he authored the unpublished "Mémoire sur les conditions de l'intervention" (Memoir on the conditions of the intervention), in which he identified critical issues: The strength of the Continental army, resource availability, and public support for independence had all been overstated by Congress and US leaders. Compounding these problems were inaccuracies in US maps and lingering mistrust of the French among the population. To bridge these gaps, Chastellux proposed that several "French and American officers would traverse the country, evaluate the army, and gauge public sentiment, simultaneously gathering intelligence and building trust between the allies." From November 1780 through January 1781, Chastellux led an extensive reconnaissance mission through Rhode Island, Connecticut, New York, New Jersey, Pennsylvania, Delaware, Maryland, and Virginia, including the Chesapeake Bay—a mission that today is overlooked. Accompanied by aides-de-camp, mapmakers, and French officers, he inspected military depots, assessed supply routes, and consulted with key US leaders such as Washington, Hamilton, and Lafayette. Beyond his reconnaissance, Chastellux leveraged social activities—dinners, balls, and hunts—to break down cultural barriers and strengthen camaraderie among the allies. These efforts succeeded in gathering vital intelligence and fostering trust, laying the foundation for closer Franco-American cooperation.[10]

Drawing on his findings, he evaluated two key options: an assault on British-held New York and a campaign in the South. As an experienced strategist, particularly in European siege warfare, Chastellux brought valuable insights that even Washington lacked. After inspecting British defenses at Fishkill, Stony Point, and West Point, he concluded that attacking New York would be excessively complex and unlikely to succeed. He highlighted obstacles such as the sandbanks at Sandy Hook, which would prevent large French ships from entering the harbor. Yet, acknowledging Washington's determination, he recommended additional intelligence gathering, noting the challenges posed by the region's Loyalist strongholds, which he described as "infected with Tories." Turning his attention southward, Chastellux identified Virginia as a far more promising theater of war, provided that a French fleet could arrive in time. He emphasized the strategic advantages of the region, particularly its deep-water access at Hampton Roads and the James and York Rivers, which were ideal for naval support and troop deployment. Moreover, the British forces' harsh treatment of Virginians had alienated many Loyalists, while enthusiasm for the Franco-American alliance was steadily growing.[11] The urgency of action in the South became even more clear in January 1781, when news arrived that Benedict Arnold, now a British general, had burned Richmond, disrupting US supply lines and highlighting Virginia's strategic importance.[12]

Chastellux first shared his findings with La Luzerne in Philadelphia during an intense two-week visit at his private residence, and through a written report he sent to Rochambeau in Newport. Both men fully endorsed his recommendations but recognized that Washington's agreement was essential in order to move forward.[13] Chastellux presented his assessments to Washington during a meeting at the general's headquarters in New Jersey. Washington, though still inclined to focus on targeting New York, remained skeptical that the South could deliver a decisive victory. Nevertheless, he listened with great interest to Chastellux's insights. These discussions proved to be a pivotal moment in their relationship. The collaboration between the two men deepened, evolving into a profound and lasting friendship. Washington later expressed his admiration in a heartfelt letter to Chastellux, writing, "Never in my life did I part with a man to whom my soul clave more sincerely than it did to you."[14]

As winter gave way to spring, the allies anxiously awaited news of reinforcements, as no decisive operation could be undertaken without them. Communication with Versailles was agonizingly slow: Transatlantic letters took months to arrive and were often further delayed by British naval blockades. Similarly, Washington had received no word from Congress. In the interim, the allies briefly shifted their focus to a smaller-scale operation in the Chesapeake, where Benedict Arnold's raids demanded immediate attention. In February 1781, Washington dispatched Lafayette with 1,200 Continental soldiers to counter Arnold and, if possible, capture him. A small French naval squadron from Newport was sent to support Lafayette, but the mission failed due to insufficient resources and adverse winds.[15] In March, Washington traveled to Newport to plan another naval operation targeting the Chesapeake, but this, too, faltered, forcing the French fleet to retreat and leaving the British in control of the region.[16] But these efforts yielded critical intelligence about the Chesapeake Bay that would prove invaluable in the future military operation conducted by the French and American generals. Meanwhile, the arrival of General William Phillips in Virginia strengthened British control, deepening the crisis. Frustrated by the inability to take decisive action, Washington wrote, "We are at the end of our tether. Now or never, deliverance must come."[17] These setbacks underscored the urgent crucial need for a larger French fleet to challenge British dominance. For the time being, however, the allies could only wait.

News Arrives: La Luzerne's Advice

In mid-April 1781, in Philadelphia, La Luzerne received the long-awaited correspondence from Versailles—weeks ahead of Rochambeau. Louis XVI had decided against sending the two thousand additional troops requested for North America, citing the substantial British presence and the escalating financial strain of countering potential British reinforcements. Instead, the king authorized the deployment of a formidable French fleet under Admiral François-Joseph Paul, Comte de Grasse, departing from Saint-Domingue (modern-day Haiti) and expected to arrive in the summer.[18] While the promise of naval reinforcements offered hope, the decision not to send additional troops heightened La Luzerne's sense of urgency. Two failed campaigns and the prolonged inactivity of Rochambeau's army had fueled skepticism about the Franco-American alliance. A failure in their next campaign could push the Americans into negotiating a truce with Britain—an outcome France could not afford. Decisive action was essential. In a private letter to Chastellux, La Luzerne dismissed an attack on New York as "madness" and expressed hope for an alternative strategy. He also revealed instructions from Versailles to "coordinate directly with De Grasse on operations."[19]

Acting on these orders, La Luzerne drafted a strategic memorandum for De Grasse, drawing heavily on Chastellux's reconnaissance and recent intelligence from the Chesapeake Bay. His argument was precise: "It is in the Bay of Chesapeake that it seems urgent to bring all the King's naval forces with such force of land as will be deemed suitable by the generals. . . . It is probable that the evacuation of Virginia will be the result of this movement." La Luzerne reinforced his case with Chastellux's insights into Virginia's geography, topography, and resources, alongside naval reports highlighting the region's strategic vulnerabilities. Unlike heavily fortified New York, Virginia lacked the time or means for sufficient British defenses, making it a far more promising target.[20] To ensure that the memorandum reached its destination, La Luzerne sent it via the French fleet's commander in Newport, De Barras, who forwarded it to Admiral De Grasse. Simultaneously, La Luzerne shared the proposal with Rochambeau, urging him to present it to Washington directly through a new meeting. Importantly, La Luzerne framed the memorandum as a suggestion rather than a directive, emphasizing that the final decision rested with Washington and Rochambeau. This diplomatic tack was aimed at preserving the cohesion of the Franco-American alliance. Rochambeau, already doubtful about the feasibility of attacking New York, fully endorsed La Luzerne's proposal. From this point forward, La Luzerne collaborated closely with Rochambeau and Chastellux to subtly guide Washington toward the Chesapeake strategy. This effort relied not only on La Luzerne's memorandum but also on a series of carefully orchestrated diplomatic initiatives that would gradually unfold.[21]

The Wethersfield Meeting: Trying to Determine Strategy Once More

In early May 1781, Rochambeau and Chastellux received the news of Admiral De Grasse's impending arrival through reports from La Luzerne and the Vicomte de Rochambeau, the general's son, recently returned from Versailles.[22] They arranged a meeting with Washington, scheduled for May 22–23 in Wethersfield, Connecticut. Although invited, La Luzerne was unable to prepare in time to attend—much to his chagrin.[23] Determined to influence the discussions despite his absence, La Luzerne adopted indirect but deliberate measures. Under orders from King Louis XVI, De Grasse's plans were not to be disclosed to Washington in writing, lest they fall into British hands. Likely with Rochambeau's tacit approval, La Luzerne encouraged Chastellux to write to Washington directly. Chastellux did and opened his April 29 letter with, "As my zeal for your country and my attachment for your Excellency knows no limits, I hazard, dear general, a step that may be conceived as a transgression." Stressing the need for discretion, he urged Washington to destroy the letter after reading it. Chastellux revealed the expected arrival of a "convoy from the West Indies." This letter was far more than a gesture of trust—it was a calculated move to earn Washington's confidence.[24]

Chastellux wrote a second secret letter on the eve of the Wethersfield meeting. He presented a detailed proposal for a coordinated campaign targeting the Chesapeake Bay, closely aligning with La Luzerne's earlier memorandum. Chastellux suggested positioning the French army between the Hudson and Delaware Rivers while awaiting De Grasse's fleet. Once the fleet arrived, heavy artillery and supplies could be transported by sea to the Chesapeake, while the army advanced overland to Virginia. To preserve Washington's leadership, Chastellux recommended framing the plan "as a sudden and newborn thought," allowing Washington to present it as his own idea during the conference with Rochambeau. This careful phrasing ensured that the proposal appeared to originate from Washington rather than being influenced by Chastellux. This delicate exercise in diplomacy preserved Washington's authority while advancing the southern strategy favored by both Chastellux and Rochambeau.

Despite these efforts, however, the Wethersfield meeting revealed Washington's continued skepticism. While acknowledging the strategic merits of a southern campaign, he voiced concerns about poor road conditions, oppressive summer heat, and the prevalence of disease. He reiterated his preference for targeting New York but agreed to consider the South as a contingency if New York proved unfeasible.[25] Washington's writings from this period reflect his cautious optimism. "We are now called upon to make our last desperate struggle to pave the way to that peace and independence for which we have so long contended," he wrote, adding his hope for reinforcements to arrive: "While an opportunity presents itself of striking the enemy a fatal blow, I will persuade myself, the concurring exertions of Congress, of the several States immediately concerned, and of every individual in them, who is well affected to our cause, will be united in yielding every possible aid on the occasion."[26] Interestingly, both Washington and Chastellux penned letters during this period proposing New York as the intended target, and both letters were intercepted by the British. Were these genuine reflections of strategy or calculated efforts to mislead British intelligence as the allies increasingly leaned toward a southern pivot? The truth likely lies in a careful balance of both, as the allies continued to navigate uncertainties regarding reinforcements and the timing of De Grasse's fleet.[27]

During the meeting, with the decision still not made, Chastellux proposed an ambitious intelligence-gathering operation building on his previous winter's reconnaissance efforts. The operation had two primary goals: to assess the feasibility of an attack on New York and to determine whether such a plan could realistically succeed. Recognizing that earlier letters and meetings had not fully swayed Washington, Chastellux approached this effort as a potential turning point—an opportunity to either alter Washington's perspective or confirm the feasibility of an attack on New York, defying prevailing skepticism. The plan, known as the Grande Reconnaissance, was approved by Washington and Rochambeau and scheduled for July. This large-scale operation would bring the Franco-American armies together near Manhattan to gather critical intelligence, evaluate strategic possibilities, and finalize their course of action.[28]

Meanwhile, the situation in the South continued to deteriorate. In May, General William Phillips succumbed to illness, leaving the command of British forces to General Cornwallis, whose arrival significantly heightened the threat in the region. Benedict Arnold, however, departed the southern theater around this time, having been reassigned to New York, where he would no longer play a role in the unfolding events. Leading the US forces in Virginia, Lafayette voiced his growing apprehension in a letter to his uncle, Chastellux: "Cornwallis causes me devilish fear." La Luzerne echoed Lafayette's concerns, warning Chastellux, "It is impossible for Lafayette to resist for long unless maritime forces come to his aid." Washington, acutely aware of these escalating challenges, also increasingly turned his attention to the South.[29]

This critical moment catalyzed decisive action from Rochambeau, aligning him with the behind-the-scenes efforts of La Luzerne and Chastellux, who were subtly advocating for a shift to a southern strategy. On May 28, Rochambeau wrote to Admiral De Grasse, presenting a flexible two-phase plan that exemplified strategic foresight and adaptability. For the first phase, Rochambeau urged De Grasse to deliver a decisive strike in Virginia, targeting British positions at Portsmouth to disrupt logistics, relieve pressure on Lafayette, and weaken British operations. Concentrating naval and land forces in the Chesapeake Bay, he argued, would exploit British vulnerabilities and deliver a significant blow to their southern campaign. Rochambeau emphasized this preference clearly, writing, "The southwesterly winds and the state of distress in Virginia will probably make you prefer the Chesapeake Bay, and it will be there where we think you may be able to render the greatest service." The second phase, contingent on favorable conditions, allowed for a potential pivot to New York, using smaller French vessels to secure Sandy Hook and block British reinforcements.[30] Historians often point to this letter as evidence of Rochambeau's determination to prioritize the Chesapeake, crediting it with steering Washington southward. Such interpretations, however, overlook the nuanced nature of Rochambeau's plan. He furthermore ensured transparency by sharing his letter with Washington, who echoed this dual approach in his own correspondence with De Grasse. While Washington emphasized New York as the primary target, he acknowledged the need for adaptability, writing, "The second object, in case we should find our force and means incompetent to the first, is the relief of Virginia, or such of the southern States as the enemy may be found in."[31] Ultimately, Rochambeau and Washington aligned on maintaining flexibility. They awaited further intelligence on their own forces and British movements before finalizing their strategy.[32]

In subsequent letters, Rochambeau highlighted the dire financial situation of the allied forces, urging De Grasse to secure 1.2 million livres to fund the campaign and deliver additional war supplies, as both he and Washington were critically short on resources. Rochambeau also requested reinforcements from Saint-Domingue to strengthen the allied forces for the challenges ahead. With weeks required for De Grasse's reply to arrive, the allied leaders remained in suspense, turning their attention to the planned reconnaissance efforts in New York.[33]

Determining Arguments: The Grande Reconnaissance of New York

By mid-June 1781, preparations were underway for the move to New York, and for the Grande Reconnaissance. On June 18, Rochambeau's

4,800 troops began their march from Newport, Rhode Island, toward New York, aiming to unite with Washington's forces who were mobilizing from the Hudson Highlands. Rochambeau left a portion of his troops and artillery behind to protect Newport and the small French fleet stationed there, which awaited its opportunity to join Admiral De Grasse's forces. The French and US armies converged on July 6, establishing camps at the Philipsburg Encampment in Greenburgh, Westchester County, positioned only about ten miles from the British stronghold. Rochambeau headquartered at the nearby Odell House (still standing today), while Washington established his headquarters at the Appleby Farm.[34] By mid-July, Ambassador La Luzerne joined the allied commanders, contributing to the strategic discussions that would follow.[35] The armies would finally remain in the encampment for six weeks and two days, conducting intelligence gathering and strategizing. They also organized numerous dinners and social events to strengthen the French-American alliance. While the camps were separated, the troops conducted joint training sessions during this period, solidifying their coordination.[36]

Days before the arrival of French forces, Washington attempted to gather intelligence through a smaller reconnaissance mission. Unfortunately this effort ended in failure, with the loss of several members of his personal guard. During these initial attempts, Washington estimated the British troop strength to be around eight thousand men—a number he later realized was too low.[37] By mid-July, plans for a larger joint reconnaissance mission were underway. But heavy rainfall caused delays, prompting a smaller reconnaissance operation on July 18, involving Washington, Rochambeau, and several officers, in which they gathered useful information. Two days later, Washington and Rochambeau held a formal meeting. Washington expressed frustration over critical challenges, including insufficient recruits, poor communication from key states, and a lack of resources. He remarked that "the uncertainties under which we labour" made it impossible to finalize a definitive plan. Their strategy ultimately hinged on gathering intelligence and assembling resources ahead of the French fleet's arrival, making the planned reconnaissance mission all the more critical.[38]

On July 21, the Grande Reconnaissance commenced. This large-scale "reconnaissance in force" aimed to simulate an attack, compelling the enemy to respond and thereby revealing their positions, defenses, and weaknesses. Approximately four thousand troops advanced toward Manhattan to evaluate British fortifications and gauge their readiness for an actual confrontation. The mission was initiated and led by Chastellux, who commanded the forces with the support of several French and American officers. Both Rochambeau and Washington joined the operation, accompanied by their aides and staff officers. Observing from a distance, they took notes and closely monitored the movements. Marching through the night on muddy roads, the troops reached their positions undetected. On the morning of July 22, Chastellux led the forces toward British Redoubt Number 8 near King's Bridge. Initially appearing abandoned, the redoubt was revealed to be manned and supplied via boats from Manhattan. As the allied troops advanced, British soldiers opened fire, triggering a skirmish in which a French officer tragically lost his leg. The allies withdrew, but not before gathering critical intelligence on nearby positions, including Fort Tryon and Fort Laurel Hill.

That afternoon, Washington and Rochambeau, accompanied by engineers and staff officers, conducted a closer survey of British defenses along the Harlem River, encountering enemy troops near Montresor's Island. Another skirmish ensued, though the allies suffered no further casualties. The reconnaissance resumed at dawn on July 23, focusing on potential landing sites at Throgs Neck. Exhausted, Washington and Rochambeau briefly rested on the peninsula but were startled by British ship cannons as the rising tide transformed the area into an island. Narrowly escaping capture, they made a daring retreat to the mainland. That evening, Chastellux led the troops back to their Philipsburg camp, completing the grueling two-day operation without further interference. The Grande Reconnaissance, the first land operation of its scale conducted jointly by the French and American armies, provided invaluable training and enhanced coordination for future campaigns.[39]

Following the operation, allied officers analyzed the gathered intelligence and produced several detailed reports, in which La Luzerne was also involved. Among these, Chastellux's *Réflexions sur l'attaque de New York* (Reflections on the attack on New York), accompanied by two detailed maps of the greater New York area and northern Manhattan, stood out as the most comprehensive. The report outlined a strategy for simultaneous assaults on five critical positions: "It would be advantageous if the attacks could be conducted simultaneously: 1) on the northern part of the island of New York, 2) on the fortifications of Long Island, 3) on the works at Paulus Hook, 4) on Staten Island, and finally, 5) on the tip of Sandy Hook." But Chastellux tempered his proposal with caution: "It is not doubtful that if these five attacks were performed together with vigor and supported by a sufficient number of troops, we could eventually promise a prompt success. But it must be admitted that they would require much superior means than those we can and could dispose of. . . . The enemy could make our best hopes vanish in an instant."[40]

The report starkly outlined the challenges the allies faced. British forces in Manhattan numbered between 10,000 and 14,000—far exceeding Washington's earlier estimate of 8,000. Chastellux calculated that a successful assault on New York would require approximately 35,000 troops, yet the allies could muster only 11,500. Moreover, the operation would rely heavily on the French fleet, which had not yet arrived and was unlikely to provide sufficient reinforcements to close the gap. These observations led Chastellux to describe New York as an "impenetrable fort," reinforcing his earlier convictions.[41] With significantly more intelligence at hand, Chastellux grew increasingly confident in his advice against attacking the city. Other officers, such as Antoine Jean Louis Lebègue de Presle Duportail, a distinguished French engineer serving in the Continental army, reached similar conclusions.[42]

These conclusions, combined with his own assessments and the realization that no new recruits would arrive in time, forced Washington to confront the harsh realities of his position. He wrote on August 1, "Everything would have been in perfect readiness to commence the operation against New York, if the States had furnished their quotas of men agreeably to my requisition. . . . I could scarce see a ground upon which to continue my preparations against New York; especially as there was much reason to believe that part (at least) of the troops in Virginia were recalled to reinforce New York and therefore I turned my views more seriously (than I had done before) to an operation to the Southward."[43]

At last the French had achieved a crucial diplomatic success. Through careful arguments and subtle diplomacy, La Luzerne, Rochambeau, and Chastellux had successfully guided Washington toward their preferred strategy without overstepping their roles or compromising the fragile Franco-American alliance. They had managed to align their goals while respecting US autonomy, a testament to their diplomatic finesse and their respect for Washington's leadership. Equally, Washington deserves recognition for his pragmatic assessment of the challenges and his ability to integrate the insights of his allies into a cohesive strategy. He demonstrated a rare balance of humility and authority, valuing the expertise of the French commanders while maintaining ultimate

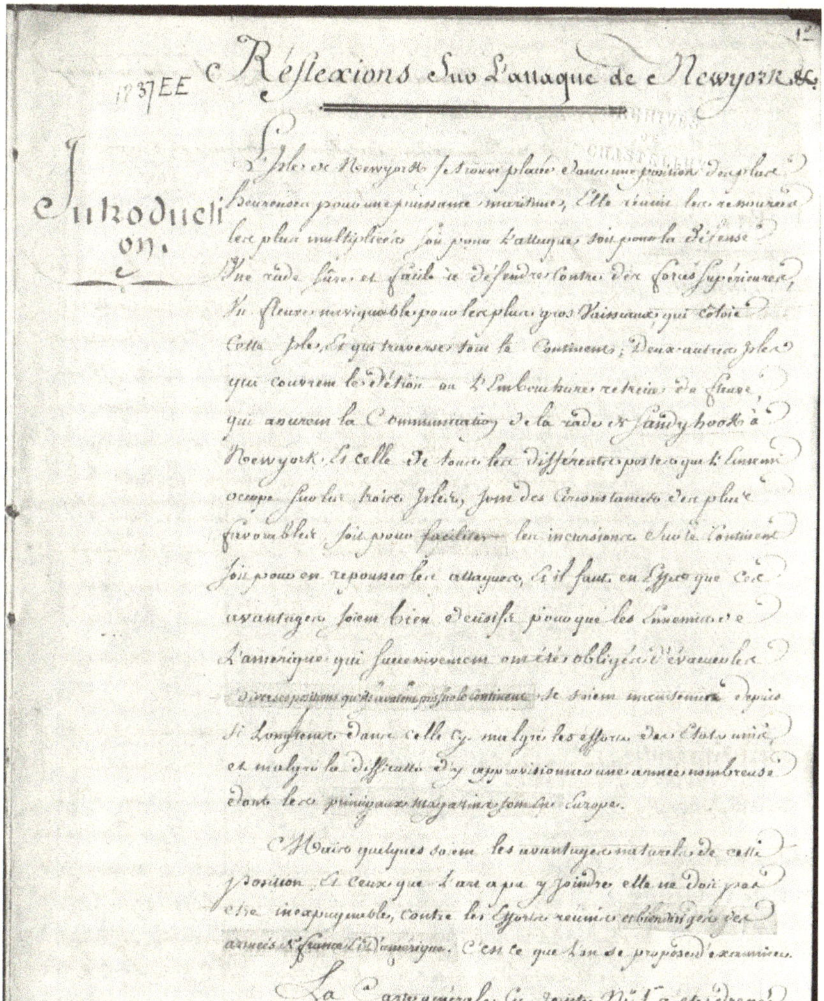

1737EE Réflexions sur l'attaque de Newyork &c. 12

Introduction.

L'Isle de Newyork se trouve placée dans une position des plus heureuses pour une puissance maritime, elle réunit les ressources les plus multipliées soit pour l'attaque, soit pour la défense. Une rade sûre et facile à défendre contre des forces supérieures, un fleuve navigable pour les plus gros vaisseaux qui côtoie cette isle, et qui traverse tout le continent; deux autres isles qui couvrent le détroit ou l'embouchure retrécie du fleuve qui assurent la communication de la rade de Sandy hook à Newyork et celle de toutes les différentes postes que l'ennemi occupe sur les trois isles, sont des circonstances des plus favorables soit pour faciliter les incursions sur le continent soit pour en repousser les attaques, et il faut en effet que ces avantages soient bien décisifs pour que les ennemis de l'amérique qui successivement ont été obligés d'évacuer les diverses positions qu'ils avaient prises sur le continent se soient maintenus depuis si longtemps dans celle cy malgré les efforts des Etats unis, et malgré la difficulté d'y approvisionner une armée nombreuse dont les principaux magazins sont en Europe.

Mais quelques soient les avantages naturels de cette position et ceux que l'art a pu y joindre elle ne doit pas être inexpugnable contre les efforts réunis et bien dirigés des armées de France et d'amérique. C'est ce que l'on se propose d'examiner.

La carte générale cy jointe No. 1 a été dressée en partie suivant [illegible] qui nous a été remise, et que nous avons rectifiée sur diverses indications données par des gens qui connaissent les lieux. Le plan No. 2 a été construit d'après la reconnaissance immédiate que nous avons faite sur le terrein les 21, 22 juillet et 6 aoust derniers. C'est d'après ces différentes

FIGURE 6.4. François-Jean Beauvoir, Chevalier de Chastellux, *Réflexions sur l'attaque de New York*, manuscript, n.p., ca. July 1781. Courtesy of the Mount Vernon Ladies' Association. Gift of Richard H. Brown and Mary Jo Otsea, 2024.

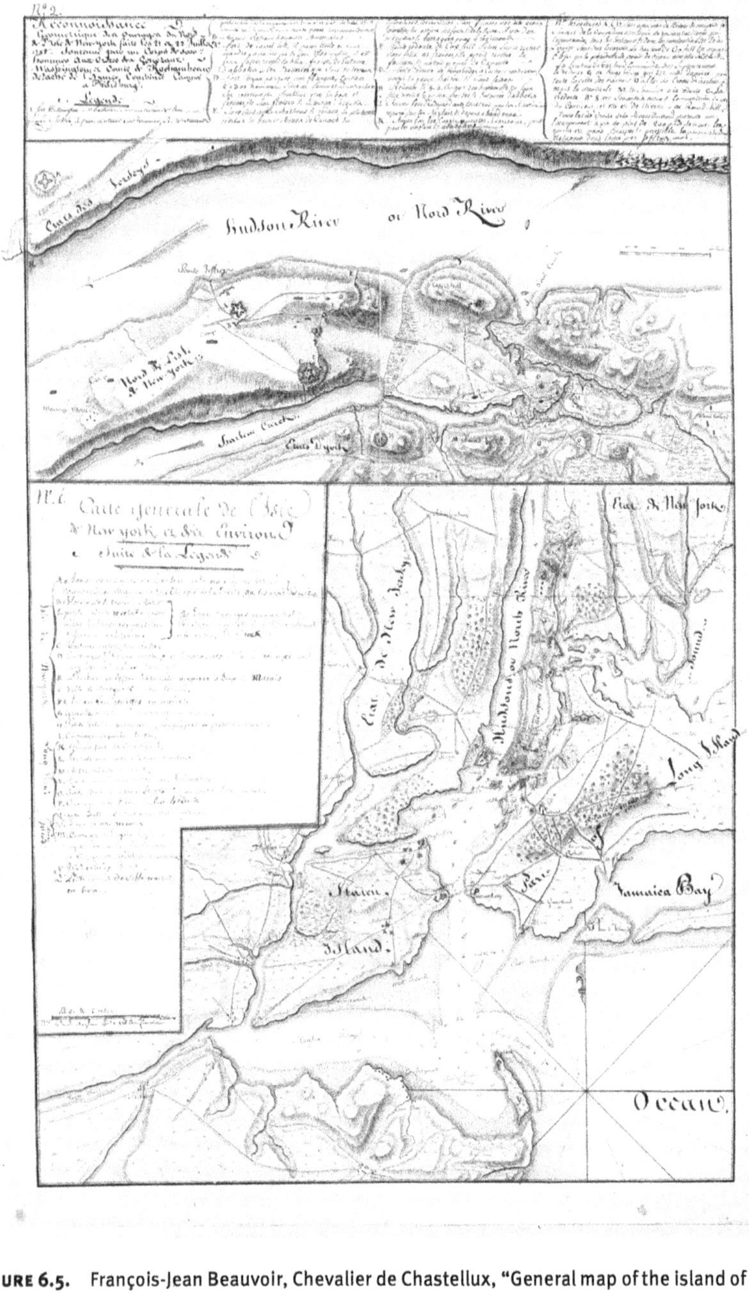

FIGURE 6.5. François-Jean Beauvoir, Chevalier de Chastellux, "General map of the island of New York and its surroundings . . . no. 2. Geometric reconnaissance of the northern works of the island of New York, conducted on July 21 and 22, 1781. Supported by a force of 5,000 men under the command of Generals Washington and Count de Rochambeau, detached from the combined army camped at Philipsburg)," n.p., ca. 1781–82. Courtesy of the Mount Vernon Ladies' Association. Gift of Richard H. Brown and Mary Jo Otsea, 2024.

responsibility for the alliance's direction. Yet uncertainty still loomed. The allies lacked concrete information about De Grasse's fleet: Its timing, location, and intended destination remained unclear. Compounding this uncertainty were the possibilities of British reinforcements and hurricanes that could delay or jeopardize De Grasse's arrival. Again, united in their determination, the allies pressed forward with preparations, ready to adapt as events unfolded.

The Confirmation of the Shift to the South

Finally, on August 14, 1781, Rochambeau, stationed at the Odell House, received news from De Grasse, who confirmed his decision to sail to the Chesapeake Bay. He would arrive in late August or early September. De Grasse also provided three critical updates: His fleet would include twenty-nine ships of the line, he would bring 3,500 additional land troops from the West Indies along with artillery and siege equipment, and he had secured 1.2 million livres from Cuban merchants to fund the campaign, as Rochambeau had requested. But De Grasse imposed a significant constraint—his fleet could remain in North America only until October 15 due to orders from Louis XVI to return to the West Indies for another campaign. This limited time frame left the allies just four to five weeks to execute their plan in Virginia, effectively ruling out New York as a secondary target, as previously proposed by Rochambeau and Washington.[44]

Contrary to the often-repeated claim that De Grasse forced Washington's hand—either through his own initiative or via Rochambeau's influence—his decision was based on collective advice. De Grasse attributed his decision to the recommendations of "MM. de Rochambeau, M. Washington, La Luzerne, and De Barras." He had received letters from both Rochambeau and Washington, as well as La Luzerne's memorandum, which was relayed through De Barras. Skillfully synthesizing these diverse inputs, De Grasse blended diplomatic advice with his naval expertise. Practical factors, such as favorable wind patterns for the Chesapeake, further influenced his selection. De Grasse later acknowledged that La Luzerne's memorandum, in particular, had shaped his decision.[45] Moreover, rather than dictating the course of action, De Grasse confirmed the feasibility of moving south. By the time his letter arrived, Washington had already embraced the southern strategy as the most promising path to victory, and preparations for the march were well underway. The allies were prepared to take the calculated risk of proceeding with or without confirmation of the fleet's arrival.

Significant uncertainties remained, however. Despite De Grasse's announcement, his arrival was not guaranteed, given the potential for delays or interference en route. Additionally, the precise location of the land campaign was unclear due to limited intelligence on British Lord Cornwallis's movements. On August 16, Lafayette delivered extraordinary news that changed everything: Cornwallis had relocated his troops to Yorktown and Gloucester by late July, fortifying his position in Virginia. At last, fortune had smiled on the Franco-American alliance. Cornwallis's move created the vulnerability that Washington and Rochambeau could only have dreamed of. His position left him exposed to a coordinated Franco-American blockade—a weakness Chastellux had identified through earlier reconnaissance and insights from prior French naval campaigns. Unlike New York, where British forces outnumbered the allies, Virginia now favored the Franco-American forces. Bolstered by De Grasse's reinforcements, the allied forces would total around seventeen thousand against Cornwallis's eight thousand. Recognizing the opportunity, Washington called it "the luckiest Circumstance in the World."[46]

At the Philipsburg Encampment, Washington and Rochambeau began organizing the march and planning the battle and siege of Yorktown. To conceal their intentions, the allies launched an elaborate deception campaign around New York City. They constructed fake bread ovens and mock boats, suggesting preparations for a prolonged assault on New York. These measures successfully misled the British. General Clinton, still reeling from the Grande Reconnaissance and convinced of an imminent attack on New York, fell into the trap. Poor intelligence sharing and divisions among British leadership compounded the confusion. Clinton's delayed responses allowed the Franco-American forces to march south unimpeded, while internal divisions later prevented effective coordination, enabling the allies to encircle Cornwallis at Yorktown.[47]

The combined Franco-American forces departed the Philipsburg Encampment on August 18. They now left New York after six weeks of research, training, negotiations, and strategizing. This period had been crucial for refining their decision-making and for strengthening cooperation between the allied commanders and their soldiers. The march south, spanning approximately six weeks, during which French and American soldiers marched in separate columns on land and sailed on water routes, was a well-coordinated effort. Reinforcements from various states steadily increased the size of the allied forces. The march itself, however, was a calculated risk by Rochambeau and Washington, as success hinged on factors beyond their control, including De Grasse's timely arrival. As Washington had anticipated, the march was arduous. Poorly maintained roads and oppressive summer heat tested the endurance of the troops.[48] Yet intelligence from Chastellux's reconnaissance, updated French maps, meticulous logistical preparations by both French and American officers, and the trust forged through recent joint operations enabled the allies to advance with remarkable efficiency.

Morale soared during the march when a letter brought extraordinary news: De Grasse's fleet had successfully reached the Chesapeake Bay. Shortly after, on September 5, De Grasse achieved a decisive victory over the British Royal Navy at the Battle of the Chesapeake, securing naval dominance and ensuring that the allies' path to Yorktown remained unobstructed. When hearing this, overcome with joy, Washington leapt into the air, waved his handkerchief, and embraced Chastellux and Rochambeau in celebration.[49] While the soldiers marched south, Lafayette succeeded in containing Cornwallis at Yorktown. By September 28, after weeks of grueling marches, the Franco-American forces arrived, merged, and commenced their siege of Cornwallis's army. Encircling the British, they effectively cut off supplies, reinforcements, and escape routes, tightening the noose around their adversary. De Grasse's control of the Chesapeake prevented any rescue by sea, while Washington and Rochambeau applied relentless pressure on land. Bad weather further worsened Cornwallis's situation, thwarting an attempted escape. Facing mounting casualties, disease, and dwindling supplies, Cornwallis had no choice but to surrender on October 19, 1781.[50]

Indeed, the plan had worked, and the world seemed turned upside down. Against all odds, the US-French army had defeated the formidable British forces. Yorktown was more than just a victory—it was a masterstroke of strategy and resolve. The decision to prioritize the southern campaign had borne fruit in spectacular fashion. But the year was not over yet. Following the triumph at Yorktown, Washington and Rochambeau resumed their deliberations, contemplating the possibility of an assault on New York. As the dust settled, however, it became clear that the southern campaign—once considered a secondary objective—had delivered the decisive blow they had long sought. With Britain overstretched on multiple fronts and war fatigue gripping the nation, Yorktown emerged as the undeniable turning point. The war's final chapter culminated in the Treaty of Paris in 1783, securing

US independence and reshaping the global balance of power. What had once seemed impossible was now reality.

The Subtle Art of Strategy and Leadership

The victory at Yorktown was not a spontaneous triumph but the culmination of months of strategic collaboration, subtle diplomacy, and resolute leadership. At its heart was an extraordinary interplay between George Washington's pragmatic and open-minded command and the nuanced guidance of his French allies—Rochambeau, Chastellux, La Luzerne, and De Grasse. Within this dynamic, New York City played a pivotal role. Although the city was initially seen as Washington's preferred target, its formidable defenses and strategic importance dominated every discussion, becoming the crucible where the coalition's decision-making process was tested and refined. The Grande Reconnaissance and the extensive deliberations at the Philipsburg Encampment revealed the immense challenges of attacking New York, ultimately steering the allies toward the southern strategy. Thus, New York was not only a potential military target but also the setting where the campaign's most consequential decisions were made.

The Franco-American leaders, despite their inherent challenges, succeeded because they prioritized collaboration over individual ambition, pragmatism over rigidity, and mutual respect over dominance. Together they navigated the complexities of coalition warfare, achieving a rare and powerful synergy. Yorktown was more than a battlefield victory; it was a testament to the power of collaboration and the transformative potential of shared vision. This triumph offers a timeless lesson in the art of coalition building and the enduring strength of alliances forged in adaptability, trust, and shared purpose.

CHAPTER 7

"Standing on Their Own Soil"

The Struggle for Emancipation in Western New York

Lucien Holness

In late September 1837, Charles B. Ray, a journalist and subscription agent for the Black newspaper *The Colored American*, arrived in the western New York town of Geneva. In a letter detailing his efforts to find subscribers for the New York City–based newspaper, Ray remarked that Geneva's Black residents were elderly, "brought here by their masters as slaves, and retained in slavery for some time afterwards." During his visit he met an elderly man who was brought to the region as a enslaved person from Virginia. After he was released from servitude, the man went on to become a landowning farmer. According to Ray, most of Geneva's Black townspeople, including this farmer, lived in "generally uncomfortable circumstances" yet resided "in their own houses, standing on their own soil" as free people. Ray's description of Geneva's Black community raises several questions. First, why did Southern slaveholders migrate to western New York in the first place? How did slavery's presence in western New York impact abolitionists' efforts in bringing about total abolition throughout the state and nation? Finally, how were these formerly enslaved people able to achieve their freedom? Although these questions are unanswered in Ray's account, they are worth considering because of the insights they can provide into the revolutionary era's complicated antislavery legacy and the challenges that abolitionists faced in eradicating slavery from New York soil.[1]

How slavery was abolished in New York has received considerable attention from historians. An early influential work was Arthur Zilversmith's *The First Emancipation* (1967), which challenged the long-held belief that New York and other Northern states decided to gradually end slavery through legislative action because it was unprofitable. Instead, Zilversmith contends that Northern support for gradual abolition can be attributed to several factors: the growing number of nonslaveholders who viewed slavery as a threat to their communities and their personal interest, the ideals of the American Revolution that were concerned with the rights of man, and the influence of humanitarian reformers who viewed slave ownership as a sin.[2]

Statewide studies on abolition have allowed historians to ask new questions and provide new interpretations about New York emancipation. For example, David N. Gellman connects the end of slavery in New York to larger questions about citizenship, race, political identity, and which voices belonged in the public sphere. For Gellman, the proliferation of print culture was important in building support across the state for emancipation because of its role in shaping public opinion. According to Gellman, "Support for statewide abolition was generated publicly rather than being orchestrated quietly by early national-era elites." Gelleman concludes that the successful passage of a gradual abolition law in the state legislature was the result of a combination of "ideological discourse, activism, and electoral alignment." Despite this outpouring of scholarship on emancipation in the Empire State, however, there is still much to be written on abolition in New York.[3]

Studies of emancipation in New York generally mention the western portion of the state in passing.[4] This chapter places western New York at the center of the story of emancipation in the Empire State.[5] Doing so not only underscores the point made by scholars that abolitionists faced a daunting task in eradicating slavery in the state, but forces us to rethink several widely cited political, economic, and social developments as well as underemphasized factors that made ending slavery in the state so difficult. I argue that enslaved people in the western portion of the state adopted long-held tactics and seized on new strategies in their attempts to liberate themselves from bondage and protect their freedom—tactics and strategies that were afforded to them thanks in part to the state's gradual abolition law. In some instances, the actions of abolitionists in western New York mirrored those of antislavery activists from other corners of the state. The state's western counties, however, had a unique political environment. Slaveholders who migrated to the region after the American Revolution waged a determined effort to plant and grow slavery in western New York. The failure of New York to immediately abolish slavery following the revolution provided an opening for slavery to gain a foothold in the region. Also contributing to slavery's reach into western New York was the fact that the state's leading antislavery organization, the New York Manumission Society (NYMS), was headquartered in New York City and, according to the historian Shane White, "was very much a city organization with little impact on the rest of the state." The NYMS's limited geographic reach forced enslaved and free African Americans to look for other allies and avenues in their quest to bring an end to Black bondage in the region.[6]

Focusing on western New York also offers new insights into the rise of the immediate abolitionist movement in the region. Historians often attribute the origins of this movement to the evangelical movements that emerged in the 1820s and 1830s.[7] The spiritual fervor was so intense that this region was referred to as the "burned-over district." This chapter, however, points to another, equally important development in the emergence of immediate abolition: the free Black communities of formerly enslaved people and free Blacks that developed in towns in western New York in the 1810s and 1820s. These free Black communities provided a crucial base of support for activists like Ray who were seeking to advance immediate abolition and who would later aid freedom seekers from the South fleeing from bondage and serve as a bulwark against slavery's influence in their local community. Yet before the American Revolution, there was nothing to suggest that western New York would become a focal point for immediate abolition or that slavery would one day be abolished across the state.

The Revolutionary Era and the Path from Gradual Abolition to Uncertain Freedom

On the eve of the American Revolution, enslaved people could be found across New York in three major regions: Long Island, New York City, and the Hudson River Valley. The enslaved experience was different in each region. For instance, in Long Island, most enslaved people could be found in the agricultural, craft, and maritime industries. In the dynamic transatlantic port city of New York, enslaved people, men in particular, had unique opportunities for mobility laboring in the city's seaport economy. As a major urban center, New York City afforded African Americans opportunities to socialize and build community in the city's markets and taverns, at times in defiance of their enslavers. North of Manhattan were the counties along the Hudson River, which were home to some of the largest slaveholding estates, sprawled over several acres. The number of enslaved people laboring on each of these estates ranged between twenty and forty. This was exceptional, however, as most enslavers in this region owned between two and three people. Whether on large or small estates in the Hudson Valley, most of the enslaved worked in agriculture, producing cereal grains, milling, iron manufacture, and commerce on the Hudson River. Although enslaved people's experiences varied across New York, in all three regions, Black bondage provided much-needed labor in a colony where free white laborers were in short supply.[8]

Although white settlers were slowly pushing westward between the late eighteenth century and the turn of the nineteenth, slaveholders were deterred from settling in western New York for several reasons. First, a portion of the region was controlled by a confederation of Iroquois (Haudenosaunee)-speaking Indigenous nations. The Six Nations were an obstacle for white settler colonialists pushing westward. Second, the region was also a site of several armed conflicts that threatened the stability of the slave system by providing enslaved people with the opportunity to escape and seek asylum in Indigenous settlements. Slaveholders on the New York frontier faced considerable risk of losing their human property. Although slavery failed to gain a foothold in the region, a series of political developments between the late eighteenth and early nineteenth century would determine whether this would continue to be the case.

The late eighteenth century witnessed the most serious challenge to slavery in New York and throughout British mainland North America. The Enlightenment, Protestant evangelical revivals, and Black resistance to slavery, along with the language of the American Revolution concerning liberty and natural rights, led a growing number of white Americans to raise moral questions about the long-held right to hold people as property. At the same time, however, paradoxically, the intellectual movement of the Enlightenment and the ideology of the American Revolution presented obstacles to immediate abolition. Many white Americans were committed to protecting private property rights, including slave ownership, and were skeptical that formerly enslaved people could become virtuous citizens. Along with these intellectual, political, and religious movements, the social upheaval of the Revolutionary War destabilized the authority of enslavers throughout much of New York and North America, providing enslaved people with opportunities to flee from bondage and with pathways to freedom. Enslaved men, women, and children were assisted in their quest for freedom by the first organized antislavery societies, which were established during this period.[9]

In 1785, the NYMS was founded in New York City. Its members were some of the state's most prominent men in business, law, and finance. A great deal of the NYMS's time was spent lobbying the legislature to adopt laws that restricted slavery and protected Black rights. By the end of the 1780s, antislavery activists had achieved mixed success. The same year that the NYMS was founded, the legislature prohibited slave traders from importing enslaved people into the state to be sold. Three years later, in 1788, the state prohibited New Yorkers from selling their bondspeople to buyers in another state and also forbade any slaveholder who brought an enslaved person into the state for their own personal use from selling that person. Enslavers who broke these laws would have their human property emancipated. The state also made manumission much easier by allowing slaveholders to free their slaves without posting bond "if the slave was under fifty years of age and not likely to become a public charge." Despite these legislative achievements, these antislavery laws had several shortcomings. One flaw was that they reaffirmed slaveholders' property rights by punishing anyone who was found harboring an enslaved runaway. Another limitation was that thousands of enslaved people and their descendants were still held in bondage. The NYMS faced an uphill battle against entrenched slaveholding interests in its fight to secure the adoption of a gradual abolition law, which the society believed would put slavery on the path to extinction in New York and transform formerly enslaved people into citizens.[10]

Two years after the American Revolution concluded, antislavery lawmakers introduced a bill that would gradually abolish slavery throughout the state. To encourage reluctant legislators to act, proponents of abolition cited the action taken by Pennsylvania in 1780 and Connecticut and Rhode Island in 1784; those states had passed their own gradual emancipation laws. Lawmakers could also find hope in the broad support that gradual abolition enjoyed among many New Yorkers. Unfortunately, antislavery lawmakers fell short. Proslavery lawmakers seized on the fears of many whites that gradual abolition would upset the state's longstanding racial order, and that formerly enslaved people in New York would not have a place in civil society. It was not until the late 1790s that another gradual abolition bill was introduced by antislavery legislators. Historians have cited several political events during this period that aided abolitionist lawmakers in securing a legislative victory. Yet one development that proved especially crucial was the allocation of additional seats to the state's western and northern counties, which provided the margin of victory in passing the gradual abolition bill.[11]

New York's 1799 gradual abolition law marked an important milestone. The law stipulated that any child born to an enslaved mother after July 4, 1799, would be considered a servant or term slave, required to labor for their mother's enslaver until they reached the age of twenty-eight, if they were male, and twenty-five, if they were female. To safeguard the future freedom of this generation, the law required slaveholders to record the name, age, and sex of the child, as well as their own name, with the city or town clerk within nine months after the child's birth. This information was meant to ensure that when a child reached the age of twenty-eight or twenty-five, slaveholders would not be able to claim that the child was enslaved for life. Enslavers would automatically be penalized if they failed to comply with the law. Although no enslaved people were freed when the gradual abolition law was adopted, the act did include a process for slaveholders to emancipate them by simply signing a sealed certificate. Despite this legislative victory, many slaveholders from the Upper South and elsewhere viewed western New York as an attractive destination in which to settle.[12]

Slavery's Rise in Western New York

Western New York afforded Maryland and Virginia enslavers numerous economic opportunities at a time when the soil on many plantations in the Upper South was nearly exhausted and the local economies stagnant. After the American Revolution, additional lands became open to white settlement with the removal of Indigenous sovereignty over much of the region. Maryland and Virginia slaveholders left the Upper South to either settle on vast tracts of land or engage in land speculation. Although slaveholders were greatly outnumbered by New England settlers who favored free labor over slavery, Maryland and Virginia enslavers had political and economic influence in their communities.

For instance, John Nicolas emigrated from Virginia in 1803 with several of his slaves and served as an Ontario County judge. Many of the region's slaveholders, such as William Helm, had distinguished military careers. Nathaniel Rochester achieved military distinction in the Revolutionary War and founded several towns and cities, including Rochester. The influence that enslavers commanded had an impact on the enforcement of New York's antislavery laws in the region. Historical evidence suggests that in western New York, children who were born to enslaved mothers in the early 1800s were not registered until the 1810s, long past the required deadline under state law. The ability of enslavers to ignore the registration clause for so long could be explained in part by the sway they held over local affairs and the concentration of organized abolitionist activity in New York City. For enslaved people who were relegated to a lifetime or period in bondage, the experience could be just as brutal and dehumanizing as it was in the South.[13]

For enslaved people, the journey from the Upper South to western New York was long and arduous. In late October 1803, the Nicholas family and their relatives left Hampstead Plantation, in Stafford County, Virginia, taking with them their human property. They forced several of their bondspeople to make the journey on foot; those unable to walk the long distance were taken in four horse-drawn wagons. Some slave owners had their enslaved nurse or house servant travel along with them in their stagecoach, where the servant was tasked with providing domestic comfort and care on the slave owners' long journey. Enslaved people were forced to travel directly northward over the Allegheny Mountains to New York under the supervision of an overseer.[14]

There is no doubt that Pennsylvania law and local officials played a role in slavery's growth in western New York by safeguarding routes that brought enslaved Virginians and Marylanders into the region. Pennsylvania allowed slaveholders to travel through the state under certain conditions. Enslavers were prohibited from bringing enslaved people into the state to sell; however, they could keep their slaves on Pennsylvania soil for up to six months. If a slaveholder was found guilty of violating the law, their slave(s) would be emancipated. To guard against such an accusation, William B. Rochester, a Maryland slaveholder and son of Nathaniel Rochester, acquired a signed and certified affidavit from John Holliday, the Franklin County justice of the peace, and John Findlay, clerk of courts. In his statement, Rochester swore that he had no intention of selling an enslaved woman named Nance along with Ned, an enslaved boy, and two other unnamed children who were traveling with him in Pennsylvania. His purpose, he declared, was to bring these enslaved people to New York. Rochester passed through Pennsylvania with Nancy, Ned, and the two enslaved children without incident. Rochester and other slaveholding migrants from the Upper South could rest assured that Pennsylvania officials like Holliday and Findlay would protect their property rights and provide them with the necessary legal documentation with which to thwart a freedom suit by an enslaved person as they traveled through the state on their way to New York.[15]

Once enslaved people arrived in western New York, they were put to work, playing a crucial role in the development and cultivation of numerous acres of farmland and contributing to the household economy. Enslaved people could be found clearing land for settlement and were largely engaged in agricultural and domestic labor. Enslaved people's labor allowed slaveholders to turn their attention to other entrepreneurial pursuits. John Nicholas and his brother-in-law profited from the labor of their slaves to maintain their large farm, which allowed them to devote a portion of their time to breeding sheep. Although slavery in western New York and the wider North seems milder compared to the tobacco, rice, sugar, and cotton fields of the South, there were some similarities.[16]

One striking resemblance between the two regions was that Northern slaveholders could be just as cruel and violent as those in the South. Thomas James was eight years old when his enslaver, Asa Kimball, sold his mother, brother, and sister to a buyer in Smithtown, over two hundred miles away from the Kimball farm in Canajoharie. James never saw his mother and sister again, although years later, he would reunite with his brother. To be torn away from his family must have been a traumatic experience for James. Several years after he acquired his freedom, Austin Steward recalled in his autobiography that there was little difference between slavery in Virginia, where he was born, and western New York. He "found it just as hard to be beaten over the head with a piece of iron in New York, as it was in Virginia," he wrote, adding that "whips and chains" were "everywhere necessary to degrade and brutalize the slave, in order to reduce him to that abject and humble state which slavery requires." Slaveholders, in their attempt to command the labor of their human property, force them to submit to their authority, and advance their financial interests, engaged in acts of brutality. As slavery's importance to the region continued to grow, so, too, did the enslaved population, which caused concern for many New Yorkers.[17]

By 1800, enslaved people could be found across New York's vast western region. According to Shane White, "most townships had at least one or two owners of slaves." Between 1800 and 1810, the enslaved population in the region increased from 351 to 975 and was concentrated in Ontario, Steuben, and Seneca Counties. The growth of the enslaved population is proof of the importance of enslaved people's labor in the region. Although the number of enslaved people in western New York was minuscule compared to that in other regions of the state, legislators grew concerned about the growth of the enslaved population in the area. In 1810, they passed a law that allowed slaveholders in the counties of Ontario, Steuben, and Seneca who brought slaves to this part of western New York after 1800 to hire out their slaves, but only for seven years, on the condition that they would be freed. Although this law provided enslaved people with a path to freedom, it also kept a significant number of African Americans trapped in bondage. These enslaved people turned to extralegal measures, making them the region's first immediate abolitionists.[18]

Fighting for Freedom and Against Slavery

Enslaved western New Yorkers sought to liberate themselves from servitude by running away. Absconding was a tactic that was long used by enslaved people throughout New York, but enslaved people brought to western New York in the early nineteenth century could no longer look to the Indigenous nations in the West as a possible refuge from bondage. The loss of Indigenous sovereignty over much of these lands forced enslaved people to seek out new destinations.

Many enslaved people fled to other towns in the region. One night in September 1807, Thomas Hill decided that the time was right to abscond from his enslaver, Samuel Baker, in the town of Bath. Baker believed that Hill was joined by another enslaved man named David who lived about forty-five miles from Hill in Geneva. Baker guessed that both men might have fled to Geneva, but he did not rule out the possibility that Hill and David could be in another town. He offered a reward of one hundred dollars for each man if they were captured and returned, or fifty dollars if they were held in any New York state jail. It is almost certain that Hill and David knew each other and plotted their escape together. It is possible that both men may have crossed paths while living in Bath, laboring alongside each other or hired out to another white New Yorker in need of additional labor. Regardless of

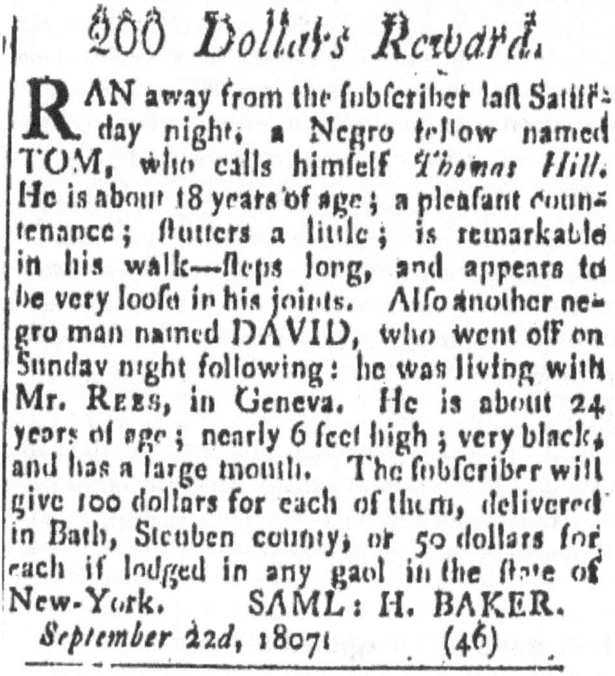
200 Dollars Reward.

RAN away from the ſubſcriber laſt Saturday night, a Negro fellow named TOM, who calls himſelf *Thomas Hill.* He is about 18 years of age; a pleaſant countenance; ſtutters a little; is remarkable in his walk—ſteps long, and appears to be very looſe in his joints. Alſo another negro man named DAVID, who went off on Sunday night following: he was living with Mr. REES, in Geneva. He is about 24 years of age; nearly 6 feet high; very black, and has a large mouth. The ſubſcriber will give 100 dollars for each of them, delivered in Bath, Steuben county, or 50 dollars for each if lodged in any gaol in the ſtate of New-York. SAML: H. BAKER.

September 22d, 1807. (46)

FIGURE 7.1. Notice in *The Expositor*, October 7, 1807. Available via Google News.

how they met, both men were able to keep their plans of escape hidden from their enslavers, and their likely collaboration indicates that enslaved people forged partnerships with other freedom seekers to ensure the greatest possibility of success.[19]

Around the same time that Hill and David made their escape, two other enslaved men, Jacob and Charles, absconded from their owners in Geneva. Their enslavers, Polydore B. Wisner and Herman H. Bogert, believed that both men were traveling with a group of freedom seekers. In a notice of their escape that appeared in the town newspaper, *The Expositor*, Wisner and Bogert indicated that the runaways traveled only at night, which was a good way to avoid detection by slave catchers and local authorities. The two enslavers never mentioned a possible intended destination (or destinations) of this group of bondspeople. The only thing they knew for certain was that the runaways were somewhere in New York. They promised a reward of twenty dollars for each runaway if they were captured and either returned to their enslavers or placed in any jail in the state.[20]

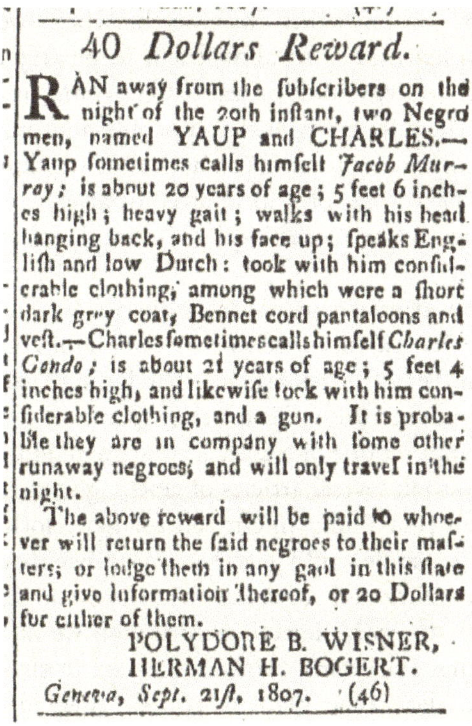

40 Dollars Reward.

RAN away from the ſubſcribers on the night of the 20th inſtant, two Negro men, named YAUP and CHARLES.—Yaup ſometimes calls himſelf *Jacob Murray;* is about 20 years of age; 5 feet 6 inches high; heavy gait; walks with his head hanging back, and his face up; ſpeaks Engliſh and low Dutch: took with him conſiderable clothing, among which were a ſhort dark grey coat, Bennet cord pantaloons and veſt.—Charles ſometimes calls himſelf *Charles Condo;* is about 21 years of age; 5 feet 4 inches high, and likewiſe took with him conſiderable clothing, and a gun. It is probable they are in company with ſome other runaway negroes, and will only travel in the night.

The above reward will be paid to whoever will return the ſaid negroes to their maſters; or lodge them in any gaol in this ſtate and give information thereof, or 20 Dollars for either of them.

POLYDORE B. WISNER,
HERMAN H. BOGERT.

Geneva, Sept. 21ſt, 1807. (46)

FIGURE 7.2. Notice in *The Expositor*, October 7, 1807. Available via Google News.

The decision of Jacob and Charles to travel with a group may have been driven by several considerations. First, Wisner and Bogert described Jacob as having a heavy gait that severely hampered his mobility. If the group of freedom seekers were discovered, the enslaved group could help Jacob, as well as one another, fend off any attempt at recapture and a return to bondage. The danger of being found and captured was not lost on the group of freedom seekers. To avoid such an outcome, Charles decided to take a gun with him. For enslaved people who were unfamiliar with the local geography, traveling with a group could also help them navigate the terrain so they could successfully elude their pursuers. Finally, escaping with a group meant that runaways could carry with them more supplies. Wisner and Bogert stated in their notice that both of the runaways had taken a considerable amount of clothing with them. These clothes could be used to hide their identities, along with those of their fellow travelers, or they could be sold to help the men reach their destination. Fugitive slave notices in local newspapers, across New York and in other states where slavery continued to exist, mention freedom seekers taking clothing that they would later wear to conceal their identities or to allow them to portray themselves as freedpeople. This strategy took on extra importance in western New York, given that there were few enslaved people and only a small free Black population in many towns. The arrival of freedom seekers in a town in western New York, or a local attempt at escape, would likely have drawn suspicion from some local white residents, some of whom were enslavers.[21]

When an enslaved man named Harry absconded from his owner, David Naglee, in Geneva, he carried with him a light-colored coat and pants "and a number of other articles that he may use alternatively to avoid detection," according to a newspaper notice of his escape. Four years later, another one of Naglee's bondsmen, Philip Hardy, fled. Like Harry, Philip took several articles of clothing with him, which his enslaver suspected that Philip might sell for new clothes or wear to disguise his identity so he could give the appearance that he was a free man. Naglee also cautioned residents that Hardy might also change his name in order to avoid detection. Although we may never know definitively whether Harry and Hardy succeeded in their attempts to emancipate themselves, their plans to conceal their identities were a strategy that freedom seekers in the region now had to heavily rely on, since almost all of what was the western frontier was now firmly under the authority of New York state.[22]

Although men frequently appeared in runaway slave notices in the western New York press, the region's newspapers featured several documented instances of enslaved women attempting to flee from their enslavers. In late July 1811, Esther was living with her two children in the town of Phelps. That summer, she decided to run off with the children. In a notice of the family's escape that appeared in the *Geneva Gazette*, Samuel Shekell, Esther's enslaver, did not mention why his bondswoman decided to flee with her infant and toddler. Perhaps he was planning on selling one of Esther's children, or maybe Esther was attempting to reunite with the rest of her family and kin. Although we cannot say for certain what Esther's motivations for absconding were, she may have headed to Geneva, given that Shekell placed his advertisement in the local paper. Shekell was concerned that if Esther and her family had indeed fled to Geneva, they might be sheltered, she might find employment, and she and her children might be able to live as free people. Shekell warned residents that anyone who assisted Esther or employed her did so at "their peril." Although the historical record is

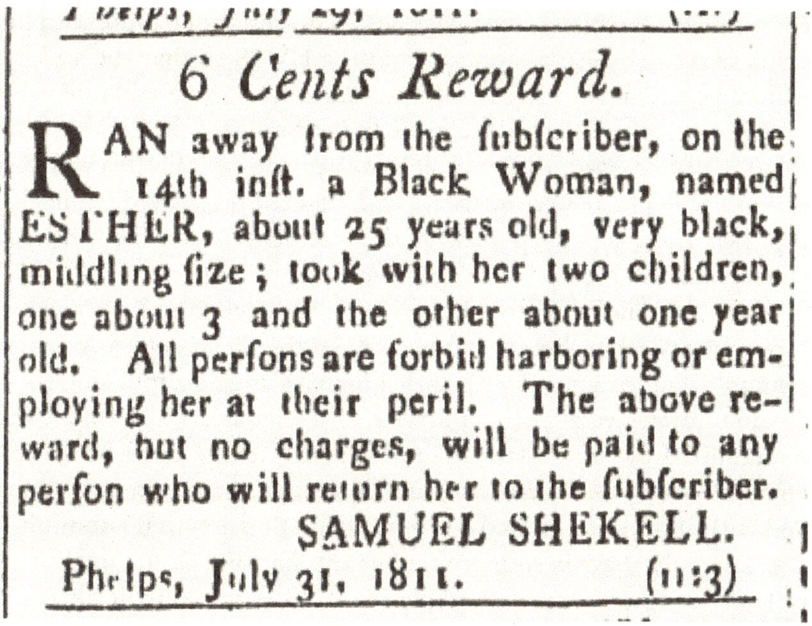

6 *Cents Reward.*

RAN away from the ſubſcriber, on the 14th inſt. a Black Woman, named ESTHER, about 25 years old, very black, middling ſize; took with her two children, one about 3 and the other about one year old. All perſons are forbid harboring or employing her at their peril. The above reward, but no charges, will be paid to any perſon who will return her to the ſubſcriber.

SAMUEL SHEKELL.

Phelps, July 31, 1811. (11:3)

FIGURE 7.3. Notice in the *Geneva Gazette*, July 31, 1811. Available via Google News.

silent on whether Esther and her children evaded capture, the odds that they succeeded were not entirely favorable. Childbearing and childcare responsibilities seriously limited Black women's mobility. Traveling with children also had its own challenges, as the cries of a hungry or exhausted child could risk alerting slavecatchers to runaways' hiding places. But these challenges did not stop women from attempting to escape from bondage.[23]

In late spring 1807, Dine and her six-month-old son fled from their enslaver, Isaac Mitchell, who held them bondage in Albany. Dine had a long history of expressing her opposition to her continued enslavement by engaging in defiant behavior. For instance, she once fled from her previous owner to Connecticut, where she was later caught and returned to New York. When Mitchell purchased Dine, he had found it impossible to discipline her. Initially he had promised her that he would manumit her after six years of service if she was well behaved, but Dine rejected this offer. After two months, an exasperated Mitchell presented Dine with the opportunity to find a new enslaver. Dine spurned Mitchell's proposal and instead decided to flee with her son. Mitchell surmised that Dine may have been lured onto a ship bound for New York City or may have joined a group of Black people traveling westward up the Mohawk

River, where her children had been sold. The desire to reunite with her children or seek legal assistance from the NYMS so that she and her children could live as a free family must have been a powerful motivator for Dine to escape, and it may explain her resistance to the demands and offers of her enslavers. Although enslaved women typically fled with just their children, there were instances where an entire enslaved family fled together. These actions underscore the great lengths to which enslaved people went to keep their families from being torn apart.[24]

Slave flight failed to topple slavery in the region and throughout New York state, but this act of resistance, or the threat of fleeing, forced slaveholders to negotiate with their lifetime slaves by promising them freedom after several years of service. In December 1799, Ginna was manumitted by her enslaver, Timothy Allyn, in the town of Seneca, Ontario County. According to Ginna's freedom certificate, her "good and faithful services" played a role in Allyn's decision to manumit her. Allyn may also have been motivated by the fear that Ginna might successfully escape, but such an admission in a freedom certificate would call into question Allyn's mastery over his human property. In their private letters, however, enslavers were more candid about the role this fear played in their decision to manumit. In December 1814, William Rochester wrote to his father, Nathaniel Rochester, about the constant unruly behavior of his bondsman Ned. Rochester confessed that it might "be better for him to leave Bath, on account of the number of free negroes about them who will doubtless put disorderly notions into his head." Those "disorderly notions" were that Ned was a free man. Despite Rochester's attempts to discipline his bondsman, Ned refused to submit to Rochester's authority. In late December or early January, Ned was placed in the local jail. Rochester believed that because Ned was so troublesome, it might be worth considering manumitting him on the condition that he purchase his freedom. Ned forced Rochester to concede that he would eventually have to free him and negotiate the terms of his manumission.[25]

Ned's resolve to become a free man came at a time of growing organized antislavery activism in western New York. During the initial years of white settlement in western New York, an organized antislavery movement was nonexistent. Until a manumission society was established, enslaved people had to look hundreds of miles to the east, to an overburdened and underresourced NYMS in New York City, or to local abolitionists, for assistance in securing their freedom. In 1797, Sylvia's enslaver had her taken from western New York to New York City,

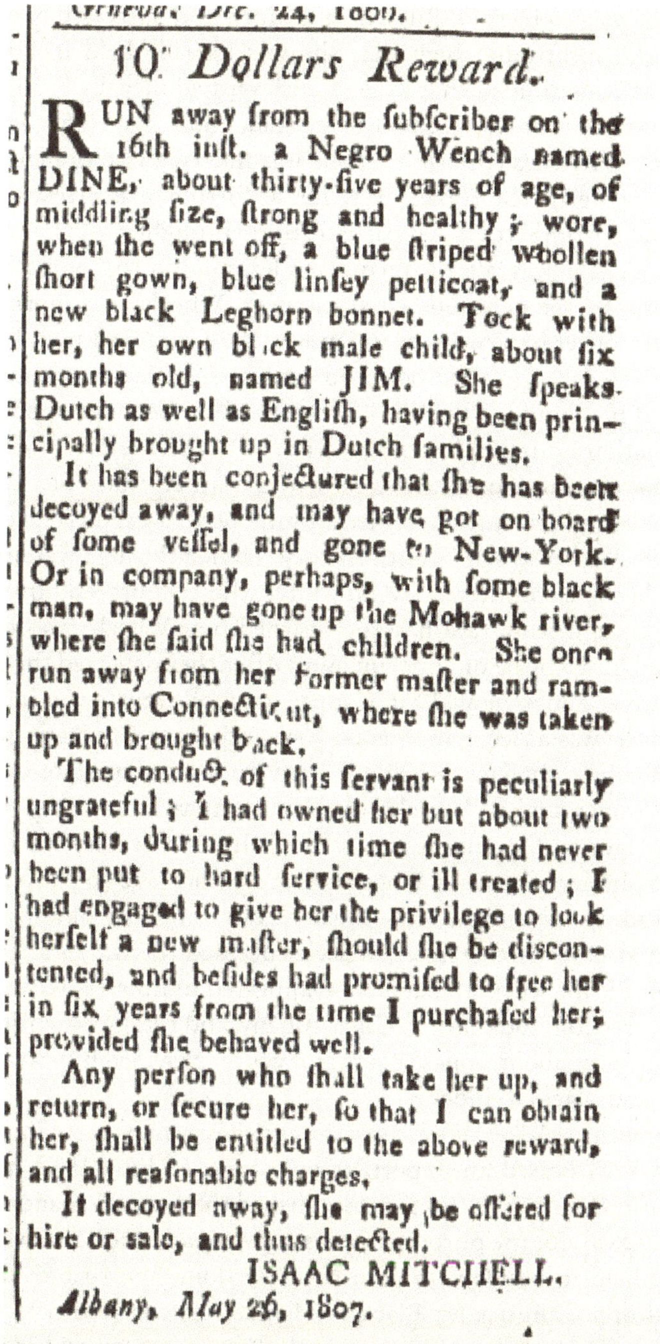

10 Dollars Reward.

RUN away from the ſubſcriber on the 16th inſt. a Negro Wench named DINE, about thirty-five years of age, of middling ſize, ſtrong and healthy; wore, when ſhe went off, a blue ſtriped woollen ſhort gown, blue linſey petticoat, and a new black Leghorn bonnet. Took with her, her own black male child, about ſix months old, named JIM. She ſpeaks Dutch as well as Engliſh, having been principally brought up in Dutch families.

It has been conjectured that ſhe has been decoyed away, and may have got on board of ſome veſſel, and gone to New-York. Or in company, perhaps, with ſome black man, may have gone up the Mohawk river, where ſhe ſaid ſhe had children. She once run away from her former maſter and rambled into Connecticut, where ſhe was taken up and brought back.

The conduct of this ſervant is peculiarly ungrateful; I had owned her but about two months, during which time ſhe had never been put to hard ſervice, or ill treated; I had engaged to give her the privilege to look herſelf a new maſter, ſhould ſhe be discontented, and beſides had promiſed to free her in ſix years from the time I purchaſed her; provided ſhe behaved well.

Any perſon who ſhall take her up, and return, or ſecure her, ſo that I can obtain her, ſhall be entitled to the above reward, and all reaſonable charges.

If decoyed away, ſhe may be offered for hire or ſale, and thus detected.

ISAAC MITCHELL.

Albany, May 26, 1807.

FIGURE 7.4. Notice in *The Expositor*, June 17, 1807. Available via Google News.

where she was to be sold. But Sylvia escaped and successfully reached the NYMS, informing them that she was illegally held in bondage. The NYMS determined that Sylvia's enslaver had illegally brought her into the state from Connecticut to be sold, and the society convinced the agent of Sylvia's enslaver that she was indeed a free woman. Many enslaved western New Yorkers were not as fortunate as Sylvia and had to seek help from settlers sympathetic to their plight.[26]

Peter Wheeler was taken from his New Jersey home to Cayuga County, New York, under nefarious circumstances. Wheeler was born to an enslaved mother in New Jersey in January 1789, and he was still a child when his enslaver, Job Mather, died. In his will, Mather manumitted Peter and his family. Although he was free, Wheeler continued to live in the Mather household until the death of Job Mather's widow. Afterward, the unscrupulous executors of the Mather estate put Wheeler up for sale and sold him to Gideon Morehouse, a cabinetmaker, who took Wheeler to Cayuga County. As they traveled through western New York, Wheeler encountered several whites who encouraged him to flee. For instance, when a tavern keeper learned how Wheeler was treated, she asked him why he did not run away. After they departed the tavern, Wheeler met a man named Mr. Cooper, an abolitionist, who informed him that he was a free man because New York was a free state and that it was against "the law to bring a slave from another state into this state." Cooper advised Wheeler to flee his enslaver once they reached Cayuga County. Morehouse was a fiendish enslaver who inflicted all sorts of physical abuse on Wheeler. The violence was so extreme that it shocked residents, and Morehouse was found guilty of abusing his bondsman. Shortly thereafter, Wheeler decided the time was right to make his escape when a solar eclipse appeared in June 1806. Wheeler's route to freedom took him to Utica, Albany, and finally New York City. Along the way, abolitionists (Black and white) provided him with food, shelter, and places to hide.[27]

Six years after Wheeler's escape, the antislavery movement in western New York witnessed an important milestone. In June 1812, a group of Ontario County abolitionists established the Ontario Manumission Society (OMS) for the purpose of assisting African Americans who were illegally held in bondage to gain their freedom, and to provide educational opportunities for Black residents. One enslaved person who sought the help of the OMS was Austin Stewart, who had been living in bondage for some time in the town of Bath. One day he happened to learn, through word of mouth, about New York's antislavery laws. He quickly sought legal advice from a nearby lawyer, who was convinced that Steward could not be held as a slave under state law. The lawyer encouraged him to seek help from the OMS. With the aid of James B. Moore, one of the society's directors, Steward was able to secure his freedom. The group was also likely involved in an 1818 case where a slaveholder sought to leave western New York and take his bondspeople with him, violating New York law. The enslaved New Yorkers refused to go and filed suit, and their enslaver was indicted and found guilty of kidnapping. This enslaver's decision to risk leaving New York with his human property was likely inspired by a landmark antislavery bill that the state assembly had passed the previous year.[28]

Emancipation and the Making of an Immediate Abolitionist Movement in Western New York

In 1817, New York abolitionists secured a legislative victory when the state assembly declared that all enslaved New Yorkers born before July 4, 1799, or brought into the state before that date, would be freed on July 4, 1827. This law was seen by many as the culmination of abolitionist efforts to bring an end to slavery once and for all throughout New York, and as the fulfillment of emancipation that went unrealized during the revolutionary era. Slaveholders, however, continued to cling to their property claims on human beings. In September 1826, less than a year before the 1817 law was to take effect, Abraham Van Gelder placed an advertisement in the *Geneva Gazette*, offering a reward of just one penny if his bondsman Harry was returned to him. Van Gelder claimed that Harry was about twenty years old and had just eight years left to serve. The regional press recognized the limited nature of the 1817 emancipatory act: The editors of the *Geneva Palladium* cautioned their readers that if they read the law closely, they would find that it did not free all slaves in the state. But the symbolism of selecting July 4 as the date on which a substantial number of enslaved people would be freed was not lost on New Yorkers.[29]

As they emerged from bondage, freed African Americans worked hard to establish independent households and institutions such as churches to improve their lives and the lives of their children. The efforts by Black western New Yorkers to acquire economic and social independence as well as engage in community building created a foundation that supported the immediate abolitionist movement. Thomas James was born sometime in the early 1800s to an enslaved mother in Canajoharie. He was about nineteen years old when he fled from bondage and settled in Rochester, where he labored for a company that hauled goods across New York. James joined and supported the African Methodist Episcopal Church, and when Peter Webb purchased his freedom in 1818, he went on to help establish the African Methodist Episcopal Zion Church in Ithaca. Black churches were important institutions in the fight against slavery, serving as meeting spaces for abolitionists and stops on the Underground Railroad. Although most free Blacks lived modestly or close to the margins, they built new lives for themselves and communities that provided a foundation for the immediate abolitionist movement, which had begun in the late 1820s and sought to fulfill the American Revolution's promise of freedom and liberty for all people.[30]

When Charles B. Ray arrived in western New York in September 1837, a generation of African Americans had been "standing on their own soil" as a free people for several years. For many of these people, freedom was not immediate. Emancipation in the region and across New York occurred piecemeal through the passage of several emancipatory acts. But some enslaved people did not wait for freedom: They took it upon themselves to hasten their liberation by absconding or by working with antislavery activists and organizations. Yet in early western New York, enslaved people faced daunting challenges in their quest to be free. Following the American Revolution, slavery began to gain a foothold in the region, and slaveholders, although a minority, exercised considerable influence.

Before the 1810s, the abolitionist movement was based in New York City, hundreds of miles away from enslaved people in the state's western counties. African Americans in western New York had relied on forging ties with sympathetic residents who could assist them, and some had attempted to flee from bondage. The actions of enslaved people did not end slavery in the region, but they did weaken it. Over the course of the early nineteenth century, the free Black community continued to grow. Although the evangelical zeal that arose in the 1820s and 1830s and the arrival of New England settlers were pivotal in turning western New York into a hotbed of support for immediate abolition, the region's first generation of freedpeople also played a critical role in creating and sustaining this movement through the communities and institutions they established. For them, the fight to realize the ideas of the American Revolution continued.

Editor Acknowledgments

With the 250th anniversary of the American Revolution and Declaration of Independence approaching, we believed there should be some form of scholarly recognition of this momentous event in New York, the state that was at the center of the revolutionary conflict. After considering various possibilities, we decided to pursue a book of essays based on the most recent scholarship exploring the different meanings of the American Revolution for the many people in New York who participated in it. The result was this volume. We want to thank and acknowledge all of the authors who contributed to the book. They made the task of editing it a very enjoyable one.

It is a pleasure to have the opportunity to thank the people who worked on this project, making it stronger, clearer, and, most important, better! Meagan Pier Levinson at Cornell University Press provided strong encouragement right from the start. Her support continued throughout. India Miraglia took over the helm with Meagan's departure and was a delight to work with—supportive, responsive, and very forgiving of missed deadlines. Their efforts and attention improved the book considerably. Also, special thanks to Tisha Dunstan, operations director at the Hudson River Valley Institute, for her excellent attention to detail and keen technological skills.

Scholars of New York history enthusiastically answered our request for assistance to review the chapters. Our thanks to Thomas Beale, Thomas Chambers, Michael Crowder, Zachary Deibel, Michael Diaz, Marcus Gallo, Michael Groth, Kelly Hopkins, Thomas Humphrey, James M. Johnson, Sung Yup Kim, Gabriel Loiacono, Edward L. Moran III, Andrea Mosterman, William Offutt, Brett Palfreyman, Reynolds J. Scott-Childress, Seanegan Sculley, Robert Selig, Timothy Shannon, Andrea Smith, and Colin J. Williams.

This book is dedicated to the late Edward Countryman, the "dean" of American Revolution studies in New York, whose superb work on New York in the revolution inspired many of its chapters.

NOTES

The American Revolution in New York Revisited

I would like to thank Andrew Villani and Christopher Pryslopski of the Hudson River Valley Institute for their careful reading of this chapter and for their thoughtful suggestions for improvement.

1. Otis quoted in Alan Taylor, *American Revolutions: A Continental History, 1750–1804* (W. W. Norton, 2016), 50-51; Fred Anderson, *The Crucible of War: The Seven Years' War and the Fate of Empire in British North America, 1754–1766* (Vintage, 2000); Edward Countryman, *The American Revolution* (Hill & Wang, 2003), 31.

2. On the battle for New York, see George C. Daughan, *Revolution on the Hudson: New York City and the Hudson River Valley in the American War for Independence* (W. W. Norton, 2017), 22–42; Barnett Schecter, *The Battle for New York City* (Walker, 2002), 82-193; Robert Middlekauff, *The Glorious Cause: The American Revolution, 1763–1789* (Oxford University Press, 1982), 339-58.

3. For overviews of the years following the 1763 Treaty of Paris, see Countryman, *American Revolution*, 30-33; Colin G. Colloway, *The Scratch of a Pen: 1763 and the Transformation of North America* (Oxford University Press, 2006), 92–111; Gordon Wood, *The American Revolution: A History* (Modern Library, 2003), 22–23; Taylor, *American Revolutions*, 50–52; Robert Allison, *The American Revolution: A Concise History* (Oxford University Press, 2011), 1–15.

4. The classic account of colonists' response to Parliament's plan to tax remains Edmund Morgan and Helen Morgan, *The Stamp Act Crisis: Prologue to Revolution* (University of North Carolina Press, 1953). Also see Justin DuRivage, *Revolution Against Empire: Taxes, Politics, and the Origins of American Independence* (Yale University Press, 2017); Edward Countryman, *People in Revolution: The American Revolution and Political Society in New York, 1760–1790* (Johns Hopkins University Press, 1981), 3-70. On England's attempt to better regulate and oversee imperial trade, see Thomas M. Truxes, *The Overseas Trade of British America: A Narrative History* (Yale University Press, 2021), 191-263. On limits to western expansion and attempts on the part of the British to better regulate trade, see Bernhard Knollenberg, *Origin of the American Revolution: 1759–1766* (Free Press, 1960), 42, 98–102; Taylor, *American Revolutions*, 6–9.

5. Leading "Progressive" interpretations include Carl Becker, *History of Political Parties in the Province of New York, 1760–1776* (University of Wisconsin Press, 1909); Charles Beard, *An Economic Interpretation of the Constitution* (Macmillan, 1914); and Merrill Jensen, *The New Nation: A History of the United States During the Confederation, 1781–1789* (Northeastern University Press, 1950).

See Michael D. Hattem's informative "The Historiography of the American Revolution," digital timeline, https://bit.ly/AmRevHistTL. Becker is quoted in Alfred Young, ed., *Beyond the American Revolution: Explorations in the History of American Radicalism* (Northern Illinois University Press, 1993), 4.

6. Daniel Boorstin, *The Genius of American Politics* (University of Chicago Press, 1953), 70. Other neoconservative studies that critiqued the Progressive School include Robert E. Brown, *Middle-Class Democracy and the Revolution in Massachusetts, 1691–1780* (Cornell University Press, 1955); and Clinton Rossiter, *Seedtime of the Republic: The Origin of the American Tradition of Political Liberty* (Harcourt & Brace, 1953).

7. See T. H. Breen, Kathleen Duval, Leslie M. Harris, Michael D. Hattem, and Serena Zabin, "The Revolution at 250: A Conversation," *Journal of the Early Republic* 44, no. 4 (2024): 513–74.

8. A sampling of this more inclusive historical literature includes the essays in Young, *Beyond the American Revolution*; Kathleen DuVall, *Independence Lost: Lives on the Edge of the American Revolution* (Random House, 2015); Countryman, *American Revolution*; Ray Raphael, *A People's History of the American Revolution: How Common People Shaped the Fight for Independence* (New Press, 2001); Gary Nash, *The Unknown American Revolution: The Unruly Birth of Democracy and the Struggle to Create America* (Penguin Books, 2005); Ira Berlin, *Many Thousands Gone: The First Two Centuries of Slavery in North America* (Harvard University Press, 1998); Woody Holton, *Liberty Is Sweet: The Hidden History of the American Revolution* (Simon & Schuster, 2022). The quote is from Jesse Lemisch, "The American Revolution Seen from the Bottom Up," in *Towards a New Past: Dissenting Essays in American History*, ed. Barton J. Bernstein (Vintage Books, 1967), 29.

9. Taylor notes the higher percentage of refugees from the American Revolution as compared to the French in *American Revolutions*, 1–9; Colin Calloway, *The American Revolution in Indian Country: Crisis and Diversity in Native American Communities* (Cambridge University Press, 1995); A. Lynn Smith, *Memory Wars: Settlers and Natives Remember Washington's Sullivan Expedition of 1779* (University of Nebraska Press, 2023).

10. Taylor, *American Revolutions*, 2–4; William L. Kidder, *Defending Fort Stanwix: A Story of the New York Frontier in the American Revolution* (Cornell University Press, 2024); Paul B. Moyer, *Wild Yankees: The Struggle for Independence Along Pennsylvania's Revolutionary Frontier, 1750–1820* (Cornell University Press, 2007); Ronald Hoffman, Thad W. Tate, and Peter J. Albert, eds., *An Uncivil War: The Southern Backcountry During the American Revolution* (University Press of Virginia, 1985).

11. Edward Countryman, "From Revolution to Statehood, 1776–1825," in *The Empire State: A History of New York*, ed. Milton Klein (Cornell University Press, 2001), 234; Paul Gilje, *The Road to Mobocracy: Popular Disorder in New York City, 1763–1834* (University of North Carolina Press, 1987), 37–68. Some "young women" in the upper Hudson Valley seized and tarred a suspected loyalist and "coated him well." *New York Gazette and Weekly Mercury*, October 2, 1775.

12. James Johnson, *Key of America: Fortress West Point and the Highlands Department in the American Revolution* (West Point Press, 2025).

13. Middlekauff, *Glorious Cause,* 336–49; Kevin J. Weddle, *The Compleat Victory: Saratoga and the American Revolution* (Oxford University Press, 2021), 361–90; Joseph R. Fischer, *A Well-Executed Failure: The Sullivan Campaign Against the Iroquois, July–September 1779* (University of South Carolina Press, 1997).

14. The economic deprivations of the Hudson Valley are discussed in Staughton Lynd, "Who Should Rule at Home? Dutchess County, New York, in the American Revolution," *William and Mary Quarterly* 18 (Spring 1961): 330–59; Jacob Judd, "Westchester County," in *The Other New York: The American Revolution Beyond New York City, 1763–1787,* ed. Joseph Tiedemann and Eugene R. Fingerhut (State University of New York Press, 2005), 107–26.

15. Tiedemann and Fingerhut, *Other New York,* 1–4; Cathy Matson, *Merchants and Empire: Trading in Colonial New York* (Johns Hopkins University Press, 1998).

16. The population numbers are in Tiedemann and Fingerhut, *Other New York,* 13. For unrest on the estates, see Thomas Humphrey, *Land and Liberty: Hudson Valley Riots in the Age of Revolution* (Northern Illinois University Press, 2004), 68–78; Patricia Bonomi, *A Factious People: Politics and Society in Colonial New York* (Columbia University Press, 1971), 211–23; Sung Bok Kim, *Landlord and Tenant in Colonial New York: Manorial Society, 1664–1775* (University of North Carolina Press, 1978), 346–415.

17. Michael Groth, *Slavery and Freedom in the Mid-Hudson Valley* (State University of New York Press, 2017), 31–33; 44–45. The quotation on the "largest slave society" is on page 5. See also David Gellman, *Emancipating New York: The Politics of Slavery and Freedom, 1777–1827* (Louisiana State University Press, 2006).

18. Groth, *Slavery and Freedom,* 21–41; Judd, "Westchester County," 122–24.

19. Christopher Minty, *Unfriendly to Liberty: Loyalist Networks and the Coming of the American Revolution in New York City* (Cornell University Press, 2023); Russell Shorto, *Revolution Song: A Story of American Freedom* (W. W. Norton, 2018), 1–3.

20. See Groth, *Slavery and Freedom,* 81–82.

1. "The Propriety of a Vigorous Government"

Much of the research and writing for this chapter was made possible by a David Library of the American Revolution short-term fellowship at the American Philosophical Society (APS). Special thanks to Brenna Holland at the APS. I am grateful to Edward Countryman for comments I received on this project. I also owe thanks to the anonymous reviewers who provided highly constructive feedback. I am particularly grateful for the input provided by my colleague Matt White, and to John L. Brooke for his mentorship and encouragement, and for reading multiple versions of this chapter. Last, I thank my wife, ElizaBeth Streifeneder, who heard more than she ever wanted to about Udny Hay.

1. *Laws of the State of N.Y.* (hereafter *N.Y. Laws*), 1st sess., chap. 29, 59.

2. Udny Hay to Nathanael Greene, February 10, 1779, series 1, oversized box 4, 63, Nathanael Greene Papers, American Philosophical Society, Philadelphia (hereafter Greene Papers).

3. On contemporary understandings of the title "officer," see Asheesh Kapur Siddique, *The Archive of Empire: Knowledge, Conquest, and the Making of the Early Modern British World* (Yale University Press, 2024), 6–14.

4. I have adopted Michael Braddick's framework for the state as a "coordinated and territorially bounded network of agencies exercising political power." Michael J. Braddick, *State Formation in Early Modern England, c. 1550–1700* (Cambridge University Press, 2000), 9, 17–18; Steve Hindle, *The State and Social Change in Early Modern England, 1550–1640* (Palgrave Macmillan, 2002); John L. Brooke, "Patriarchal Magistrates, Associated Improvers, and Monitoring Militias: Visions of Self-Government in the Early American Republic, 1760–1840," in *State and Citizen: British America and the Early United States*, ed. Peter Thompson and Peter S. Onuf (University of Virginia Press, 2013), 181–88. For the most recent overview, see Gabriel J. Loiacono's introduction to the forum "Local Governance in the Early Republic," *Journal of the Early Republic* (hereafter *JER*) 44 (Summer 2024): 217–28.

5. Michael Mann, "The Autonomous Power of the State: Its Origins, Mechanisms, and Results," *European Journal of Sociology* 25 (November 1984): 185–212; Johannes Lindvall and Jan Teorell, "State Capacity as Power: A Conceptual Framework," STANCE Working Paper Series, 2016, 6–24; Jonathan K. Hanson and Rachel Sigman, "Leviathan's Latent Dimensions: Measuring State Capacity for Comparative Political Research," *Journal of Politics* 83 (October 2021): 1495–510.

6. Norma Landau, *The Justices of the Peace, 1679–1760* (University of California Press, 1984); Norma Landau, "The Changing Persona of the Justices and Their Quarter Sessions," in *The Oxford Handbook of English Law and Literature, 1500–1700*, ed. Lorna Hutson (Oxford University Press, 2017), 239–56; Brendan Gillis, "Conduits of Justice: Magistrates and the British Imperial State, 1732–1834" (PhD diss., Indiana University, 2015); Julius Goebel Jr. and T. Raymond Naughton, *Law Enforcement in Colonial New York: A Study in Criminal Procedure (1664–1776)* (Patterson Smith, 1970); Sung Yup Kim, "Justices of the Peace, Lawyers, and the People: Local Courts and the Contested Professionalization of Law in Late Colonial New York" (PhD diss., Stony Brook University, 2016).

7. Nicholas Varga, "The Development and Structure of Local Government in Colonial New York," in *Town & County: Essays on the Structure of Local Government in the American Colonies*, ed. Bruce C. Daniels (Wesleyan University Press, 1978), 186–215; Patricia U. Bonomi, "Local Government in Colonial New York: A Base for Republicanism," in *Aspects of Early New York Society and Politics*, ed. Jacob Judd and Irwin H. Polishook (Sleepy Hollow Restorations, 1974), 29–50.

8. Brooke, "Patriarchal Magistrates," 184.

9. Andrew Shankman, "Toward a Social History of Federalism: The State and Capitalism to and from the American Revolution," *JER* 37 (Winter 2017): 619–24.

10. Jack P. Greene, "State Formation, Resistance, and the Creation of Revolutionary Traditions in the Early Modern Era," in *Revolutionary Currents: Nation Building in the Transatlantic World*, ed. Michael A. Morrison and Melinda Zook (Rowman & Littlefield, 2004), 4–5; Jack P. Greene, "Negotiated Authorities:

The Problem of Governance in the Extended Polities of the Early Modern Atlantic World," in *Negotiated Authorities: Essays in Colonial Political and Constitutional History* (University Press of Virginia, 1994), 15–16; Shankman, "Toward a Social History," 615–17, 619–24, 627.

11. Christopher R. Pearl, *Conceived in Crisis: The Revolutionary Creation of an American State* (University of Virginia Press, 2020), 40; Douglas Bradburn, "The Rise of the States: Governance, Institutional Failure, and the Causes of American Independence," paper presented at meeting of the American Historical Association, Washington, DC, January 5, 2008, 1–19; see also "A Political System in Decay," chap. 3 in Edward Countryman, *A People in Revolution: The American Revolution and Political Society in New York, 1760–1790* (Johns Hopkins University Press, 1981), 72–98.

12. Dillon L. Streifeneder, "'The Propriety of a Vigorous Government': State Formation in New York, 1740-1795" (PhD diss., Ohio State University, 2022), 95–114, 129–47; Douglas Edward Leach, *Roots of Conflict: British Armed Forces and Colonial Americans, 1677–1763* (University of North Carolina Press, 1986), 76–106; Douglas Greenberg, *Crime and Law Enforcement in the Colony of New York, 1691–1776* (Cornell University Press, 1974), 188–236.

13. Bradburn, "Rise of the States," 18.

14. Oscar Handlin and Mary Flug Handlin, *Commonwealth: A Study of the Role of Government in the American Economy, Massachusetts, 1774–1861*, rev. ed. (Belknap Press of Harvard University Press, 1969), xii. For an overview of the field, see the forum "Taking Stock of the State in Nineteenth-Century America," *JER* 38 (Spring 2018): 61–118; Gautham Rao, "William J. Novak's *The People's Welfare* and the New Historiography of the Early Federal State," *American Journal of Legal History* 57 (June 2017): 226–31; William J. Novak and Steven Pincus, "Revolutionary State Formation: The Origins of the Strong American State," in *State Formations: Global Histories and Cultures of Statehood*, ed. John L. Brooke, Julia C. Strauss, and Greg Anderson (Cambridge University Press, 2018), 138–55.

15. Novak and Pincus, "Revolutionary State Formation," 147–49, 153.

16. Novak and Pincus, "Revolutionary State Formation," 153; James A. Henretta, "Magistrates, Common Law Lawyers, Legislators: The Three Legal Systems of British America," in *The Cambridge History of Law in America*, ed. Michael Grossberg and Christopher Tomlins, vol. 1, *Early America, 1780–1815* (Cambridge University Press, 2008), 586.

17. Max M. Edling, "Shaping the Constitution," in *The Cambridge History of The Age of Revolutions*, ed. Wim Klooster, vol. 1, *The Enlightenment and the British Colonies* (Cambridge University Press, 2023), 460.

18. Novak and Pincus, "Revolutionary State Formation," 148.

19. The exception is Pearl's study on Pennsylvania, *Conceived in Crisis.*

20. Hugh Hastings, *Public Papers of George Clinton* (hereafter *PPGC*), 10 vols. (New York, 1899-1910), 4:550-52.

21. Henretta, "Magistrates," 586–87; Novak and Pincus, "Revolutionary State Formation," 148–53.

22. See sessions 1–6 in *N.Y. Laws.*

23. Countryman, *People in Revolution*, 184–87.

24. Willi Paul Adams, *The First American Constitutions: Republican Ideology and the Making of the State Constitutions in the Revolutionary Era* (University of North Carolina Press, 1980), 27–48; "The Constitution of New York, April 20, 1777" (Samuel Loudon, 1777).

25. "Constitution of New York"; Novak and Pincus, "Revolutionary State Formation," 153.

26. *PPGC*, 2:876–79.

27. *N.Y. Laws*, 1st sess., chap. 29, 55–60. For a comparison with other state impress laws and the role of local officials, see chap. 4 in E. Wayne Carp, *To Starve the Army at Pleasure: Continental Army Administration and American Political Culture, 1775–1783* (University of North Carolina Press, 1984), 74–98.

28. This number is based on a comparison of prewar and postwar lists of JPs and Loyalists.

29. On New York's colonial JPs, see Kim, "Justices of the Peace," 100–122.

30. Streifeneder, "Propriety of a Vigorous Government," 237–43.

31. Index to Council of Appointment Minutes, New York State Department of State, 1777-1786, A1846, New York State Archives, Albany.

32. For example, between January and August 1778, fifty-seven judges and justices were appointed in Westchester County. A surviving roll of justices from May 1779 indicates only twenty serving. Index to Council of Appointment Minutes, 1777–1786; "A List of Justices in Westchester," microfilm reel no. 3, Alexander McDougall Papers, 1756-1795, American Philosophical Society, Philadelphia (hereafter McDougall Papers).

33. *PPGC*, 3:132–33. "Qualification" required swearing an oath before the county clerk at an appointed time and place. Those who failed to qualify were not authorized to act in an official capacity.

34. *PPGC*, 3:369.

35. *PPGC*, 4:128–29.

36. *PPGC*, 3:259.

37. Index to Council of Appointment Minutes, A1846.

38. Nathanael Greene to George Washington, November 14, 1778, *Founders Online*, National Archives, https://founders.archives.gov/documents/Washington/03-18-02-0146.

39. This justice was likely Cornelius or Martin Wiltsie of Rombout Precinct.

40. Bogart to Bancker, March 6, 1779, series 2, box 7, folio 8a, Greene Papers; Storm to Bancker, March 10, 1779, series 2, box 7, folio 8n, Greene Papers.

41. *PPGC*, 4:566–67.

42. Hay to Greene, February 10, 1779.

43. Dutchess County Court of Common Pleas Minute Books, 1779, Dutchess County Clerk's Office, Poughkeepsie, NY; Hay to Greene, February 23, 1779, series 1, box 2, Greene Papers; Clinton to Hay, February 10, 1779, *PPGC*, 4:558.

44. Greene to Hay, February 16, 1779, in *The Papers of General Nathanael Greene*, ed. Richard K. Showman (University of North Carolina Press, 1976), 3:263–65.

45. Greene to Hay, February 16, 1779.

46. Hay to Clinton, January 20, 1779, series 1, box 2, folio 56, Greene Papers; Hay to Greene, January 21, 1779, *Papers of Nathanael Greene*, 3:175–76.

47. *PPGC*, 4:541–43.

48. *PPGC*, 4:546.

49. McDougall to Benson, February 9, 1779, microfilm reel no. 2, McDougall Papers.

50. Scott to McDougall, February 11, 1779, microfilm reel no. 2, McDougall Papers.

51. Benson to McDougall, March 29, 1779, microfilm reel no. 2, McDougall Papers.

52. *N.Y. Laws*, 2nd sess., chap. 32, 134–36.

53. *PPGC*, 4:750.

54. *N.Y. Laws*, 3rd sess., chap. 4, 148–50.

55. *PPGC*, 5:475–77, 482, 621–22, 846–52; see also Hay's letters to the Assembly regarding acquisition of supplies, and the ensuing statute passed by the legislature addressing Hay's concerns. Hay to Greene, February 10, 1779, and Greene to Hay, February 16, 1779; Major General William Heath to George Washington, December 27, 1779, *Founders Online*, National Archives, https://founders.archives.gov/documents/Washington/03-23-02-0566; Hay to Heath, January 28, 1780, *The Heath Papers* (Massachusetts Historical Society, 1904), 3:24–26; McDougall circular, May 22, 1779, microfilm reel 3, McDougall Papers; Hay to McDougall, June 14, 1779, microfilm reel 3, McDougall Papers.

56. *N.Y. Laws*, 3rd sess., chap. 41 and chap. 67, 208–10, 264–65.

57. Alison G. Olson, "Eighteenth-Century Colonial Legislatures and Their Constituents," *Journal of American History* 79 (September 1992): 543–67; Aaron Graham, "Legislatures, Legislation and Legislating in the British Atlantic, 1692–1800," *Parliamentary History Yearbook Trust* 37 (October 2018): 369–88.

58. Asheesh Kapur Siddique, "Governance Through Documents: The Board of Trade, Its Archive, and the Imperial Constitution of the Eighteenth-Century British Atlantic World," *Journal of British Studies* 59 (May 2020): 267–68; also, on the importance of the emergence of standardized and professional administrative procedures for the British fiscal-military state, see John Brewer, *The Sinews of Power: War, Money, and the English State, 1688–1783* (Alfred A. Knopf, 1988), 64–87.

59. McDougall to Holt, December 30, 1778, microfilm reel 2, McDougall Papers.

60. This had been a perennial problem for the colonial regime, which struggled greatly to provide its agents copies of statutes or other central directives, failing to print even a consolidated digest of New York's laws until 1774. "An Act to Revise Digest and Print the Laws of This Colony," March 24, 1772, in *The Colonial Laws of New York from the Year 1664 to the Revolution* (Albany, 1894), 5:355–57; Peter Van Schaack, *Laws of New-York: From the Year 1691, to 1773 Inclusive* (Hugh Gaine, 1774).

61. McDougall to Holt, December 30, 1778.

62. Holt's *The New-York Journal; or, the General Advertiser*, and Loudon's *The New York Packet, and the American Advertiser*.

63. *New-York Journal*, April 12, 1779.

64. Hay to Greene, May 11, 1779, vol. 7, folio 72, calendar, 84–85, Greene Papers.

65. Hay to Greene, January 29, 1780, in Showman, *Papers of General Nathanael Greene*, 5:323–26. On the "phases of logistical support," see Erna Risch, *Supplying Washington's Army* (Center of Military History, 1981), 23–26.

66. Lieutenant Colonel Udny Hay to George Washington, March 11, 1780, *Founders Online*, National Archives, https://founders.archives.gov/documents/Washington/03-25-02-0015.

67. *PPGC*, 5:846–52.

68. John Shy, "Logistical Crisis and the American Revolution: A Hypothesis," in *Feeding Mars: Logistics in Western Warfare from the Middle Ages to the Present*, ed. John A. Lynn (Westview, 1993), 161–79.

69. Hay to George Washington, March 11, 1780.

70. Gary Gerstle, *Liberty and Coercion: The Paradox of American Government from the Founding to the Present* (Princeton University Press, 2015), 345; Gary Gerstle, "The Resilient Power of the States Across the Long Nineteenth Century," in *The Unsustainable States*, ed. Lawrence Jacobs and Desmond King (Oxford University Press, 2009), 61–87.

71. Laura F. Edwards, *The People and Their Peace: Legal Culture and the Transformation of Inequality in the Post-Revolutionary South* (University of North Carolina Press, 2009), 26–53; see also the forum "Local Governance in the Early Republic," *JER* 44 (Summer 2024): 217–83.

72. On the persistence of localism in New York, see Sung Yup Kim, "'Every Cord That Binds Together the People to the Government': Local Magistracy and the Making of an Adjudicatory State in Early New York," *JER* 44 (Summer 2024): 258. See also Brian Murphy's observation that in 1784, some New Yorkers expressed fears that the state government had once again become "weak, unsettled," having lost the "spirit of enterprise" given it by the revolution. Brian Murphy, *Building the Empire State: Political Economy in the Early Republic* (University of Pennsylvania Press, 2015), 5.

73. Murphy, *Building the Empire State*, 5–6.

74. This interpretation goes against some prominent studies of early US governance, particularly those focused on legal history—Laura Edwards's book on the persistence of local legal culture in the Carolinas (*People and Their Peace*) being the most influential. In a similar vein, Kim, "Every Cord That Binds Together,'" asserts that New York state authorities struggled to control or influence local governance well into the 1820s, and that oversight occurred primarily via the Supreme Court and "a jurisprudence of local governance," which he calls an "adjudicatory state" (252–53). But this ignores the important role the Northern states played in political economy and internal development and the fact that statutes did force local officials to conform with centralized direction. John L. Brooke has shown that a new civil landscape emerged in the decades after the revolution, upending "former habits" where local oligarchs (and their lawyers) controlled the mechanisms of state power for personal gain alone. This new civil society consisted of a thriving print culture and associations that facilitated a "thickening" of

communication between every locality and the legislature, serving as a "flywheel" that turned populist demands for public improvement and "good government and police" into statute laws. See John L. Brooke, *Columbia Rising: Civil Life on the Upper Hudson from the Revolution to the Age of Jackson* (University of North Carolina Press, 2010), chaps. 2-3. See also Pearl's book on Pennsylvania. He notes that while people "saw the need to end the revolutionary tactics of the state, such a move in no way meant the principles and goals of the revolution died with it. Pennsylvanians had worked for a system of government in which they had a central place in shaping public policy," and that meant maintaining a "government that could act with efficiency, effectiveness, and authority to protect the public welfare." Pearl, *Conceived in Crisis*, 205–19. Additional comparative studies of these two regions are needed to tease out the intricacies of how they diverged. These might build on works such as Robin Einhorn's comparative study of taxation, *American Taxation, American Slavery* (University of Chicago Press, 2006); or Sean Adams's of coal industries in Pennsylvania and Virginia, *Old Dominion, Industrial Commonwealth: Coal, Politics, and Economy in Antebellum America* (Johns Hopkins University Press, 2004). On activist Northern state governments, see Murphy, *Building the Empire State*; Handlin and Handlin, *Commonwealth*; Louis Hartz, *Economic Policy and Democratic Thought: Pennsylvania, 1776–1860* (Harvard University Press, 1948); and chapter 10 in Robert H. Wiebe, *The Opening of American Society: From the Adoption of the Constitution to the Eve of Disunion* (Alfred A. Knopf, 1984), 194–208.

75. *N.Y. Laws*, 10th sess., chap. 15 and chap. 16, 371–85; 11th sess., chap. 63, 744–69.

76. Alan Taylor, *William Cooper's Town: Power and Persuasion on the Frontier of the Early American Republic* (Alfred A. Knopf, 1996), 176–80; Alfred F. Young, *The Democratic Republicans of New York: The Origins, 1763–1797* (University of North Carolina Press, 1967), 308–10, 315.

77. Young, *Democratic Republicans*, 304.

78. Young, *Democratic Republicans*, 305; *N.Y. Laws*, 10th sess., chap. 15, 371–84.

79. Young, *Democratic Republicans*, 309.

80. Young, *Democratic Republicans*, 309–10; *An Impartial Statement Respecting the Decision of the Late Committee of Canvassers* (New York, 1792); Taylor, *William Cooper's Town*, 176–80.

81. Alfred B. Street, ed., *The Council of Revision of the State of New York* (Albany, 1859), 286–88.

2. "Fix It Up, in Open View"

The author thanks the editorial team and anonymous readers for their generous feedback and encouragement. Some of the research in this chapter was part of the author's dissertation at William & Mary, advised by Karin Wulf, Joshua Piker, and Nicholas Popper. The author also thanks Susan Ferber at Oxford University Press, publisher of *When the Declaration of Independence Was News* (2026).

1. *The New-York Journal; or, the General Advertiser*, July 4, 1776, 2. On newspapers and communication during the American Revolution, see Joseph M. Adelman, *Revolutionary Networks: The Business and Politics of Printing the News, 1763–1789* (Johns Hopkins University Press, 2019); Bernard Bailyn and John B. Hench, eds., *The Press and the American Revolution* (American Antiquarian Society, 1980); Robert G. Parkinson, *Thirteen Clocks: How Race United the Colonies and Made the Declaration of Independence* (Omohundro Institute of Early American History and Culture; University of North Carolina Press, 2021); Jordan E. Taylor, *Misinformation Nation: Foreign News and the Politics of Truth in Revolutionary America* (Johns Hopkins University Press, 2022).

2. On the British decision to target New York, see Rohit T. Aggarwala, "'I Want a Packet to Arrive': Making New York City the Headquarters of British America, 1696–1783," *New York History* 98, no. 1 (2017): 7–39; Phillip Papas, *That Ever Loyal Island: Staten Island and the American Revolution* (New York University Press, 2007).

3. *New-York Journal*, July 11, 1776, 2.

4. *New-York Journal*, July 11, 1776, 2. Much of the recent research on John Holt's printings of the Declaration of Independence has been done by Seth Kaller, Inc., which, in 2024, facilitated the private sale of the only known copy of the newspaper in private hands. That copy was sold through Sotheby's for $3.36 million.

5. *New-York Journal*, July 18, 1776, 3.

6. John Holt stopped printing *The New-York Journal* after August 29, 1776.

7. For what happened to New York after John Holt and the city's other printers evacuated, see Benjamin L. Carp, *The Great New York Fire of 1776: A Lost Story of the American Revolution* (Yale University Press, 2023).

8. On New York printers during the American Revolution, see Ruma Chopra, "Printer Hugh Gaine Crosses and Re-Crosses the Hudson," *New York History* 90, no. 4 (2009): 271–85; Victor Hugo Paltsits, *John Holt, Printer and Postmaster* (New York Public Library, 1920); Steven Carl Smith, *An Empire of Print: The New York Publishing Trade in the Early American Republic* (Pennsylvania State University Press, 2017), chap. 1; Isaiah Thomas, *The History of Printing in America, with a Biography of Printers*, 2nd ed. (Burt Franklin, 1967), 1:300, 303, 312.

9. *New-York Journal*, June 23, 1774, 1; Adelman, *Revolutionary Networks*, 65–66, 114; Christopher F. Minty, "'UNITE OR DIE': John Holt's *New-York Journal; or, the General Advertiser* and the Imagery of Allegiance," *The Junto: A Group Blog on Early American History*, January 21, 2016, https://earlyamericanists.com/2016/01/21/forming-his-political-principles-john-holts-new-york-journal-or-the-general-advertiser-and-the-imagery-of-allegiance/.

10. *New-York Journal*, December 15, 1774, 1.

11. Letter from "Reprobator" in response to "Mercator," *New-York Journal*, August 18, 1774, 2.

12. *Dunlap's Pennsylvania Packet, or the General Advertiser*, May 6, 1776, postscript.

13. *New-York Journal*, May 9, 1776, 2; Friederike Baer, *Hessians: German Soldiers in the American Revolutionary War* (Oxford University Press, 2022), 205–6.

14. *New-York Journal*, May 23, 1776, 1.

15. *New-York Journal,* June 6, 1776, 2.

16. *New-York Journal,* June 13, 1776, 1–2.

17. Worthington Chauncey Ford, ed., *Journals of the Continental Congress, 1774–1789,* vol. 5, *1776, June 5–October 8* (Government Printing Office, 1906), 425.

18. The New York Delegates to the New York Provincial Congress, June 8, 1776, in *Letters of Delegates to Congress, 1774–1789,* ed. Paul H. Smith, Gerald W. Gawalt, Rosemary Fry Plakas, and Eugene R. Sheridan (Library of Congress, 1940), 4:171.

19. Smith et al., *Letters of Delegates to Congress,* 4:171n1.

20. *Journals of the Provincial Congress, Provincial Convention, Committee of Safety and Council of Safety of the State of New-York, 1775–1776–1777* (Albany, 1842), 1:490–91.

21. *New-York Journal,* June 13, 1776, 3.

22. *New-York Journal,* May 30, 1776, 4.

23. Arrest warrant from a secret committee of the New York Provincial Congress, June 21, 1776, in *The Papers of George Washington: Revolutionary War Series,* vol. 5, *16 June 1776–12 August 1776,* ed. Philander D. Chase (University Press of Virginia, 1991), 72–74.

24. General Orders, June 28, 1776, in Chase, *Papers of George Washington,* vol. 5, 129–30; *Constitutional Gazette* (New York), June 29, 1776, 3–4.

25. *New-York Journal,* June 27, 1776, 3.

26. *Journals of the Provincial Congress,* 1:506.

27. Philip Livingston was not included as a signatory of the letter that the New York delegates sent to the New York Provincial Congress on July 2, but he probably arrived in Philadelphia that day or on July 3.

28. *Journals of the Provincial Congress,* 1:512.

29. Jay to Livingston, July 1, 1776, in *The Selected Papers of John Jay,* vol. 1, *1760–1779,* ed. Elizabeth M. Nuxoll (University of Virginia Press, 2010), 262. Livingston was similarly "mortified" by the New York Provincial Congress's decision. Livingston to Jay, [July 6, 1776], in Nuxoll, *Selected Papers of John Jay,* vol. 1, 288.

30. Rutledge to Jay, June 8, 1776, in Nuxoll, *Selected Papers of John Jay,* vol. 1, 249–50; Rutledge to Jay, June 29, 1776, in Nuxoll, *Selected Papers of John Jay,* vol. 1, 260–62.

31. Rutledge to Jay, June 29, 1776, in Nuxoll, *Selected Papers of John Jay,* vol. 1, 263–65.

32. Jay to Rutledge, [July 6, 1776], in Nuxoll, *Selected Papers of John Jay,* vol. 1, 263–65.

33. Francis Lightfoot Lee to Richard Henry Lee, July 1, 1776, in Smith et al., *Letters of Delegates to Congress,* 4:342–43. The Maryland Convention's decision to allow their delegates to vote for independence had reached Philadelphia that morning.

34. The New York Delegates to the New York Provincial Congress, July 2, 1776, in Smith et al., *Letters of Delegates to Congress,* 4:371–72.

35. Henry Wisner to the New York Provincial Congress, July 2, 1776, in Smith et al., *Letters of Delegates to Congress,* 4:373.

36. Gerry to James Warren, July 5, 1776, in Smith et al., *Letters of Delegates to Congress*, 4:391–92.

37. Paine to Joseph Palmer, July 6, 1776, in Smith et al., *Letters of Delegates to Congress*, 4:399.

38. *New-York Journal*, July 4, 1776, 2.

39. John Hancock to Certain States, July 6, 1776, in Smith et al., *Letters of Delegates to Congress*, 4:396.

40. *Journals of the Provincial Congress*, 1:518.

41. *Journals of the Provincial Congress*, 1:518.

42. *Journals of the Provincial Congress*, 1:520–21.

43. John Alsop to the New York Convention, July 16, 1776, in *American Archives: Fifth Series; Containing a Documentary History of the United States of America, from the Declaration of Independence, July 4, 1776, to the Definitive Treaty of Peace with Great Britain, September 3, 1783*, vol. 1, ed. Peter Force (Washington, DC, 1848), 368–69.

44. In August, Phillip Livingston wrote that, before he and the other delegates received notice that the convention had accepted Alsop's resignation, they noticed only that he "had not attended for some days," and they "did not know the reason of his absenting himself." Phillip Livingston to the New York Convention, August 16, 1776, in Force, *American Archives*, vol. 1, 977.

45. New York Convention to the New York Delegates, July 22, 1776, in Force, *American Archives*, vol. 1, 977.

46. *Journals of the Provincial Congress*, 1:535–36.

47. The first documented public readings of the Declaration of Independence took place the day before, on July 8, in Philadelphia, Easton, and Reading, Pennsylvania, as well as in Trenton, New Jersey. On July 9, there were also public readings in Princeton and New Brunswick, New Jersey.

48. Wendy Bellion, *Iconoclasm in New York: Revolution to Reenactment* (Penn State University Press, 2019); Arthur A. Marks, "The Statue of King George III in New York and the Iconology of Regicide," *American Art Journal* 13, no. 3 (1981): 61–82.

49. *Constitutional Gazette*, July 10, 1776, 1–2.

50. *New-York Journal*, July 11, 1776, 3; *The New York Packet and American Advertiser*, July 11, 1776, 2; *The New-York Gazette: And the Weekly Mercury*, July 15, 1776, 1.

51. *New-York Journal*, July 11, 1776, 2.

52. *New-York Journal*, July 11, 1776, 2; John Milton, *Paradise Lost* (London, 1667), book 1.

53. *New-York Journal*, July 11, 1776, 2. One example of a British newspaper that reprinted Holt's account is *The Gazetteer and New Daily Advertiser* (London), September 25, 1776, 3.

54. *New-York Journal*, July 11, 1776, 2.

55. *New-York Journal*, July 11, 1776, 4. Holt ran this advertisement from July 4 through the suspension of his paper at the end of August. On the complicity of printers in the institution of slavery, see Jordan E. Taylor, "Enquire of the Printer: Newspaper Advertising and the Moral Economy of the North American Slave Trade, 1704–1807," *Early American Studies* 18, no. 3 (2020): 287–323.

56. Hugh Gaine, broadside of the Declaration of Independence, ca. July 1776; Samuel Loudon (attributed), broadside of the Declaration of Independence, ca. July 1776.

57. As Seth Kaller has noted, John Holt's broadsides of the Declaration of Independence probably postdate his July 11 newspaper, both because the title is off-center in the newspaper but centered on the broadside, and because of the sheer amount of labor and time required to print five hundred broadsides. Seth Kaller, Inc., "Early Printings of the Declaration of Independence," accessed August 10, 2025, https://www.sethkaller.com/dec-chrono/.

58. John Holt learned the printing business from Elizabeth's brother, William Hunter, in Williamsburg, Virginia. After John's death in 1788, Elizabeth took over his business. *The Independent Gazette; or the New-York Journal Revived*, February 19, 1784, 3.

59. Extant copies of John Holt's broadside can be found in the Cincinnati Museum Center, the Huntington Library, the New York Public Library, the Westchester County Archives, and one private collection.

60. Solomon Southwick, broadside of the Declaration of Independence, ca. July 13, 1776; Ezekiel Russell, broadside of the Declaration of Independence, ca. July 20, 1776.

61. *New Hampshire Gazette, or, Exeter Morning Chronicle*, July 16, 1776, 1.

62. *The Freeman's Journal, or New-Hampshire Gazette* (Portsmouth), July 20, 1776, 4.

63. *New-York Journal*, July 25, 1776, 3.

3. Raking the Ashes

The author wishes to thank the Early American Republic Seminar at the Graduate Center of the City University of New York as well as Claire E. Gherini for their very helpful feedback on previous drafts of this chapter. He also wishes to thank Michael D. Hattem for sharing an early copy of his book. Finally, he thanks the two anonymous readers from the press, who offered useful critiques.

1. Diedrich Knickerbocker [Washington Irving], *A History of New York, from the Beginning of the World to the End of the Dutch Dynasty* (New York, 1809), 2:187; Diedrich Knickerbocker [Washington Irving], *A History of New York* [. . .], 3rd ed. (Philadelphia, 1819), 2:259; Andrew Burstein, *The Original Knickerbocker: The Life of Washington Irving* (Basic Books, 2007), esp. 6–7, chap. 4; Elizabeth Bradley, *Knickerbocker: The Myth Behind New York* (Rutgers University Press, 2009).

2. For examples of works that highlight social conflict, see Staughton Lynd, "Mechanics in New York City Politics, 1774–1788," *Labor History* 5 (Fall 1964): 225–46; Jesse Lemisch, "Jack Tar in the Streets: Merchant Seamen in the Politics of Revolutionary America," *William and Mary Quarterly* 25 (July 1968): 381–95; Howard B. Rock, *Artisans of the New Republic: The Tradesmen of New York City in the Age of Jefferson* (New York University Press, 1979); Edward Countryman, *A People in Revolution: The American Revolution and Political Society in New York, 1760–1790* (Johns Hopkins University Press, 1981); Paul Gilje, *The Road to Mobocracy: Popular Disorder in New York City, 1763–1834* (University of North

Carolina Press, 1987); Graham Russell Hodges, *Root and Branch: African Americans in New York and East Jersey, 1613–1863* (University of North Carolina Press, 1999); Simon Middleton, *From Privileges to Rights: Work and Politics in Colonial New York City* (University of Pennsylvania Press, 2006); Joyce D. Goodfriend, *Who Should Rule at Home? Confronting the Elite in British New York City* (Cornell University Press, 2017).

3. Vincent Brown, *Tacky's Revolt: The Story of an Atlantic Slave War* (Harvard University Press, 2020), 244; Benjamin L. Carp, *The Great New York Fire of 1776: A Lost Story of the American Revolution* (Yale University Press, 2023); Benjamin L. Carp, "'The First Incendiary': A Female Firebrand and the New York City Fire of 1776," in *Women Waging War in the American Revolution*, ed. Holly A. Mayer (University of Virginia Press, 2022), 23–37. On enslaved fire setting, see Daniel Immerwahr, "Burning Down the House: Slavery and Arson in America," *Journal of American History* 110, no. 3 (2023): 449–73.

4. Alfred F. Young, *The Shoemaker and the Tea Party: Memory and the American Revolution* (Beacon, 1999), 105–7, 206; Clifton Hood, "Journeying to 'Old New York': Elite New Yorkers and Their Invention of an Idealized City History in the Late Nineteenth and Early Twentieth Centuries," *Journal of Urban History* 28, no. 6 (2002): 700.

5. Hood, "Journeying," 699–704; see also David D. Van Tassel, *Recording America's Past: An Interpretation of the Development of Historical Studies in America, 1607–1884* (University of Chicago Press, 1960), 52–53, 56, 58–59, 60, 62–64, 66, 122; Wendy Bellion, *Iconoclasm in New York: Revolution to Reenactment* (Pennsylvania State University Press, 2019); Michael Kammen, *A Season of Youth: The American Revolution and the Historical Imagination* (Cornell University Press, 1978), 219.

6. Thomas Jefferson, *Notes on the State of Virginia*, ed. David Waldstreicher (Bedford/St. Martin's, 2002), 197; Michael D. Hattem, *The Memory of '76: The Revolution in American History* (Yale University Press, 2024), 147–48; Eileen Ka-May Cheng, *The Plain and Noble Garb of Truth: Nationalism and Impartiality in American Historical Writing, 1784–1860* (University of Georgia Press, 2008), 32–34, chap. 4; Benjamin L. Carp, *Rebels Rising: Cities and the American Revolution* (Oxford University Press, 2007), epilogue; Philip Ranlet, *The New York Loyalists* (University of Tennessee Press, 1986); Milton M. Klein, "Shaping the American Tradition: The Microcosm of Colonial New York," *New York History* 59, no. 2 (1978): 173–97; Milton M. Klein, "New York in the American Colonies: A New Look," *New York History* 53, no. 2 (1972): 132–56; Alexander C. Flick, *Loyalism in New York During the American Revolution* (New York, 1901), 180–82.

7. Oscar Theodore Barck, *New York City During the War for Independence: With Special Reference to the Period of British Occupation* (Columbia University Press, 1931); Thomas J. Wertenbaker, *Father Knickerbocker Rebels* (Scribner's, 1948).

8. Graham Russell Hodges, "Black Revolt in New York City and the Neutral Zone, 1775–1783," in *Slavery, Freedom and Culture Among Early American Workers* (Routledge, 2015), 65–86; Judith L. Van Buskirk, *Generous Enemies: Patriots and Loyalists in Revolutionary New York* (University of Pennsylvania Press, 2002); Edwin G. Burrows, *Forgotten Patriots: The Untold Story of American Prisoners*

During the Revolutionary War (Basic Books, 2008); Ruma Chopra, *Unnatural Rebellion: Loyalists in New York City During the American Revolution* (University of Virginia Press, 2011); Steven H. Jaffe, *New York at War: Four Centuries of Combat, Fear, and Intrigue in Gotham* (Basic Books, 2012); Christopher Sparshott, "Loyalist Refugee Camp: A Reinterpretation of Occupied New York," in *The Consequences of Loyalism: Essays in Honor of Robert M. Calhoon*, ed. Rebecca Brannon and Joseph S. Moore (University of South Carolina Press, 2019), 62; Donald F. Johnson, *Occupied America: British Military Rule and the Everyday Experience of Revolution* (University of Pennsylvania Press, 2020).

9. John Sloss Hobart to New York Convention, September 25, 1776, in *Journals of the Provincial Congress, Provincial Convention, Committee of Safety and Council of Safety of the State of New-York, 1775–1777* (Albany, 1842), 2:222–23; Carp, *Great New York Fire*, chap. 11. See also Wayne E. Lee, *Barbarians and Brothers: Anglo-American Warfare, 1500–1865* (Oxford University Press, 2011); T. Cole Jones, *Captives of Liberty: Prisoners of War and the Politics of Vengeance in the American Revolution* (University of Pennsylvania Press, 2020).

10. John Rodgers, *The Divine Goodness Displayed, in the American Revolution: A Sermon, Preached in New-York, December 11th, 1783* [. . .] (New York, 1784), 26–27; [Samuel Williams], "History of the American Revolution," *Rural Magazine, or, Vermont Repository* 1 (August 1795): 434; [Thomas Pemberton], *An Historical Journal of the American War* (Boston, 1795), 87; James Thacher, *Military Journal During the American Revolutionary War* [. . .] (Boston, 1823), 69; Sarah J. Purcell, *Sealed with Blood: War, Sacrifice, and Memory in Revolutionary America* (University of Pennsylvania Press, 2002), chap. 2; Clifton Hood, "An Unusable Past: Urban Elites, New York City's Evacuation Day, and the Transformations of Memory Culture," *Journal of Social History* 37, no. 4 (2004): 883–913.

11. *The Annual Register, or a View of the History, Politics, and Literature for the Year 1776* (London, 1777), 180; *The Annual Register* [. . .], 2nd ed. (London, 1779), 175–76; John Adolphus, *The History of England from the Accession of King George the Third, to* [. . .] *1783* (London, 1802), 2:427; Robert Beatson, *Naval and Military Memoirs of Great Britain, 1727–1783* (London, 1804), 4:166–67.

12. William Gordon, *The History of the Rise, Progress, and Establishment, of the Independence of the United States of America: Including an Account of the Late War* [. . .] (London, 1788), 2:330–31. See also William Gordon, *The History of the Rise* [. . .] (New York, 1789), 2:127; Van Tassel, *Recording America's Past*, 74; Malcolm Freiberg, "The Reverend William Gordon's Autumn 1776 Tour of the Northeast," *New England Quarterly* 65, no. 3 (1992): 479. For absolution of Washington, see John Marshall, *Life of George Washington, Commander in Chief of the American Forces* [. . .] (Philadelphia, 1804), 2:475–76n; Jared Sparks, ed., *The Writings of George Washington* (Boston, 1834), 4:100n; William B. Reed, ed., *Life and Correspondence of Joseph Reed* (Philadelphia, 1847), 1:239n; Washington Irving, *Life of George Washington* (New York, 1855), 2:361–62.

13. Duke de la Rouchefoucault-Liancourt, *Travels Through the United States of North America* [. . .] *in the Years 1795, 1796, and 1797* [. . .], 2nd ed. (London, 1800), 4:228; [Samuel Latham Mitchill], *The Picture of New-York, or The Traveller's Guide Through the Commercial Metropolis of the United States* [. . .] (New York, 1807), 131–32.

14. David Humphreys, "An Elegy on the Burning of Fairfield, in Connecticut [. . .]," in *Poems* (Philadelphia, 1789), 1–2; Inventories of Damages by the British and Americans in New Jersey, 1776–1782, Records of the Legislature, New Jersey State Archives, Trenton; William W. Williams, *History of the Fire Lands Comprising Huron and Erie Counties, Ohio* [. . .] (Cleveland, 1879), 10–20; Robb K. Haberman, "Burning Memories: The Destruction of Kingston and the Gubernatorial Election of 1798," *New York History* 100, no. 3 (2020): 19–29.

15. John F. Watson, "Appendix: Containing Olden Time Researches and Reminiscences of New York City," in *Annals of Philadelphia* [. . .] (Philadelphia and New York, 1830), 57–58 (second pagination); Benjamin L. Carp, "David Grim's Fairy Tale: The New York City Fire in Myth," *Gotham: A Blog for Scholars of New York City History*, February 15, 2023, https://www.gothamcenter.org/blog/david-grims-fairy-tale-the-new-york-city-fire-in-myth; Van Tassel, *Recording America's Past*, 104; Young, *Shoemaker*, pt. 2, chap. 5; Purcell, *Sealed with Blood*, 192–94; Hood, "Unusable Past," 884, 892–95; Hattem, *Memory of '76*, chap. 3.

16. Watson, *Annals of Philadelphia*, 57 (second pagination).

17. Watson, *Annals of Philadelphia*, 47, 56, esp. 57–58 (second pagination); Grant Thorburn Sr., "Old Down Town Churches," *New-York Observer*, November 4, 1858. See also Deborah Dependahl Waters, "Philadelphia's Boswell: John Fanning Watson," *Pennsylvania Magazine of History and Biography* 98, no. 1 (1974): 12n10, 21, 25–26; William Dunlap, *History of New Netherlands, Province of New York, and State of New York, to the Adoption of the Federal Constitution* (New York, 1840), 2:78–79; John W. Barber and Henry Howe, *Historical Collections of the State of New York* [. . .] (New York, 1841), 303–4; George Bancroft, *History of the United States from the Discovery of the American Continent* (Boston, 1866), 9:129.

18. Watson, *Annals of Philadelphia*, 57 (second pagination); "A Soldier of Seventy-Six," "Annals of New-York: Reminiscences of the American Revolution," *New-York Mirror* 9, no. 32 (February 11, 1832): 249; Daniel Curry, *New-York: A Historical Sketch of the Rise and Progress of the Metropolitan City of America* (New York, 1853), 135; Benson J. Lossing, *Life of Washington: A Biography Personal, Military, and Political* (New York, 1860), 2:300, 300n; Charles Burr Todd, *The Story of the City of New York* (New York, 1888), 336; Martha J. Lamb, *History of the City of New York: Its Origin, Rise and Progress*, vol. 2 (New York, 1880), 136.

19. [John Pintard], *New-York Advertiser*, August 25–28, 1826, [2], [3]; for attribution, see John Pintard to Eliza Noel Pintard Davidson, August 23, 1826, in *Letters from John Pintard to His Daughter, Eliza Noel Pintard Davidson, 1816–1833*, vol. 2, *1821–1827*, in *Collections of the New York Historical Society* 71 (1940): 294–95, 295n35; "Reminiscences of the Early Life of John Pintard," 1841, John Pintard Papers, New-York Historical Society, 79–81. On banalization, trivialization, and silencing, see Michel-Rolph Trouillot, *Silencing the Past: Power and the Production of History* (Beacon, 1995), esp. 26, 83, 96, 97, 102–7, 147–48.

20. James Hardie, *The Description of the City of New-York* [. . .] (New York, 1827), 85.

21. *New York Sun*, reprinted in "The Great Fire in New York," *Family Magazine, or General Abstract of Useful Knowledge* 3, no. 40 (1836): 319. Troyer Steele Anderson, *The Command of the Howe Brothers During the American Revolution* (Oxford University Press, 1936), 231, similarly argued that "little permanent

ill effect appears to have resulted" from the fire. Barck, *New York City,* 82, disagreed: "Its seriousness was its destruction of houses needed not only by the army, but for the civilians who flocked to the city."

22. William Berrian, *An Historical Sketch of Trinity Church, New-York* (New York, 1847), 144–47; E. B. O'Callaghan, ed., *The Documentary History of the State of New-York* (Albany, 1850), 3:637–46; E. B. O'Callaghan, ed., *Documents Relative to the Colonial History of the State of New York* [. . .] (Albany, 1857), 8:686–87, 798–99; Peter Force, ed., *American Archives: Fifth Series; Containing a Documentary History of the United States* [. . .], vol. 2 (Washington, DC, 1851), 120–21, 123, 135, 140, 168, 182–83, 193–94, 200, 236–38, 380, 443–45, 460–63, 465–66, 493–94, 503–4, 519, 524, 548, 719, 819–22, 921, 981–82; Peter Force, ed., *American Archives: Fifth Series; Containing a Documentary History of the United States* [. . .], vol. 3 (Washington, DC, 1853), 1012–13, 1306–7, 1424–25; D. T. Valentine, "The Great Fires in New York City in 1776 and 1778," *Manual of the Corporation of the City of New York for 1866* (New York, 1866), 766–86; "Old New York and Trinity Church," *NYHS Collections* 3 (1870), 270–76, 280–83; "A Centennial Letter," *New York Tribune,* March 4, 1876, 4; "[Carl] Baurmeister's Narrative of the Capture of New York, September 1776," *Magazine of American History with Notes and Queries* 1, no. 1 (1877): 33–39; [Ewald Shewkirk], "Occupation of New York City by the British, 1776: Extracts from the Diary of the Moravian Congregation," ed. A. A. Reinke, *Pennsylvania Magazine of History and Biography* 1, no. 2–3 (1877): 133–48, 250–62; Henry P. Johnston, *The Campaign of 1776 Around New York and Brooklyn* (Brooklyn, 1878), 1:262, 2:117–19; Van Tassel, *Recording America's Past,* chap. 11, pp. 124–25.

23. Benson J. Lossing, *The Pictorial Field-Book of the Revolution* (New York, 1851), 2:819; *Phelps' New York City Guide; Being a Pocket Directory* [. . .] (New York, 1853), 10; George Tucker, *The History of the United States from Their Colonization to* [. . .] *1841* (Philadelphia, 1856), 1:184–86; Bancroft, *History,* 9:129.

24. Hood, "Journeying," 702; Mary L. Booth, *History of the City of New York from Its Earliest Settlement to the Present Time* (New York, 1859), 2:540–42, 541; Harriet Prescott Spofford, "Mary Louise Booth," in *Our Famous Women: An Authorized Record of Their Lives and Deeds* (Hartford, CT, 1884), 121. See also Hugh Macatamney, *Cradle Days of New York, 1609–1825* (Drew and Lewis, 1909), 70; on British hearings in 1776 and 1783, see Carp, *Great New York Fire,* chaps. 10, 14.

25. Lamb, *History,* 2:116–19, 135, 136; Charles Hemstreet, *The Story of Manhattan* (Charles Scribner's Sons, 1901), 167.

26. Cheng, *Plain and Noble Garb,* 86–87, 209; George Rapelje, *A Narrative of Excursions, Voyages, and Travels* [. . .] (New York, 1834), 13, 14, 15; Carp, *Great New York Fire,* 44–46, 50–51.

27. Thomas Jones, *The History of New York During the Revolutionary War* [. . .], ed. Edward Floyd De Lancey (New York, 1879), 1:84, 85, 120, 121, 314–15, 2:307, 308, 309–15.

28. William L. Stone, *History of New York City from the Discovery to the Present Day* (New York, 1872), 250–53, 250, 252, 253n; Hood, "Unusable Past," 898; James C. Scott, *Weapons of the Weak: Everyday Forms of Peasant Resistance* (Yale University Press, 1985). See also Matilda Despard, *Old New York, from the Battery to Bloomingdale* (New York, 1875), 83–84; Theron Brown, "Who Burned

New York?," *Independent* (New York), July 20, 1876. Augustine E. Costello, *Our Firemen: A History of New York Fire Departments* [. . .] (New York, 1887), 37, 200, 201–4, gives a mixed answer by recapitulating both Watson and Stone. Brigadier General Theophilus F. Rodenbough advanced both explanations: "The consensus of opinion seems to ascribe the beginning of the fire to accident, and its violence and extent to the want of a fire department, and to the opportunities afforded by the circumstances to irresponsible incendiaries." "New-York During the Revolution, 1775–1783," in *The Memorial History of the City of New-York from Its First Settlement to the Year 1892*, ed. James Grant Wilson (New York, 1892), 2:527. See also Theodore Roosevelt, "New York," in *Historic Towns*, ed. Edward A. Freeman and William Hunt (London, 1891), 132–33, 137–39, 141; Charles Royster, *The Destructive War: William Tecumseh Sherman, Stonewall Jackson, and the Americans* (Knopf, 1991), esp. chap. 8.

29. William Henry Shelton, *The Jumel Mansion: Being a Full History of the House on Harlem Heights* [. . .] (Houghton Mifflin, 1916), chaps. 4–5, pp. 24–25, 44, 52, 63, 65.

30. William Henry Shelton, "New York Fought Fire Under Washington's Eye," *New York Times*, February 28, 1926, XX12; William Henry Shelton, "Nathan Hale Execution and the New York Fire," *New York Times*, September 22, 1929, XX13. See also Bethany Andreasen, "Treason or Truth: The New York City Textbook Controversy, 1920–1923," *New York History* 66, no. 4 (1985): 406, 410–11; Joseph Moreau, *Schoolbook Nation: Conflicts over American History Textbooks from the Civil War to the Present* (University of Michigan Press, 2003), esp. chap. 5; Mary Beth Baker, "Nathan Hale: Icon of Innocence," *Connecticut History* 45, no. 1 (2006): 1–30; Hattem, *Memory of '76*, 151–55.

31. Van Tassel, *Recording America's Past*, 179; Randall Mason, *The Once and Future New York: Historic Preservation and the Modern City* (University of Minnesota Press, 2009), xxvi, xxvii; Rufus Rockwell Wilson, *New York: Old and New; Its Story, Streets, and Landmarks*, 2nd ed. (J. B. Lippincott, 1903), 1:259; Henry Collins Brown, *Glimpses of Old New-York* (Lent and Graff, 1917), 130, 131; Hood, "Journeying," 703–4, 709–10.

32. Hattem, *Memory of '76*, 138; Hood, "Journeying," 707–9.

33. Barck, *New York City*, 79–82, 81–82; I. N. Phelps Stokes, ed., *The Iconography of Manhattan Island, 1498–1909* (Robert H. Dodd, 1916, 1926), 1:324, 5:1006, 1020–24, 1168–69; "Societies," *Magazine of American History with Notes and Queries* 23, no. 6 (1890): 509; Max Page, *The Creative Destruction of Manhattan, 1900–1940* (University of Chicago Press, 1999), chap. 7.

34. Wertenbaker, *Father Knickerbocker Rebels*, 98–102; Willard M. Wallace, *Appeal to Arms: A Military History of the American Revolution* (Harper and Brothers, 1951), 118; Bayrd Still, *Mirror for Gotham: New York as Seen by Contemporaries from Dutch Days to the Present* (New York University Press, 1956), 42.

35. John C. Fitzpatrick, ed., *The Writings of George Washington* [. . .] (US Government Printing Office, 1940), 37:531–33, first made available George Washington's letter to Lund Washington on October 6, 1776, where Washington expresses his approval of the burning of New York City.

36. Stephen Conway, *The War of American Independence, 1775–1783* (Edward Arnold, 1995), 247.

4. Long Island Loyalties

Research for this chapter was supported by funding from the Robert David Lion Gardiner Foundation. The authors would like to thank Heath Bowen, Kathryn Curran, Terry Tirado, Jennifer E. Stertzer, Erica Cavanaugh, Katie Blizzard, Andreas Meyris, William M. Ferraro, Todd Braisted, Mark Sternberg, Nadine Delia, Liam McClinsey, Michael Keegan, Erica Soto, Robert Ingoglia, Robert Murray, Kaitlyn Pacella, Harriet Gerard Clark, Theresa Skvarla, Justinne Lake-Jedzinak, Jessica Pearl, and Heather Minty for their support. They would also like to thank Thomas S. Wermuth, Jennifer Lemak, Devin Lander, and the anonymous reviewers, all of whom made our piece much stronger.

1. Wickes to Washington, September 10, 1778, in *Papers of George Washington: Revolutionary War Series* (hereafter *PGW*), vol. 16, *1 July 1778–14 September 1778*, ed. David R. Hoth (University of Virginia Press, 2006), 564.

2. Tryon to Germain, September 5, 1778, CO 5/1108, ff. 262–70 (esp. 262–64), National Archives of the United Kingdom (hereafter UK-KeNA).

3. See Frederic Gregory Mather, *The Refugees of 1776 from Long Island to Connecticut* (J. B. Lyon, 1913); see also Lora Horton Higgins, "Seven Years in Exile: The Long Island Refugees, 1776–1783" (MA thesis, University of Georgia, 2009), https://getd.libs.uga.edu/pdfs/higgins_lora_200905_ma.pdf.

4. Tryon to Germain, September 5, 1778.

5. Wickes to Washington, August 25 and 27, 1778, in *PGW*, 16:377, 391.

6. Tryon to Germain, October 8, 1778, CO 5/1108, f. 279, UK-KeNA.

7. Brookhaven was a name used for the modern community of Setauket on the north coast of Long Island. It should not be confused with the current town of Brookhaven, nearer the south coast.

8. For the oath, see CO 5/1109, ff. 2–49, UK-KeNA. For histories of the Culper ring, see Morton Pennypacker, *General Washington's Spies on Long Island and in New York* (Long Island Historical Society, 1939); and Alexander Rose, *Washington's Spies: The Story of America's First Spy Ring* (Bantam Books, 2006).

9. See, for example, "Evolution of Espionage in America: Revolutionary America; The Culper Spy Ring," Office of the Director of National Intelligence, accessed July 31, 2024, https://web.archive.org/web/20240206212331/https://www.intel.gov/evolution-of-espionage/revolutionary-war/culper-spy-ring.

10. For a robust overview of the Culper ring, see *PGW*, vol. 22, *1 August–21 October 1779*, ed. Benjamin L. Huggins (University of Virginia Press, 2013), 42–45.

11. Edward Larkin, "What Is a Loyalist?," *Common-Place: The Journal of Early American Life* 8, no. 1 (2007): https://commonplace.online/article/what-is-a-loyalist/. Larkin's piece has been cited in numerous books and articles, including Maya Jasanoff, *Liberty's Exiles: American Loyalists in the Revolutionary World* (Knopf, 2012); Emma Stapely, *Afterlives of the American Revolution* (Palgrave Macmillan, 2024); and Philip Gould, *Writing the Rebellion: Loyalists and the Literature of Politics in British America* (Oxford University Press, 2013).

12. Jasanoff, *Liberty's Exiles*, 5–8; Liam Riordan and Jerry Bannister, *The Loyal Atlantic: Remaking the British Atlantic in the Revolutionary Era* (University of Toronto Press, 2012), 5–6.

13. Stapely, *Afterlives*, 126.

14. See, for example, Joseph S. Tiedemann, *Reluctant Revolutionaries: New York City and the Road to Independence* (Cornell University Press, 1997); Ruma Chopra, *Unnatural Rebellion: Loyalists in New York City During the Revolution* (University of Virginia Press, 2011); Christopher F. Minty, *Unfriendly to Liberty: Loyalist Networks and the Coming of the American Revolution in New York City* (Cornell University Press, 2023).

15. Lee to Washington, February 19, 1776, in *PGW*, vol. 3, *1 January–31 March 1776*, ed. Philander D. Chase (University Press of Virginia, 1988), 339–41; William Fielding to the Earl of Denbigh, December 29, 1776, in *The Lost War: Letters from British Officers During the American Revolution*, ed. Marion Balderston and David Syrett (Horizon, 1975), 113–14.

16. The Palmer School of Library and Information Science at Long Island University, thanks to grants from the Robert David Lion Gardiner Foundation, has digitized thousands of documents that have gone a long way to increasing access to Long Island's history. Over eighty-three thousand images are available from at least fifty historical organizations. See https://liu.access.preservica.com/ (accessed September 30, 2024).

17. John G. Staudt, "'A State of Wretchedness': A Social History of Suffolk County, New York in the American Revolution" (PhD diss., George Washington University, 2005), 25–27.

18. Staudt, "'State of Wretchedness,'" 28.

19. For more about the Presbyterian and religious influence on the creation of Suffolk County, see Staudt, "'State of Wretchedness,'" 52–60.

20. Staudt, "'State of Wretchedness,'" 64.

21. Staudt, "'State of Wretchedness,'" 66–67.

22. Staudt, "'State of Wretchedness,'" 67–68. For a full list of those who signed and did not, see Mather, *Refugees*, 1054–65.

23. Staudt, "'State of Wretchedness,'" 71.

24. Staudt, "'State of Wretchedness,'" 73. See also Thomas Bayles, *During the Revolution in Brookhaven Town* (Town of Brookhaven, 1976), 7; Mather, *Refugees*, 989–1013.

25. Staudt, "'State of Wretchedness,'" 81–82.

26. Harrison to Hancock, August 27, 1776, in *PGW*, vol. 6, *13 August–20 October 1776*, ed. Philander D. Chase and Frank E. Grizzard Jr. (University Press of Virginia, 1994), 140–44.

27. Council of War, August 29, 1776, in *PGW*, 6:153–55; see also General Orders, August 31, 1776, in *PGW*, 6:171–77.

28. Trumbull to Washington, September 5, 1776, in *PGW*, 6:226–27; Livingston to Washington, September 11, 1776, in *PGW*, 282–84. A mutilated, illegible copy of an oath of allegiance from September 4, 1776, is in Dominick-Floyd Papers, box 4, f. 60, Long Island Museum. For more on Gardiner, see Mather, *Refugees*, 116–17, 351–52, 770–71.

29. John Adams to Abigail Adams, September 4, 1776, in *Adams Family Correspondence*, vol. 2, *1 June 1776–31 March 1778*, ed. L. H. Butterfield, Wendell D. Garrett, and Marjorie E. Sprague (Harvard University Press, 1963), 117–18.

30. Adams to Cooper, September 4, 1776, in *Papers of John Adams*, vol. 5, *29 August 1776–9 March 1778*, ed. Robert J. Taylor, Gregg L. Lint, and Celeste Walker (Harvard University Press, 1983), 11.

31. William Howe, "A Proclamation," August 23, 1776, in *American Archives: Fifth Series; Consisting of a Collection of Authentick Records, State Papers, Debates, and Letters and Other Notices of Public Affairs, the Whole Forming a Documentary History of the Origin and Process of the North American Colonies; of the Causes and Accomplishment of the American Revolution; and of the Constitution of Government for the United States, to the Final Ratification Thereof*, ed. Peter Force, vol. 1 (Washington, DC, 1848), 1121.

32. William Erskine to the Inhabitants of the County of Suffolk, August 28, 1776, in Force, *American Archives: Fifth Series*, vol. 1, 1211–12.

33. Jonathan Trumbull Sr. to George Washington, September 30, 1776, in *PGW*, 6:439–40; Trumbull to Washington, October 13, 1776, in *PGW*, 6:559–61.

34. *New-York Gazette: And the Weekly Mercury*, November 11, 1776, 1.

35. CO 5/1109, ff. 2–49, UK-KeNA.

36. Nehemiah Marks to Oliver DeLancey, December 21, 1780, Henry Clinton Papers, vol. 134, f. 26, William L. Clements Library, University of Michigan. The first known place to identify the Roes as supporters of the Culper ring is Corey Ford, *A Peculiar Service* (Little, Brown, 1965), 266. Ford quotes Marks's letter. See also Linda Elten Barber, "Community Formation and Patterning in Historic Old Mans, Long Island" (PhD diss., State University of New York at Stony Brook, 1992), 418, 537, 539, 545–46, 554, 578. Whereas many believed that the Culper ring operated in Setauket and Oyster Bay, Marks's letter indicates that its reach extended beyond those towns and into what is now Port Washington, Long Island. And the Roe family had deep roots in the community. They had lived in Drowned Meadow since the late seventeenth century and were among its first residents.

37. For those who signed the Continental Association, see "Signers in Brookhaven, Suffolk County" and "Brookhaven Association," July 1775, in *American Archives: Fourth Series; Containing a Documentary History of the English Colonies in North America, from the King's Message to Parliament, of March 7, 1774, to the Declaration of Independence by the United States*, ed. Peter Force, vol. 3 (Washington, DC, 1840), 614–15. For the oath of allegiance, see CO 5/1109, UK-KeNA.

38. "Islip Precinct," June 29, 1775, in Force, *American Archives: Fourth Series*, vol. 3, 612.

39. "Signers in Southold, Suffolk County," June 23, 1775, in Force, *American Archives: Fourth Series*, vol. 3, 618.

40. "Signers in Easthampton, Suffolk County," [1775], in Force, *American Archives: Fourth Series*, vol. 3, 611–22; Staudt, "'State of Wretchedness,'" 67.

41. "Signers in Smithtown, Suffolk County," [1775], in Force, *American Archives: Fourth Series*, vol. 3, 617.

42. "Suffolk County Association," July 19, 1775, in Force, *American Archives: Fourth Series*, vol. 3, 613–14.

43. See CO 5/1109, UK-KeNA.

44. See Staudt, "'State of Wretchedness,'" 67.

45. For the oath, see CO 5/1108, UK-KeNA. For more on Allicocke, see Minty, *Unfriendly to Liberty*.

46. See Christopher F. Minty, "'Of One Hart and One Mind': Local Institutions and Allegiance During the American Revolution," *Early American Studies* 15, no. 1 (2017): 99–132, https://doi.org/10.1353/eam.2017.0003; Donald F. Johnson, "Ambiguous Allegiances: Urban Loyalties During the American Revolution," *Journal of American History* 104, no. 3 (2017): 610–31, https://doi.org/10.1093/jahist/jax311.

47. Staudt, "'State of Wretchedness,'" 89–90; Benjamin Tallmadge to George Washington, April 6, 1781, in *PGW*, vol. 31, *7 March–5 May 1781*, ed. Jennifer E. Stertzer, William M. Ferraro, Thomas E. Dulan, et al. (University of Virginia Press, 2023), 295–97. For a description of Fort Slongo, see Robert B. Roberts, *New York's Forts in the Revolution* (Fairleigh Dickinson University Press, 1980), 252–54. A hand-drawn map of the fort is filed with Tallmadge to Lemuel Trescott, September 25, 1781, Papers of George Washington, series 4, Library of Congress, Washington, DC.

48. Thomas Jones, *History of New York During the Revolutionary War, and of the Leading Events in the Other Colonies at That Period* (Printed for the New-York Historical Society, 1879), 2:26–27.

5. From Defeated People to Sovereign Nation

The author would like to thank Maeve Kane and the History Department at Marist University for their comments. She would also like to thank the editors of this volume, particularly Thom Wermuth, as well as the reviewers for their feedback and guidance.

1. "Journal of Lieut. Thomas Blake," in *Journals of the Military Expedition of Major General John Sullivan Against the Six Nations of Indians in 1779 with Records of Centennial Celebrations*, ed. Frederick Cook (Auburn, NY, 1887) (hereafter *Expedition Journals*), 39.

2. For more on the Haudenosaunee in the revolution, see Colin G. Calloway, *The American Revolution in Indian Country: Crisis and Diversity in Native American Communities* (Cambridge University Press, 1995); Barbara Graymont, *The Iroquois in the American Revolution* (Syracuse University Press, 1975); Anthony F. C. Wallace, *The Death and Rebirth of the Seneca* (Vintage Books, 1972). For scholars who focus on the Sullivan-Clinton Expedition as genocide, see Barbara Alice Mann, *George Washington's War on Native America* (Praeger, 2005); Rhiannon Koehler, "Hostile Nations: Quantifying the Destruction of the Sullivan-Clinton Genocide of 1779," *American Indian Quarterly* 42 (Fall 2018): 427–53.

3. The Oneida and many Tuscarora allied with the Continental army.

4. Thomas Jefferson et al., copy of the Declaration of Independence, July 4, 1776, Thomas Jefferson Papers, Library of Congress, Washington, DC.

5. Graymont, *Iroquois*, 193.

6. For more on the campaign's goal of claiming Haudenosaunee lands, see Koehler, "Hostile Nations," 436, 442; A. Lynn Smith, *Memory Wars: Settlers and*

Natives Remember Washington's Sullivan Expedition of 1779 (University of Nebraska Press, 2023), 4.

7. For more on the military failures of the expedition, see Graymont, *Iroquois*; Joseph R. Fischer, *A Well-Executed Failure: The Sullivan Campaign Against the Iroquois, July–September 1779* (University of South Carolina Press, 1997).

8. Cornplanter, Half Town, and Big Tree, "To the Great Council of the Thirteen Fires: The Speech of Corn Plant, Half Town, and Big Tree, Chiefs and Counsellors of the Seneca Nation, 1794," in *Documents Relative to Indian Affairs* (New York, 1817), n.p., Buffalo History Museum, Buffalo, NY.

9. Cornplanter, Half Town, and Big Tree, "To the Great Council," n.p.

10. See William N. Fenton, "Toward the Gradual Civilization of the Indian Natives: The Missionary and Linguistic Work of Asher Wright (1803–1875) Among the Senecas of Western New York," *American Philosophical Society Proceedings* 100, no. 6 (1956): 567–81; David Preston, *The Texture of Contact: European and Indian Settler Communities on the Frontiers of Iroquoia, 1667–1783* (University of Nebraska Press, 2009); Alan Taylor, *The Divided Ground: Indians, Settlers, and the Northern Borderland of the American Revolution* (Alfred A. Knopf, 2006); Wallace, *Death and Rebirth*, 184. Wallace and Matthew Dennis focus on the postrevolution revitalization of Seneca society through the teachings of the Seneca prophet Handsome Lake. Matthew Dennis, *Seneca Possessed: Indians, Witchcraft, and Power in the Early American Republic* (University of Pennsylvania Press, 2010). Alyssa Mt. Pleasant's work focuses on the revitalization of the Buffalo Creek community as a Haudenosaunee space after the expedition. Alyssa Mt. Pleasant, "After the Whirlwind: Maintaining a Haudenosaunee Place at Buffalo Creek, 1780–1825" (PhD diss., Cornell University, 2007).

11. Emilie Connolly, "Strategies of Succession and the 1797 Treaty of Big Tree," *William and Mary Quarterly* 80, no. 1 (2023): 130; Wallace, *Death and Rebirth*, 195–96.

12. Other Haudenosaunee nations faced significant land cessions in the postrevolutionary period. The resale of Oneida land made up a significant portion of public revenue for New York state in the early 1790s. See Chad Anderson, *The Storied Landscape of Iroquoia: History, Conquest, and Memory in the Native Northeast* (University of Nebraska Press, 2020), 50, 117.

13. Nancy Shoemaker, "The Rise or Fall of Iroquois Women," *Journal of Women's History* 2, no. 3 (1991): 44.

14. Anderson, *Storied Landscape of Iroquoia*, 8.

15. "Washington Outlines Indian Campaign, Philadelphia 31 January 1779," in *The Sullivan-Clinton Campaign in 1779: Chronology and Selected Documents* (University of the State of New York, Division of Archives and History, 1929) (hereafter *SCC*), 71.

16. "Journal of Major Jeremiah Fogg," in *Expedition Journals*, 97.

17. "General Sullivan's Report of the Campaign to John Jay, President of Congress, Teaogo, September 30, 1779," in *SCC*, 167.

18. *By the King, a Proclamation* (London, 1763), Gilder Lehrman Institute of American History, New York.

19. This boundary was readjusted in the 1768 Treaty of Fort Stanwix between Britain and the Haudenosaunee. Preston, *Texture of Contact*, 260–61.

20. Scholars recognize the American Revolution as a war of territorial aggrandizement against Native peoples. See Stuart Banner, *How the Indians Lost Their Lands: Law and Power on the Frontier* (Belknap Press of Harvard University Press, 2005), 121–22; Ned Blackhawk, *The Rediscovery of America: Native Peoples and the Unmaking of U.S. History* (Yale University Press, 2023); Calloway, *American Revolution*, xv; Colin G. Calloway, *The Indian World of George Washington: The First President, the First Americans, and the Birth of the* Nation (Oxford University Press, 2018), 6; Edward Countryman, *The American Revolution* (Hill & Wang, 1985), 232; Allan Greer, *Property and Dispossession: Natives, Empires and Land in Early Modern North America* (Cambridge University Press, 2018), 406–7; Max M. Mintz, *Seeds of Empire: The American Revolutionary Conquest of the Iroquois* (New York University Press, 1999), 1.

21. "Governor Clinton Urges Washington to Make an Indian Expedition, Poukeepsie 15th October 1778," in *SCC*, 69.

22. Rachel B. Hermann, *No Useless Mouth: Waging War and Fighting Hunger in the American Revolution* (Cornell University Press, 2019), 51.

23. "General Sullivan Outlines the Indian Expedition to Washington, Mill Stone, 16 April, 1779," in *SCC*, 79.

24. Anderson, *Storied Landscape of Iroquoia*, 50.

25. "Instructions of Washington to General Sullivan, Head-Quarters, 31 May, 1779," in *SCC*, 90–92.

26. Graymont, *Iroquois*, 213.

27. Koehler, "Hostile Nations," 430.

28. "General Sullivan Reports to Washington on the Chemung Skirmish Teago—August 15th 1779," in *SCC*, 127–128.

29. Banner, *Indians Lost Their Lands*, 121.

30. Franklin B. Hough, *Proceedings of the Commissioners of Indian Affairs, Appointed by Law for the Extinguishment of Indian Titles in the State of New York* (Albany, 1861), 57.

31. See Mann, *George Washington's War*, 37, 109; Mintz, *Seeds of Empire*, 114.

32. "Journal of Dr. Jabez Campfield," in *Expedition Journals*, 54.

33. "Washington Offers the Command of the Indian Expedition to Major-General Gates, Middlebrook, 6 March 1779," in *SCC*, 73.

34. "Washington Congratulates General Sullivan on Success at Newtown, Head Quarters, West Point, 15 September 1779," in *SCC*, 151.

35. "Journal of Lieutenant Robert Parker, of the Second Continental Artillery, 1779," in *SCC*, 205.

36. "Journal of Major John Burrowes," in *Expedition Journals*, 45.

37. "Gen. Sullivan's Address to the Army, Aug. 30, 1779," in *Letters and Papers of Major-General John Sullivan, Continental Army*, vol. 3, *1779–1795*, ed. Otis G. Hammond (New Hampshire Historical Society, 1939), 112.

38. "Journal of Dr. Jabez Campfield," 60.

39. "General Sullivan's Report," 159.

40. "Journal of Major Jeremiah Fogg," 98.

41. "Journal of Major Jeremiah Fogg," 98.

42. "Journal of Lieutenant William Barton," in *Expedition Journals*, 8.

43. According to Rachel Hermann, the year 1779 had the right conditions for a food crisis. Warfare targeting food supplies and the harsh winter led to a more significant refugee crisis. Hermann, *No Useless Mouth*, 52; Wallace, *Death and Rebirth*, 195.

44. Wallace, *Death and Rebirth*, 168; Mann, *George Washington's War*, 108–9.

45. Mt. Pleasant, "After the Whirlwind," 37.

46. Reginald Horsman, *Expansion and American Indian Policy, 1783–1812* (Michigan State University Press, 1967), 10.

47. Philip Schuyler, quoted in Banner, *Indians Lost Their Lands*, 112.

48. "Treaty with the Six Nations, October 22, 1784," in *Documents of United States Indian Policy*, 3rd ed., ed. Francis Paul Prucha (University of Nebraska Press, 2000), 5; Horsman, *Expansion*, 19. Treaty negotiations were confusing, as New York state commissioners attended to sign a separate treaty with the Haudenosaunee. New York officials believed they should control Indian affairs. See Connolly, "Strategies of Succession," 126.

49. Horsman, *Expansion*, 55.

50. Washington to James Duane, September 7, 1783, in Prucha, *Documents*, 1.

51. "Report of the Committee on Indian Affairs, October 15, 1783," in Prucha, *Documents*, 4.

52. Horsman, *Expansion*, 20.

53. Michael Leroy Oberg, *Peacemakers: The Iroquois, the United States, and the Treaty of Canandaigua, 1794* (Oxford University Press, 2016), 32.

54. Banner, *Indians Lost Their Lands*, 127. These treaty terms were later confirmed at the Treaty of Fort Harmar in 1789. "The Speech of the President of the United States of America to Cornplanter, Half-Town and Big-Tree, Chiefs of the Seneca Nation of the Indians, 1791," box 19, doc. 40, Paul G. Reilly Indian Collection, Archives & Special Collections Department, E. H. Butler Library, SUNY Buffalo State.

55. Banner, *Indians Lost Their Lands*, 128.

56. "Minutes of the Proceedings at Fort Stanwix," 1784, Wayne Manuscripts Indian Treaties 1778–1795, box 45, doc. 6, Paul G. Reilly Indian Collection; Taylor, *Divided Ground*, 156.

57. "The Charter of the Colony of Massachusetts Bay in New England, 1628–9," in New York State Legislature, Assembly, doc. 51, *Report of the Special Committee to Investigate the Indian Problem of the State of New York*, appointed by the Assembly of 1888 (Albany, 1889), 94.

58. "Grant to the Duke of York, Dated 12th March, AO. 16, Car. 2D, 1664," in *Report of the Special Committee*, 101.

59. "From Liber One of Miscellaneous Records, in the Office of the County Clerk of the County of Cattaraugus," in *Report of the Special Committee*, 107.

60. "From Liber One," 107.

61. Massachusetts first sold the preemption right to Oliver Phelps and Nathaniel Gorham, who extinguished Native title to the eastern third of the land grant area, a part of Iroquoia that belonged to other Haudenosaunee nations. The preemption right to portions of Seneca land remained in place for the nineteenth century. For more on the Phelps and Gorham purchase, see

Laurence M. Hauptman, *Conspiracy of Interests: Iroquois Dispossession and the Rise of New York State* (Syracuse University Press, 1999), 88.

62. For example, Georgia entered into a compact with the United States in 1802 in which Georgia gave up western land claims to the US in exchange for federal assistance with extinguishing Native title within state boundaries in the future. See Theda Perdue and Michael D. Greene, *The Cherokee Nation and the Trail of Tears* (Penguin Books, 2007), 55.

63. Taylor, *Divided Ground*, 10.

64. "From Liber One," 107.

65. Alyssa Mt. Pleasant, "Independence for Whom? Expansion and Conflict in the Northeast and Northwest," in *The World of the Revolutionary American Republic*, ed. Andrew Shankman (Routledge, 2014), 118.

66. George Washington, "The Reply of the President of the United States, to the Speech of the Corn Plant, Half Town, and Big Tree, Chiefs and Counsellors of the Seneca Nation of Indians," in *Documents Relative to Indian Affairs*, n.p.

67. Washington, "Reply of the President," n.p.

68. Oberg, *Peacemakers*, 66.

69. Henry Knox, "Instructions to Major General Anthony Wayne Relatively to a Proposed Treaty with the Indians Northwest of the Ohio, April 4, 1794," Wayne Papers, Historical Society of Pennsylvania, Philadelphia, Paul G. Reilly Indian Collection.

70. Red Jacket, "Treaty of Canandaigua Oct 19–November 12, 1794," in *The Collected Speeches of Sagoyewatha, or Red Jacket*, ed. Granville Ganter (Syracuse University Press, 2006), 64–65.

71. Hauptman, *Conspiracy of Interests*, 90; Oberg, *Peacemakers*, 114.

72. "Treaty with the Six Nations, 1794," in *Indian Affairs: Laws and Treaties*, vol. 2, ed. Charles J. Kappler (US Government Printing Office, 1904), 35.

73. Although the United States and New York state ignored the promises made in the Treaty of Canandaigua for most of the nineteenth century in order to force land cessions, extend jurisdiction over Haudenosaunee lands, and tax them, the Iroquois still used the treaty to assert their sovereignty. See Jack Campisi and William A. Starna, "On the Road to Canandaigua: The Treaty of 1794," *American Indian Quarterly* 19, no. 4 (1995): 487.

74. Many Haudenosaunee today continue to view the treaty this way. Robert W. Venables, "Some Observations on the Treaty of Canandaigua," in *Treaty of Canandaigua, 1794: 200 Years of Treaty Relations Between the Iroquois Confederacy and the United States*, ed. G. Peter Jemison and Anna M. Schein (Clear Light, 2000), 87.

75. On the memory of the expedition, see Smith, *Memory Wars.*

76. "Historical Address of Rev. David Craft," in *Expedition Journals*, 336.

6. "The Last Desperate Struggle"

I am deeply grateful to Susan Seal, president of the Friends of Odell House Rochambeau Headquarters, and Constance Kehoe, president of Revolutionary Westchester 250, for informing me of the opportunity to contribute to this volume on New York in the American Revolution and for helping bring the story to life by personally guiding me through the sites of the Grande Reconnaissance. My sincere thanks also go to George Washington's Mount Vernon for its continuing support of my work, and to the Karsh Institute of Democracy at the University of Virginia, whose support during my two-year postdoctoral fellowship made the research and writing of this chapter possible. Finally I wish to thank the Chastellux family, especially Hugues and Philippe, for their enduring generosity in granting me access to their family archive and supporting my research.

1. On "gamble," see Richard M. Ketchum, *Victory at Yorktown* (Henry Holt, 2004), 152; Harold Atkins Larabee, *Decision at the Chesapeake* (CN Porter, 1964); Larrie D. Ferreiro, *Brothers at Arms: American Independence and the Men of France and Spain Who Saved It* (Alfred A. Knopf, 2016). On Rochambeau's forceful role, or even "manipulation," see Thomas Fleming, *Beat the Last Drum: The Siege of Yorktown, 1781* (H. Wolff, 1963), 89; John Ferling, *Almost a Miracle: The American War of Independence* (Oxford University Press, 2007), 504–5; Nathaniel Philbrick, *In the Hurricane's Eye: The Genius of George Washington and the Victory at Yorktown* (Viking, 2018), 238. For analyses that mainly credit De Grasse, see Norman Desmarais, *Washington's Engineer: Louis Duportail and the Creation of an Army Corps* (Prometheus Books, 2021); Tom Shachtman, *How the French Saved America* (St. Martin's, 2017). In Olivier Chaline and Jean-Marie Kowalski, *L'Amiral de Grasse et l'indépenance américaine* (Sorbonne University Press, 2023), the authors do not clearly state the reason why De Grasse decided to go to the Chesapeake Bay.

2. Chastellux has not been recognized for this role except in Iris de Rode, *François-Jean de Chastellux (1734–1788): Un soldat-philosophe dans le monde atlantique à l'époque des Lumières* (Honore Champion, 2022). La Luzerne has been overlooked, except in Lee Kennet, *The French Forces in America* (Bloomsbury, 1977), and in Jean Berenger, "Le Siege de Yorktown," in *La France et independence Americaine*, ed. Olivier Chaline, Philippe Bonnichon, and Charles-Philippe de Vergennes (Sorbonne University Press, 2008).

3. The correspondence between Chastellux and La Luzerne is held by the Chastellux family, in the Chateau de Chastellux, to which the author of this chapter has exclusive access. It will be referred to hereunder as PAC (Private Archive Chastellux). See de Rode, *François-Jean de Chastellux*, 17–21. It will be available in scan at George Washington's Mount Vernon in 2025.

4. Following de Ternay's death in Newport in the winter of 1780, his role was successively assumed by Charles-René-Dominique Sochet, Chevalier Destouches, and later Jean-Melchior Saint-Laurent, Comte de Barras.

5. Lee Kennett, "Le bilan d'une rencontre, l'armée française en Amérique, 1780–1783," *Annales historiques de la Révolution française*, no. 226 (October–December 1976): 529–42; T. Cole Jones, "Displaying the Ensigns of Harmony: The French Army in Newport, Rhode Island, 1780–1781," *New England Quarterly* 85, no. 3 (2012): 430–67. For full context, see William C. Stinchcombe, *The American Revolution and the French Alliance* (Syracuse University Press, 1969).

6. Laura Aurricchio, *The Marquis de Lafayette Reconsidered* (Random House, 2014); de Rode, *François-Jean de Chastellux*, part 1; Arnaud Blondet, *Jeux de*

guerre, l'histoire de l'armée de Rochambeau au secours des États-Unis, 1780–1781, preface by Iris de Rode, vol. 1 (Éditions Jean-Jacques Wuillaume, 2024); George L. Sioussat, "The Chevalier de La Luzerne," *Pennsylvania Magazine of History and Biography* 60, no. 4 (1936): 391–418.

7. See, for context, Christoper Ward, *The War of the Revolution* (Skyhorse, 2011).

8. "Notes for the Hartford Conference," September 1780, *Founders Online*, https://founders.archives.gov/documents/Washington/03-28-02-0173-0003.

9. Marquis de Lafayette, "Rapport sur la trahison d'Arnold," Private Archive Chastellux (PAC), EE 139, Chateau de Chastellux. For full context on Arnold, see Nathanael Philbrick, *Valiant Ambition: George Washington, Benedict Arnold, and the Fate of the American Revolution* (Viking, 2016).

10. Chastellux, "Mémoire sur les conditions de l'intervention," October 1780, PAC, EE 37.

11. "Chastellux to the Marquise de la Tournelle (His Sister)," February 2, 1782, PAC, EE 140; Washington to Chastellux, December 14, 1782, *Founders Online*; and Chastellux, "Mémoire sur l'Amérique" and "Mémoire sur la guerre actuelle," n.d. (estimate 1780), PAC, EE 26–27. For details, see de Rode, *François-Jean de Chastellux*, 423–28.

12. Philbrick, *Valiant Ambition*, 91.

13. La Luzerne to Chastellux, December 9, 1780, PAC, EE 211.

14. Washington to Chastellux, December 14, 1782, *Founders Online*, https://founders.archives.gov/documents/Washington/99-01-02-10201.

15. On this campaign, see James L. Nelson, *George Washington's Great Gamble and the Sea Battle That Won the American Revolution* (McGraw Hill, 2010), 37–47.

16. Larrie D. Ferreiro, "The Race to the Chesapeake Between Destouches and Arbuthnot, March 1781," *Society for Nautical Research*, November 2018; Nelson, *George Washington's Great Gamble*, 48–71.

17. Washington to John Laurens, April 9, 1781, *Founders Online*.

18. "Correspondance de la Luzerne avec le Ministre des Affaires Etrangeres," Philadelphia, April 1, 1781, 230 PAAP/3, Archives Diplomatiques de France, La Courneuve.

19. La Luzerne to Chastellux, June 10, 1781, PAC, EE 211.

20. The memorandum has several versions: Rochambeau, papers 14, 104, Manuscript Division, Library of Congress, Washington, DC; Series B4—"Campagnes," archive identifier GA 191, 159–60, Archives de la Marine deposited at Archives Nationales de France, Paris; archive identifier GA 3736, 97–100, Archives du Ministère des Affaires Etrangères, Paris. See also de Rode, *François-Jean de Chastellux*, 321–27.

21. Correspondance Politique, Etats-Unis, vol. 19, no. 4, fol. 9, Archives du Ministère des Affaires Étrangères.

22. Rochambeau to La Luzerne, April 23, 1781, archive identifier GA 3736, 102, Archives du Ministère des Affaires Etrangères.

23. La Luzerne to Chastellux, April 28, 1781, PAC, EE 211.

24. Chastellux to Washington, April 29, 1781, *Founders Online*, https://founders.archives.gov/documents/Washington/03-31-02-0399.

25. Rochambeau, *Mémoires militaires, historiques et politiques de Rochambeau, ancien maréchal de France, et grand officier de la Légion d'honneur*, ed. Luce de Lancival (Paris, 1809), 273.

26. "Conference at Wethersfield with Rochambeau," May 23, 1781 *Founders Online*, https://founders.archives.gov/documents/Washington/99-01-02-05842; Washington to John Sullivan, May 29, 1781, Founders Online, https://founders.archives.gov/documents/Washington/99-01-02-05898.

27. De Rode, *François-Jean de Chastellux*, 325–26; Randolph G. Adams, *The Burned Letter of Chastellux*, Franco-American Pamphlet Series 7 (William L. Clements Library, 1935).

28. Chastellux to Marquise de La Tournelle, May 28, 1781, PAC, EE 140.

29. La Fayette to Chastellux, July 10, 1781, PAC EE 260; and La Luzerne to Chastellux, March 12, 1781, PAC, EE 211.

30. Rochambeau to De Grasse, May 28, 1781, Archives du Ministère des Affaires Etrangères G.A. A1, 3734, 32. Almost no historian has focused on that part of this crucial letter, except Lee Kennett, *The French Forces in America* (Greenwood, 1977), 108–9.

31. Washington to De Grasse, July 21, 1781, *Founders Online*, https://founders.archives.gov/documents/Washington/99-01-02-06471.

32. Washington to Rochambeau, June 10, 1781, *Founders Online*, https://founders.archives.gov/documents/Washington/99-01-02-06027; Rochambeau to Washington, June 12, 1781, *Founders Online*, https://founders.archives.gov/documents/Washington/99-01-02-06050; Rochambeau to De Grasse, May 28, 1781, quoted in Henri Doniol, *Histoire de la participation de la France à l'établissement des États-Unis d'Amérique: Correspondance diplomatique et documents*, vol. 5 (Paris, 1892), 520–22.

33. Rochambeau to De Grasse, June 10 and June 11, 1781, quoted in Doniol, *Histoire de la participation*, vol. 5, 521.

34. Rochambeau's headquarters at the Odell House, located at 425 Ridge Road in Hartsdale, still stands today as a museum (https://www.odellrochambeau.org/). Washington's headquarters at the Joseph Appleby House, once located on Secor Road in Scarsdale, no longer exists. For this encampment, see Robert Selig, *The Franco-American Encampment in the Town of Greenburgh, 6 July–18 August 1781: A Historical Overview and Resource Inventory* (Town of Greenburgh, 2020), https://greenburghny.com/CivicAlerts.aspx?AID=570&ARC=716.

35. Waldo G. Leland, ed., "Letters from La Fayette to La Luzerne, 1780–1782," *American Historical Review* 20 (1915): 22.

36. Chastellux to Marquise Tournelle, August 13, 1781, PAC, EE 321.

37. Washington to Samuel Huntington, July 6, 1781, *Founders Online*, https://founders.archives.gov/documents/Washington/99-01-02-06303; George Washington, diary entry, July 18, 1781, *Founders Online*, https://founders.archives.gov/documents/Washington/01-03-02-0007-0003-0014; Ludwig von Closen, *The Revolutionary Journal of Baron Ludwig von Closen, 1780–1783*, trans. and ed. Evelyn M. Acomb (University of North Carolina Press, 1958), 97. See also Joseph Stolz III, "Documenting a Proposed 1781 French-American Attack on New York: The Chastellux Archive and the Epic Finale

That Never Was," *Early American Studies: An Interdisciplinary Journal* 22, no. 1 (2024): 194–212.

38. Washington, diary entry, July 20, 1781, *Founders Online*, https://founders.archives.gov/documents/Washington/01-03-02-0007-0003.

39. Closen, *Revolutionary Journal*, 93–101; Rochambeau, *Mémoires militaires*, 248; Alexandre Berthier, "Journal de Berthier," in *The American Campaigns of Rochambeau's Army, 1780, 1781, 1782, 1783*, trans. and ed. Howard C. Rice Jr. and Anne S. K. Brown (Princeton University Press, 1996), 1:251; Washington, diary entry, July 23, 1781, *Founders Online*, https://founders.archives.gov/documents/Washington/01-05-02-0001-0001-0023.

40. Chastellux, *Réflexions sur l'attaque de New York*, with two maps, n.p. This work, previously held at PAC, today is at George Washington's Mount Vernon, as it was sold by the Chastellux family through Christie's New York in 2017.

41. Chastellux, *Réflexions*, n.p.

42. Antoine Jean Louis Lebègue de Presle Duportail, "Observations générales sur la manière de passer sur l'isle de New York, July 27, 1781," quoted in Norman Desmarais, *Washington's Engineer: Louis Duportail and the Creation of an Army Corps* (Prometheus Books, 2021), 164.

43. George Washington, diary entry, August 1, 1781, *Founders Online*, https://founders.archives.gov/documents/Washington/01-03-02-0007-0004-0001.

44. De Grasse to Rochambeau, July 28, 1781, quoted in Doniol, *Histoire de la participation*, vol. 5, 520–22.

45. La Luzerne to Chastellux, October 21, 1781, PAC, EE 87.

46. Washington to La Fayette, August 15, 1781, *Founders Online*, https://founders.archives.gov/documents/Washington/99-01-02-06693.

47. Stanley D. M. Carpenter, *Southern Gambit: Cornwallis and the British March to Yorktown* (University of Oklahoma Press, 2018).

48. Robert Selig, *March to Victory: Washington, Rochambeau, and the Yorktown Campaign of 1781* (Center for Military History, 2005).

49. Closen, *Revolutionary Journal*, 123.

50. For details on Yorktown, see Ketchum, *Victory at Yorktown*.

7. "Standing on Their Own Soil"

I would like to thank the anonymous reviewers for their helpful feedback, the George and Ann Richards Civil War Era Center at Penn State University for a faculty fellowship that supported this research, and the staff at the Geneva Historical Society for their assistance.

1. "For the Colored American," *Colored American*, October 14, 1837.

2. Arthur Zilversmith, *The First Emancipation: The Abolition of Slavery in the North* (University of Chicago Press, 1967), 85, 226–28.

3. Shane White, *Somewhat More Independent: The End of Slavery in New York City, 1770–1810* (University of Georgia Press, 1991), 143–49; Leslie M. Harris, *In the Shadow of Slavery: African Americans in New York City, 1626–1863* (University of Chicago Press, 2003), 70; Graham Russel Hodges, *Root and Branch: African Americans in New York and East Jersey, 1613–1863* (University of North Carolina

Press, 1999), 185–86; Michael E. Groth, *Slavery and Freedom in the Mid-Hudson Valley* (State University of New York Press, 2017), 70; David N. Gellman, *Emancipating New York: The Politics of Slavery and Freedom, 1777–1827* (Louisiana State University Press, 2006), 4, 10, 13.

4. See Edgar J. McManus, *A History of Negro Slavery in New York* (Syracuse University Press, 1966); White, *Somewhat More Independent.*

5. This chapter defines western New York as a region stretching from the lands at the edge of the Hudson River Valley to the Great Lakes of Ontario and Erie.

6. White, *Somewhat More Independent*, 84.

7. Gilbert Hobbs Barnes, *Antislavery Impulse: 1830–1844* (D. Appleton-Century, 1933); Allen Carden, *Freedom's Delay: America's Struggle for Emancipation* (University of Tennessee Press, 2014), 90; Whitney Cross, *The Burned-Over District: The Social and Intellectual History of Enthusiastic Religion in Western New York, 1800–1850* (Cornell University Press, 1950); James Brewer Stewart, *Holy Warriors: The Abolitionists and American Slavery* (1976; repr., Hill and Wang, 1996); Douglas M. Strong, *Perfectionist Politics: Abolitionism and the Religious Tensions of American Democracy* (Syracuse University Press, 1999); Milton C. Sernett, *North Star Country: Upstate New York and the Crusade for African American Freedom* (Syracuse University Press, 2002).

8. Gellman, *Emancipating New York*, 18–21.

9. Stewart, *Holy Warriors*, 12–14; Donald L. Robinson, *Slavery in the Structure of American Politics: 1765–1820* (Harcourt Brace Jovanovich, 1971), 36–37; Manisha Sinha, *The Slave's Cause: A History of Abolition* (Yale University Press, 2016), 9–10, 28–29.

10. Paul J. Polgar, *Standard Bearers of Equality: America's First Abolition Movement* (University of North Carolina Press, 2019), 53–54; A. Judd Northrup, "Slavery in New York: A Historical Sketch," *State Library Bulletin*, no. 4 (May 1900): 289; McManus, *History of Negro Slavery*, 166; "An Act Prohibiting the Importation of Slaves into New York State (1788)," Department of State, Bureau of Miscellaneous Records, Enrolled Acts of the State Legislature, Series 13036-78, New York State Archives, Albany, https://digitalcollections.archives.nysed.gov/index.php/Detail/objects/49827.

11. Gellman, *Emancipating New York*, 46, 177–78; White, *Somewhat More Independent*, 84.

12. "An Act for the Gradual Abolition of Slavery (March 1799)," *Laws of the State of New York: Passed at the Sessions of the Legislature Held in the Years 1797, 1798, 1799, and 1800*, vol. 4 (Albany, 1887), 388–89.

13. Kathryn Grover, *Make a Way Somehow: African-American Life in a Northern Community, 1790–1965* (Syracuse University Press, 1994), 13; Blake McKelvey, "Colonel Nathaniel Rochester," *Rochester History* 24, no. 1 (1962): 4–6; George S. Conover, ed., *History of Ontario County, New York: With Illustrations and Family Sketches of Some of the Prominent Men and Families*, compiled by Lewis Cass Aldrich (Syracuse, 1893), 255; Irvin W. Near, *A History of Steuben County, New York, and Its People*, vol. 1 (Lewis, 1911), 101; Dann J. Broyld, *Borderland Blacks: Two Cities in the Niagara Region During the Final Decades of Slavery* (Louisiana State University Press, 2023), 42; Sarah L. H. Gronningsater, *The Rising Generation:*

Gradual Abolition, Black Legal Culture, and the Making of National Freedom (University of Pennsylvania Press, 2024), 63–64.

14. "An Account of the Emigration of the Rose and Nicolas Families from Virginia to New York State as Given by George W. Nicholas Esq. of Geneva N.Y.," 1901, Geneva Historical Society, Geneva, NY; G. David Brumberg, *The Making of an Upstate Community: Geneva, New York, 1750–1920* (Geneva Bicentennial Commission, 1976), 38.

15. Document attesting to Nathaniel Rochester's ownership of "one woman named Nance, one boy named Ned, and two male children," September 9, 1809, Rochester Family Papers, Series 2: Financial, Legal, and Property Records, 1800–1809, University of Rochester Special Collections, Rochester, NY.

16. Ontario Repository, July 17, 1810; E. Anne Schaezte, *Slavery in the Genesee Country (also known as Ontario County), 1789 to 1827* (Afro-American Historical Association of the Niagara Frontier, 1998), 5; Conover, *History of Ontario County*, 255; Charles F. Milliken, *A History of Ontario County, New York, and Its People: Genealogical and Biographical, Illustrated*, vol. 2 (Lewis Historical, 1911), 251.

17. *Wonderful Eventful Life of Rev. Thomas James: By Himself* (Rochester, NY, 1887), 3; Austin Steward, *Twenty-Two Years a Slave and Forty Years a Freeman* (Canandaigua, NY, 1867), 107–8.

18. Shane White, "Slavery in New York State in the Early Republic," *Australasian Journal of American Studies* 14, no. 2 (1995): 7; *Public Laws of the State of New-York Passed at the Thirty-Third Session of the Legislature* (Albany, 1810), 81–82.

19. *The Expositor*, October 7, 1807.

20. *The Expositor*, October 7, 1807.

21. *The Expositor*, October 7, 1807.

22. *Geneva Gazette*, September 23, 1812; *Geneva Gazette*, August 14, 1816.

23. *Geneva Gazette*, July 31, 1811; Deborah Gray White, *Ar'n't I a Woman? Female Slaves in the Plantation South*, rev. ed. (W. W. Norton, 1999), 70–72.

24. *The Expositor*, June 17, 1807.

25. Manumission of Ginna, December 5, 1799, Geneva Historical Society; John Canfield Spencer to Nathaniel Rochester, August 17, 1814, William Beatty Rochester to Nathaniel Rochester, December 18, 1814, William Beatty Rochester to Nathaniel Rochester, January 5, 1815, Rochester Family Papers, Series 1: Correspondence, 1780–1817, University of Rochester Special Collections. It is likely that Ned was the enslaved boy that William brought to New York in the fall of 1809.

26. Polgar, *Standard Bearers of Equality*, 104–5.

27. Peter Wheeler, *Chains and Freedom: Or, The Life and Adventures of Peter Wheeler, a Colored Man Yet Living, a Slave in Chains, a Sailor on the Deep, and a Sinner at the Cross* (New York, 1839), 21, 36–38, 42, 48, 125–51.

28. "An Act to Incorporate the Ontario Manumission Society (June 1812)," in *Laws of the State of New York, Passed at the Thirty-Fifth Session of the Legislature* (Albany, 1812), 453–55; Steward, *Twenty-Two Years a Slave*, 106–9; Near, *History of Steuben County*, 101–2.

29. *Geneva Gazette and General Advertiser*, September 13, 1826; *Geneva Palladium*, July 4, 1827; *Laws of the State of New York, Passed at the Thirty-Ninth, Fortieth and Forty-First Sessions of the Legislature, Commencing January 1816 and Ending April 1818*, vol. 4 (Albany, 1818), 144.

30. Blake McKelvey, "Lights and Shadows in Local Negro History," *Rochester History* 21, no. 4 (1959): 2; Sernett, *North Star Country*, 6–7.

Contributors

Benjamin L. Carp is the Daniel M. Lyons Professor of American History at Brooklyn College. He also teaches at the Graduate Center of the City University of New York. He is the author of *The Great New York Fire of 1776: A Lost Story of the American Revolution* (Yale University Press, 2023).

Robert Chiles is a senior lecturer in the Department of History at the University at Maryland and a coeditor of the *New York History Journal.*

John Cording at St. Thomas Aquinas College specializes in Loyalist studies. He is working on an open-access database of New York Loyalists that will be launched in 2026.

Iris de Rode, postdoctoral fellow at the Karsh Institute for Democracy, University of Virginia, specializes in Franco-American relations during the American Revolution, with a focus on the intersection of military strategy, diplomacy, and Enlightenment thought. Her book, *François-Jean de Chastellux (1734–1788): Un soldat-philosophe dans le monde atlantique à l'époque des Lumières* (2022), was awarded the Prix Guizot by the Académie Française in 2023.

Lucien Holness is an assistant professor of history at Penn State University Park. He is a historian of North American slavery, abolition, and emancipation.

Elana Krischer is a visiting assistant professor of history at Marist University. She has published in the *Journal of the Early Republic* and *Iroquoia: The Journal of the Conference on Iroquois History*. Her research interests include Native American history, nineteenth-century history, and settler colonialism.

Devin Lander is the New York state historian and a coeditor of the *New York History Journal.*

Jennifer Lemak is the chief curator of history at the New York State Museum. She is also a coeditor of the *New York History Journal.*

Christopher F. Minty is a digital editor at the University of Virginia and the author of *Unfriendly to Liberty: Loyalist Networks and the Coming of the American Revolution in New York City* (Cornell University Press, 2023).

Russell Shorto is the author of *The Island at the Center of the World*, which chronicles the Dutch colony of New Netherland and its legacy. He is the author of *Taking Manhattan: The Extraordinary Events That Created Manhattan and Shaped America*, a contributing writer at the *New York Times Magazine*, and the director of the New Amsterdam Project at the New York Historical Society.

Emily Sneff is a historian and consulting curator and a leading expert on the Declaration of Independence. She is the author of *When the Declaration of Independence Was News* (Oxford University Press, 2026).

Dillon L. Streifeneder is an assistant professor of history at the United States Naval Academy in Annapolis, Maryland. His current scholarship focuses on state formation and governance in the era of the American Revolution.

Thomas S. Wermuth is the Frank T. Bumpus Chair in Hudson River Valley History at Marist University, where he teaches courses in the early United States and regional history.

Index

Page numbers in *italics* indicate illustrative material.